THE
PERFORMANCE
PARADOX

THE
PERFORMANCE
PARADOX

Turning the Power of Mindset into Action

EDUARDO BRICEÑO

Ballantine Books
New York

Published in the United States by Ballantine Books,
an imprint of Random House, a division of
Penguin Random House LLC, New York.

BALLANTINE is a registered trademark and the colophon is a
trademark of Penguin Random House LLC.

LIBRARY OF CONGRESS CATALOGING-IN-PUBLICATION DATA
Names: Briceño, Eduardo, author.
Title: The performance paradox / Eduardo Briceño.
Description: First Edition. | New York: Ballantine Group, 2023 |
Identifiers: LCCN 2023012868 (print) | LCCN 2023012869 (ebook) |
ISBN 9780593356906 (hardcover; alk. paper) | ISBN 9780593356913 (ebook)
Subjects: LCSH: Performance—Measurement. | Performance standards. |
Organizational effectiveness. | Achievement motivation. |
Organizational learning.
Classification: LCC HF5549.5.P35 B75 2023 (print) |
LCC HF5549.5.P35 (ebook) | DDC 658.3/125—dc23/eng/20230323
LC record available at https://lccn.loc.gov/2023012868
LC ebook record available at https://lccn.loc.gov/2023012869

International edition ISBN 978-0-593-72524-5

Printed in the United States of America on acid-free paper

randomhousebooks.com

First Edition

Book design by Diane Hobbing

To my mother and father, who made my sister and me their highest priority; to my beloved wife, Allison, who inspired me to develop a purpose and make the most of life; and to Carol Dweck, who believed in my ability to grow and showed me a life-changing path to do so.

CONTENTS

PART THREE:
FROM INDIVIDUAL TRANSFORMATION TO GLOBAL IMPACT

Part One:
Driving Individual Growth

Chapter 1: The Performance Paradox

BIG IDEA *While it might seem counterintuitive, constantly performing does not improve our performance. The route to success is often not a straight line.*

Anjali felt her palms grow sweaty every time her manager Salma asked, "Can I offer some feedback?"

"No!" She wanted to scream. "I'm already working as hard as I can!"

Indeed, she was, and since joining the company, she'd received positive feedback from managers and direct reports alike.

But she'd never had a manager who was also so up-front about areas where she could improve—and it was usually the logistical components of her job, which she rarely had time to stay on top of. Anjali viewed herself as an attentive, hands-on person who always put her customers first, and if she had to choose between taking a customer's call and updating the company's database, she'd pick the phone call 100 percent of the time.

Talking to Salma made her feel like a kid again, like she couldn't get it right.

The next time Salma uttered that dreaded F-word—*feedback*—and started offering suggestions on how she could do things differently, Anjali couldn't hold back. "I'm already working as hard as I can!"

After a brief but painful pause, Salma smiled at her.

"Anjali, no one wants you to work any harder. We want to figure out how we can make things *easier* for you."

Anjali had never thought about it like that—she assumed all of the feedback was a veiled warning that her job was in jeopardy.

When the phone rang, Gino Barbaro always leaped to answer it.

If he saw a bartender or waiter reaching for the receiver, he would shoo them away; after all, this was his restaurant, his reputation, his *name*. At Gino's Trattoria, if he wanted something done right, he needed to do it himself.

That's how Gino approached pretty much everything at the restaurant. Each day his mind would bounce around to whatever needed to be done next—taking orders over the phone, managing the kitchen staff, ordering supplies and ingredients, cleaning, keeping on top of financial transactions, locking up at night.

He didn't trust anyone to do these things as well as he would, and he didn't have the time to train them.

During the 2008 recession, the restaurant started to lose money. Gino responded by putting in extra hours to make sure everything was executed "perfectly," but it soon became apparent that that wasn't enough to keep the restaurant afloat. After twelve years of seventy-hour weeks, he was exhausted and couldn't envision working even harder to cut costs or promote the business to get out of this hole—there weren't enough hours in the day to stop and think about what to try differently. Something had to change.

There had to be a way to run a business that didn't leave him miserable, scrambling for time, and burnt out.

Douglas Franco was tapped by Peruvian investment firm Enfoca to change the trajectory of its new acquisition, iEduca, a Lima-based higher education company that offers courses for adults. The investment firm thought that a change in leadership would enable iEduca to grow faster.

Upon joining the company as CEO, Douglas observed that his new colleagues—especially those on the executive team—seemed to believe they were already optimizing the business. Douglas worried that this attitude was causing the company to stagnate and preventing the team from experimenting with new ideas.

To accelerate growth, iEduca would need to find new ways of doing things.

Frustrated and feeling pressure to deliver success to his investors, Douglas tried to encourage his new colleagues to think critically about opportunities for improvement. But his frustration was met with resistance. His team members dug in their heels and kept trying to prove themselves, rather than improve.

Then, when the COVID-19 pandemic broke out, student enrollment plummeted and revenues collapsed.

This was not how Douglas had envisioned his new chapter. He had to find a way to get his team to stop trying to impress him and start working with him to find new solutions—and the clock was ticking.

We'll come back to Anjali, Gino, and Douglas later, but now that you've heard a bit about their challenges, let me tell you about mine.

Early in my career, I was the youngest investment professional at the Sprout Group—then one of the oldest and largest venture capital firms in the world. I loved being exposed to different executive teams, industries, and companies at the leading edge of innovation, and I had the exciting opportunity to serve on boards of directors alongside much more experienced and knowledgeable investors and operators.

But when I think back on those days, what I remember most vividly is the incredible pressure I felt to *perform*.

We regularly sat in meetings listening to startup teams pitch their ventures. When the entrepreneurs stepped out of the room, we'd take turns voicing our impression of the opportunity. As a very junior professional just starting my career, I didn't know enough to have a strong conviction about whether an investment was attractive, but I pretended to.

As my colleagues shared their views, I would try to decide what to advocate for. When my turn came, I left my conflicting thoughts

and uncertainties unspoken to make it appear that all of my thinking pointed in one direction and that I had high confidence in my
recommendation. I would pick a side—to engage in due diligence
or turn down the opportunity, or to invest or not—and advocate
for it with certainty.

I realized that by not sharing some of my thoughts, I was with-
holding information that could have helped us make better decisions. This caused me anxiety because I wanted to help our team,
but I was handcuffed by my belief that I needed to appear knowledgeable, decisive, and confident of my opinions.

After years of this, I got very good at looking like I knew what I
was doing, but inside I felt disingenuous and inauthentic. I was
constantly pretending.

Eventually, the chronic stress of these feelings affected my body
physically. Under constant pressure, I kept my muscles contracted,
so much that, eventually, they lost their ability to relax. It turns out
that muscles are malleable, for better or for worse! Mine became
shorter and harder, preventing blood from penetrating them and
delivering the nutrients needed for proper functioning and healing.

It became painful for me to use my hands—to type, use the computer mouse, drive a car, open doors, even brush my teeth. After
seeing many specialists, I was finally diagnosed with a repetitive
strain injury called myofascial pain syndrome.

As time went on, my condition grew worse. I met people with
the same affliction who could no longer use their hands for more
than ten minutes a day, and it terrified me.

I was determined to do all I could to heal.

But I suspected that what I needed to change was more than just
my posture.

STUCK IN CHRONIC PERFORMANCE

Though the stories differ, Gino, Anjali, Douglas's colleagues, and I
were all suffering from the same condition, one I call *chronic performance:* the constant attempt to get every task done as flawlessly as
possible, and then some.

Maybe parts of our stories sound familiar to you?

Are you always racing to check tasks off a list?

Do you spend most of your time trying to minimize mistakes?

Do you suppress your uncertainties, impressions, or questions to try to appear like you always know what you're doing?

Would you rather walk over hot coals than get feedback?

These are all signs of chronic performance. While it may seem like minimizing mistakes is a reasonable use of our time or that appearing decisive is a wise career strategy, these habits can have a devastating impact on our skills, confidence, jobs, and personal lives.

Chronic performance could be the reason you might be feeling stagnant in some area of your life. You might be working more hours or putting more effort into tasks, yet you never seem to get ahead. Life feels like a never-ending game of catch-up. That's chronic performance—throwing more energy at tasks and problems yet staying at the same level of effectiveness.

MEET THE PARADOX

Most of us go about our days assuming that in order to succeed, we simply need to work hard to get things done. That's what we've been told all our lives. So what's the problem? Doesn't hard work lead to better performance? The answer is a paradox—one I call the *performance paradox.*

Maybe you're a busy professional trying to learn a difficult new skill, like giving masterful presentations, motivating colleagues, or resolving conflict, yet no matter how much you work at it, you don't seem to be getting better.

You could be a leader whose team achieves the same results month after month even though you are certain everyone is working hard.

Or perhaps you'd like to deepen your relationships with your family, friends, or colleagues, but conversations stay superficial.

The performance paradox is the counterintuitive phenomenon that if we want to improve our performance, we have to do something other than just perform. No matter how hard we work, if we only do things as best as we know how, trying to minimize mistakes, we get stuck at our current levels of understanding, skills, and capabilities.

Too often, the performance paradox tricks us into chronic performance, which leads to stagnation. We get stuck in a hamster wheel in our work, as well as in our relationships, health, hobbies, and any aspect of life. It can *feel* like we're doing our best, when in fact we're missing out on discovering better ways to create, connect, lead, and live.

Why does the paradox ensnare so many of us?

It's a seemingly logical response to feeling pressured, overwhelmed, and underwater. We think the answer is to just work harder and faster, but the way to improve our results is not to spend more time performing. It is to do something else that is a lot more rewarding and, ultimately, productive.

Understanding this paradox and how to overcome it is the subject of this book. We'll explore how pervasive the performance paradox is, and I'll show you how individuals, teams, and organizations can break through it. It's the key to surviving and thriving in the twenty-first century and beyond.

THE RIP CURRENTS OF LIFE

As the world was reopening from the COVID-19 pandemic, I attended a weeklong workshop at Modern Elder Academy, known as "the world's first midlife wisdom school," where my mentor Chip Conley was teaching some sessions.

The lessons were enriching. My cohort mates were wise and supportive. The facilities in El Pescadero, Mexico, were gorgeous, and the food was delicious. Everything was bliss, except for one thing.

Despite the beautiful beach where the campus is located, we were told not to go in the ocean due to the dangerously strong currents.

I grew up in Venezuela, forty-five minutes from the sea, and I love ocean swimming. So, in El Pescadero, I felt like I'd been placed in front of a table piled with gourmet chocolate and told not to eat any of it.

I was pretty sure if I ignored the advice and went swimming, I'd be fine. But I didn't want to miscalculate and drown, or *worse*, become *that guy* who ignored warnings, needed to be rescued, and led others into danger.

So I was relieved to learn about Playa Cerritos, a public beach a mile away where it was considered safe to swim. One morning, I woke up early to run to the public beach and get back in time for the day's workshop.

When I got there, the place looked like paradise. After a brief jog, I dove in.

The breakers were strong, but I knew what to do—dive to the sandy bottom and let the wave pass, then resurface and continue swimming away from the shore. Once the breaking waves were behind me, the ocean was calm.

I floated on my back, enjoying the sensation of being rocked back and forth. I felt present and at peace, grateful for life and for nature. It was just what I had hoped for.

Then, I lifted my head and discovered that I was very far from shore. A strong current must have been pulling me away from the coast. It was still early morning, and the beach was deserted. I was completely on my own.

Not good.

My goal suddenly changed. I went from wanting to get some exercise, reconnect with the ocean, and appreciate life to focusing on a single overarching goal: get back to land—alive.

I started swimming back to shore. After a few moments, I paused to see how much progress I had made and realized I had not moved at all. Instead, the rip current was carrying me out to sea.

Each year, in the United States alone, more than one hundred people drown in rip currents. If you get caught in one, like I did, your nervous system can switch to fight-or-flight mode. There's no way to flee, so you fight. You tell yourself to double down and give it your all to try to beat the ocean.

But continuing to fight—even fighting harder and faster—is not the best way to reach your destination.

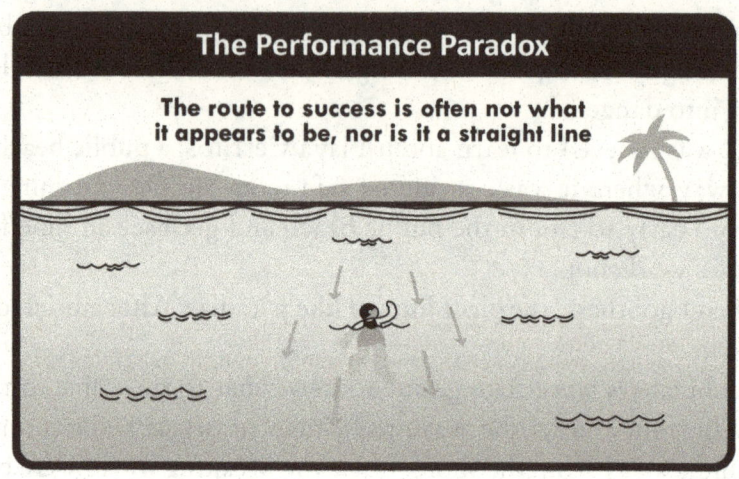

To get back to shore, I needed to *learn while doing*. I couldn't just *do*, and simply swim in a straight line toward the beach. I needed to learn what route might take me there—and I needed to do it while the pressure was on.

I turned almost ninety degrees and started swimming parallel to the coast. Initially, the rip current carried me farther out, but after a little while, the current appeared to subside, so I kept going, swimming steadily and gradually angling toward the coast. When I started getting tired, I switched to backstroke to give my worn-out muscles a rest. Eventually, I felt the waves beginning to form in front of me: I was getting closer to shore. I flipped back onto my stomach, aimed straight toward the shore, and picked up my pace.

When I got past the breakers, I took a deep breath and let a large wave tumble me toward the shore. Finally, when the wave was done with me, I collapsed onto the beach, dizzy and exhausted, but safe.

THE PERFORMANCE PARADOX

Even if you've never gotten caught in a rip current in the ocean, you've surely been caught in the rip currents of life. They are invisible and ever present. We often find ourselves in situations where pushing forward with everything we've got does not have the desired effect. I'm talking about those moments when simply doing more of the same thing prevents us from discovering better ways to make progress toward our goals.

When refusing to learn to delegate means missing out on the opportunity to grow as a leader.

When continuing to play a song the same way prevents us from learning to play it more beautifully.

When we choose executing what we already know over exploring beyond our boundaries.

At the same time, we need to perform in order to get things done: Gino had to continue taking orders and plating meals to keep his pizzeria open; I had to use all of my ocean swimming skills and stay focused on getting to shore to survive the rip current.

To prosper in today's complex and fast-changing world, we need to balance and integrate performance and learning.

Let's consider less life-threatening situations. You might think that the way to get better at writing or cooking is to simply write more words each day or cook a three-course meal every night, yet that's not the case.

That's the paradox.

If we focus *only* on performing the activity, our skills plateau and we risk becoming irrelevant, or worse.

Tricked by the performance paradox, we too often stay on autopilot rather than take on challenges, solicit feedback, and examine surprises and missteps to learn from them. For an author, that could mean asking for critiques of draft text. For a cook, it might involve experimenting with ingredients from another country's cuisine. For all of us, it means seeking out what we don't know instead of focusing solely on what we do.

To thrive, we must reconnect with the curiosity and learning habits we all had as young children, before school taught us to focus

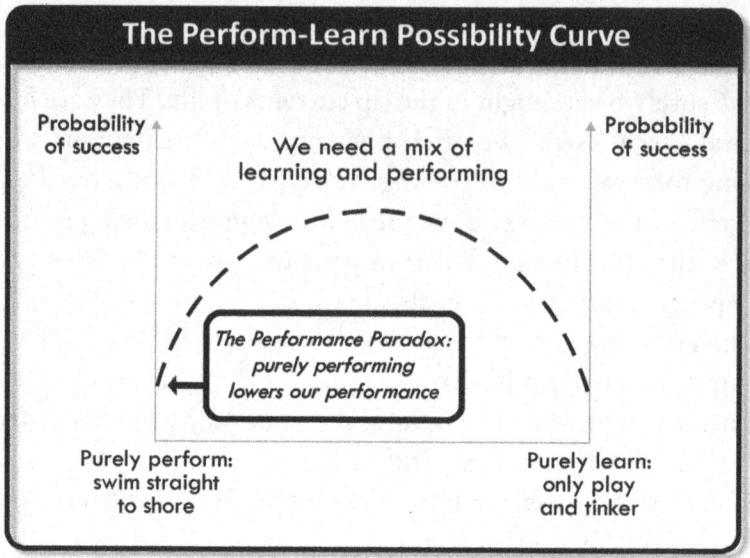

The Perform-Learn Possibility Curve

Probability of success — We need a mix of learning and performing — Probability of success

The Performance Paradox: purely performing lowers our performance

Purely perform: swim straight to shore

Purely learn: only play and tinker

on performance. This opens up boundless possibilities for what we can pursue and who we can become, preparing us to grow in our careers as our responsibilities evolve, the world changes, and new challenges and opportunities arise.

STUCK TREADING WATER

When teams and organizations get trapped by the performance paradox, the consequences are bleak. Many struggle or fail because they continue to fight the current, blindly pushing ahead, focusing on execution without developing the habit of seeking new insights and strategies.

When meetings serve only as a means for doling out tasks and don't have structures to generate questions or share lessons learned, our teams miss out on discovering and amplifying better ways of working.

When goals focus only on performance, like enlisting new clients or writing lines of code, and not on learning, like acquiring new sales skills or software integration techniques, they unintentionally lead people to get stuck in chronic performance.

When companies give in to the pressure to overly standardize processes and tell employees that there's only one right way to do things, they open the door for competitors to zip right past them. This is how businesses become irrelevant.

These problematic habits are often implemented in response to growth. As the number of employees increases, leaders tend to revert to traditional ideas of management that emerged during the Industrial Revolution, when the main concern was manufacturing widgets as cheaply as possible. Today, the main challenges in the fast-changing service economy are to identify unmet needs, drive innovation, and personalize service.

When organizations give in to command-and-control temptations, workers who ask questions—who readily admit they don't have all the answers—start to be seen as obtrusive, slow, and burdensome. People start feeling it is unsafe to share impressions, solicit feedback, or experiment. No one wants to threaten their social status and possibly hurt their career, so they learn to stay silent.

Managers start portraying themselves as infallible, but that actually hinders their growth, which ironically threatens the performance of their teams and organizations. The C-suite obsession with flawless execution inhibits true growth—even financial growth.

The reality is that organizations that are able to shift their focus from purely performing to incorporating learning become better equipped to outperform others.

A LIFE-CHANGING TURN OF EVENTS

In my youth, the school system taught me to focus on grades rather than on learning. Yours probably did, too. On the surface, this seemed to work fine, as I ended up attending a top university. I was subsequently hired to work at an investment bank on Wall Street and a prestigious venture capital firm in Silicon Valley. In my twenties, I was getting paid more than I ever thought I would.

Focusing on performing had gotten me a dream job. But I didn't like the person I had become. I detested always pretending to know more than I knew, giving advice when I didn't think I was sufficiently qualified, projecting confidence when I felt uncertain.

I didn't want to spend the next few decades in the same way, only to look back in regret. If I stayed the course, I would likely become very wealthy, but at what cost?

The threat of losing the use of my hands forced me to reflect on what I wanted to do with them. I had given my career all my time and energy, and then some, to always do the best I knew how, which had led to apparent success—but to what end? I had to make a change.

Ultimately, I decided to apply to Stanford to pursue a master's in business administration and a master's in education. I didn't get in, which was, in retrospect, a blessing in disguise because Professor Carol Dweck—the psychologist and researcher whose work has changed the way millions of people think about success and talent— wasn't there yet.

Two years later I reapplied, and this time, I was accepted. Getting to know Carol as a treasured teacher, mentor, and friend was a life-changing experience. Her pioneering work on *mindset*—the beliefs we hold about whether human qualities and abilities are fixed or can be developed—transformed my relationships, career, and life.

Once I began to study mindset in depth, I was able to reassess my life through a totally new lens. I could see how frequently I got stuck in a *fixed mindset*—believing my intelligence or abilities were static, with no room for improvement—and how this had gotten me into the habit of chronic performance at work, on the soccer field, and in my relationships. In a fixed mindset, anything less than perfection hurts our ego, so we experience more performance anxiety and are driven to *prove* rather than *improve*.

Because I believed intelligence and talent were fixed, I had focused on showing how smart and talented I was rather than trying to get smarter and better. I was striving for flawlessness.

But Carol's research told me I could break free of those habits and actually enjoy a lot more success in my life and in my career by choosing to cultivate what she coined a *growth mindset*.

THE MISSING PIECE

I learned from Carol the core insight from her findings: that we need to shift our beliefs about the nature of our abilities in order to shift our behaviors and results. But I also learned something that isn't as commonly known: It wasn't as simple as just starting to believe that I could change; I would also need to break out of my chronic performance habits.

When sharing my perspectives with colleagues, friends, and family, I would need to expose all my thoughts, rather than cherry-pick evidence, so I could learn from others' responses. When choosing classes or jobs, I would need to take on challenges I could learn from, rather than select courses or roles in which I knew I could perform best. When I made a mistake, I would need to acknowledge and discuss it rather than sweep it under the rug. And most important, I would need to always keep top of mind what I was working to improve on, and how.

I learned that as powerful as a growth mindset is, it is not a silver bullet. Growth mindset is a necessary foundation that needs to be cultivated in tandem with effective strategies and habits for growth.

A set of studies from educational psychologist Maria Cutumisu at the University of Alberta sheds light on this. Cutumisu and her team wanted to see what role growth mindset played in college students' willingness to seek critical feedback and revise their work—two strategies proven to be effective for improving skills and performance.

In an online game, the students were asked to design posters and were then given the opportunity to solicit critical feedback. After reading the feedback, they could either submit their posters as is or revise them.

Here's what may seem surprising to those of us who've witnessed the power of growth mindset. The studies found *no significant associations* between the students' mindsets and their learning choices—that is, whether they decided to solicit critical feedback and revise their work.

In other words, mindset alone did not determine whether students used effective learning techniques, which were key to creating high-quality posters.

Now, this doesn't mean that mindset isn't important. Among the students who sought critical feedback and revised their work, those who had demonstrated a growth mindset learned more from the feedback and performed better than their peers.

But the key takeaway is that just because someone is in a growth mindset, it doesn't mean they know how to learn or implement effective strategies to actually improve their skills.

Too many of us think that the way to improve is simply to work hard, but that is not true. This misunderstanding leads us to work harder in ways that don't lead to improvement, which we then take as evidence that we can't get better—a fixed mindset. Even the understanding that we can continually learn and grow is not sufficient. To effectively learn and improve, we must develop and implement habits and strategies that support growth. We may think we mastered that in school, when in fact our educational systems haven't focused on teaching people how to learn.

If we don't come to understand the performance paradox and how to overcome it, our belief in a growth mindset will remain shallow, insufficient, and vulnerable. To grow and succeed, we must develop the belief that we can change, as well as the competence for *how* to change. These two elements work hand in hand and reinforce each other.

As we will see later in the book, these are the two ingredients that Anjali, Gino, Douglas's company, and I needed to be able to change our trajectories.

FROM INDIVIDUALS TO CULTURES

Not only can individuals develop the beliefs and habits to achieve much greater growth and success, but we can create teams and organizations that do, too. In fact, we have to, because people develop their beliefs and habits by observing others around them.

I made it my mission to help organizations develop growth mindset cultures and know-how. I partnered with Lisa Blackwell—

Carol Dweck's former student and colleague—and co-founded an organization that develops and provides programs for schools to foster growth mindset cultures among educators, parents, and children. Carol Dweck, Steve Goldband, and Ellen Konar volunteered their time as advisors and mentors.

In collaboration with other growth mindset advocates, we achieved significant impact. Growth mindset is now a key principle in many schools and universities around the world.

But schools weren't the only places in need of a culture shift. Given my background, I felt called to focus my attention on the business sector and began helping professionals and leaders transform their lives, careers, and organizations.

For the past fifteen years, I have had the privilege of helping hundreds of organizations of all sizes, including some of the largest companies in the world, discover the power of growth mindset beliefs and know-how, and assisted them in building learning cultures and systems.

Learning organizations are those that prioritize the development of people—everyone comes to work every day in part to grow, and to support one another in doing so. Leaders inspire their staff to ask questions, share creative ideas that may seem unconventional, and discover different ways of seeing the world—and they lead the way. Not only are meetings geared toward getting tasks done, but they are a place to share new insights and ask questions. Performance management systems are focused not only on outcome metrics, but also on how much each person is learning and contributing to the growth of others. Learning organizations enable their people to think outside the box, innovate, and implement effectively, leading them to outperform other organizations.

In my work, I've found that people feel uplifted as they find new ways of working that are more effective, enriching, and joyful. They discover ways to let go of fear and pursue creativity, exploration, and experimentation. Instead of being guarded with their colleagues, people start sharing their thinking more transparently, which allows them to build deeper and more collaborative relationships. They also feel less chained by present realities, become more resilient, and have a greater sense of agency to drive change. As a result, they achieve greater revenue, profitability, and impact.

We gravely need these new kinds of organizations, because the prevailing work paradigm looks very different from what research has told us truly leads to improvement and high performance.

Even when we work hard, believing we can improve, too many of us remain frozen in chronic performance, and it's destroying our ability to stretch our skill sets and grow our organizational capabilities. If we are to truly achieve greater effectiveness, we need to understand the performance paradox and develop habits and cultures that free us from outmoded, ineffectual beliefs and behaviors.

Imagine what would happen if we were all able to move more fluidly between learning and performing. When we let go of the need to be in constant performance mode, we are less likely to see each interaction as an argument we must win. When we replace a fixation on being right with a passion for learning, we can discover creative ways to achieve greater progress. And when we learn how to translate our new competencies into superb performance, we are better equipped to craft solutions to society's greatest challenges.

But until we truly cultivate the habits to continue learning and growing each day of our lives, we're effectively locking ourselves and our teams into the stifling, performance-driven classrooms so many of us spent hours longing to escape as children.

Don't we want professionals who are curious to explore the unknown?

Don't we want to reignite that curiosity in ourselves, our teams, and our organizations?

What if we could all embrace how much we *don't* yet know—and then commit to doing something about it?

THE JOURNEY AHEAD

This book is the result of the lessons gained from the individuals and organizations my colleagues and I have had the privilege to serve.

I'll describe how to overcome the performance paradox, explain how to make time for learning even when we're feeling incredible pressure to perform, and share how this new way of understanding growth can help us transform ourselves, our teams, and our communities.

I'll share stories of how the strongest individuals and organizations strike a balance between learning and performing in order to foster a deep understanding of customers, continuous improvement, and innovation — and in the case of companies, how this ultimately leads to increased growth and income.

You'll meet a mother of three whose desire to lift her family out of financial hardship inspired her to embrace effective learning and performance habits, and you'll discover how that led her to become one of the most successful financial advisors in the United States.

You'll learn what effective executives in the financial services, technology, and construction industries did to help their companies bounce back after they experienced significant failure.

You'll see how a CEO who was committed to creating a diverse and inclusive workforce discovered the many ways he had to defy conventional wisdom — and his own beliefs — to achieve his goal.

You'll gain strategies for *how* to change and improve, including ways to develop greater knowledge, skills, understanding of others, and self-awareness. And you'll learn how to do these things even when your to-do list is jam-packed and your inbox overflowing.

In Part One of this book, I'll share key principles and strategies that anyone can use to overcome the performance paradox and unlock lifelong development. You'll see how Anjali, Gino, and I, as well as many others, broke out of chronic performance and changed our trajectories.

In Part Two, we'll examine what leaders, teams, and organizations do to achieve extraordinary growth, and how they toggle between learning and performing. You'll see how Douglas and many other leaders inspire their colleagues to improve and foster growth.

In Part Three, I'll show how to apply these lessons to achieve quantum leaps in your most worthy aims.

Today, given the boundless sources of learning at the tips of our fingers, we live in a learner's paradise — an ocean of knowledge and opportunity. But the fast pace of change also means non-learners get pulled into the ever-present rip currents.

Which path will you choose?

At the end of each chapter, I've included questions for you to reflect upon. Learning science tells us you will get more out of this book, and more effectively implement change, if you actively reflect along the way. I have also included a *looking forward* prompt to help you identify knowledge gaps and prepare you to get the most out of the chapter to come. You might also consider inviting a partner to join you on this learning journey.

You can find notes and resources to help you apply the strategies discussed throughout the book at briceno.com/paradox/resources/.

REFLECTION QUESTIONS

- In what areas of work or life might I be fooled by the performance paradox and stuck in chronic performance?
- How might my colleagues or loved ones be stuck in chronic performance?
- What might be some consequences?

LOOKING FORWARD

How might effort to perform be different from effort to improve?

Chapter 2: The Tournament and the Range

BIG IDEA *To overcome the performance paradox and unlock growth, we need to integrate the Learning Zone into our work and life.*

Imagine you want to get really good at chess. What would you do?

Easy. You'd play as many games of chess as possible. It's a reasonable, logical assumption.

It's also misguided.

Think about it this way. Many of us have spent countless hours typing away on our computers, yet how many of us are world-class typists? Even more puzzling—and more dangerous—research suggests that on average, the more years that general physicians practice medicine, the worse their patient outcomes become. That's what scientists at Harvard Medical School found when they analyzed sixty-two research studies on the subject.

Similarly, research on chess shows that playing a lot of games of chess is not a great way to improve. Those who spend the most time playing in tournaments are not those who reach the highest rankings.

Richard Williams understood this about tennis. So, bucking conventional wisdom, his daughters, Serena and Venus, didn't play junior tennis tournaments for years before turning professional. Instead, they were serious students, both in school and on the court. If you saw the biographical film *King Richard,* you would have seen how Richard meticulously planned for his daughters' success. Tennis time was devoted to practice rather than matches. They went on to become the best in the world.

Among many things, the Williams sisters learned that the main way to improve was not to spend all of their time playing in competitions—in other words, stuck in chronic performance.

Improvement and high performance in any domain come down to making sure we engage in two distinct but equally powerful states of mind: the *Learning Zone* and the *Performance Zone*. Each has a different purpose and requires a distinct focus and set of tools. Much like salt and pepper, the two zones can be used simultaneously to add growth and impact to the recipes of our lives—as we'll examine in Chapter 3—but they are very different.

We step into the *Performance Zone* when doing things to the best of our ability, trying to minimize mistakes, as we would in a chess or tennis tournament or when we're in a time crunch to complete a task. It's the way we get things done. We can all learn how to make the most of our time in this zone and to operate at our best—and we'll get into how to do that in this book.

But that doesn't mean we should be striving for top performance all the time; in fact, if we spend *all* our time in the Performance Zone, then stagnation, frustration, and burnout will follow. That's the very definition of chronic performance. Remember Gino from the last chapter? He was stuck in chronic performance, desperately trying to run his restaurant and never getting ahead.

That's why we must also engage in the *Learning Zone,* where we focus on growing our skills and knowledge. That could mean a chess player doing chess puzzles that challenge her just beyond her current level of ability, or a professional basketball player spending thirty minutes on his jump shot alone, or an actor working with a dialect coach to refine a proper Afrikaans accent before an audition. For a salesperson, it could mean testing different pitches as she meets with new clients and keeping track of which get the best responses. The Learning Zone is about inquiry, experimentation, making and reflecting on mistakes, and implementing adjustments on the journey toward greater excellence. It is a long-term investment that generates future dividends in the form of improved skills and stronger results.

Engaging in the Learning Zone doesn't require a significant time commitment, but it does require intention. We step into this zone

	PERFORMANCE ZONE	LEARNING ZONE
Goal	Perform	Improve
Activities designed for	Performance	Improvement
We focus on what	We have mastered	We don't know
Mistakes are to be	Avoided	Expected
Main benefit	Immediate results	Growth and future results

anytime we solicit feedback, try a new way of working, or examine how a competitor keeps landing all the accounts we've been bidding for. We embrace the Learning Zone the moment we choose not to respond in anger when someone critiques our work and decide instead to *listen* to what they are saying in an honest attempt to truly understand and learn from them.

Let's say you're a pro golfer. The Learning Zone is the work you do at the driving range—the place where you experiment with different approaches and see what works best. The golf tournament is where you'll spend time in the Performance Zone, focusing on what you do best.

Our work on the metaphorical driving range enables us to excel when the pressure is on.

Once we distinguish between the two zones, it's easy to see why so many of us get caught up in the performance paradox. Most organizations were simply not built with learning in mind. When we observe our workplaces, it's easy to conclude that the way to get promoted is to present ourselves as flawless, or as workhorses with blinders on, even if doing so prohibits innovation and true growth.

If we want to create a culture of growth—one where continuous improvement drives increasing performance—we have to make sure that growth behaviors are respected, valued, and rewarded.

We have to give ourselves and our colleagues the tournament *and* the range.

THE TRANSFORMATIVE POWER OF THE TWO ZONES

Lizzie Dipp Metzger showed up at her husband's office one morning to see if he needed help.

She walked out that afternoon with a job of her own.

Lizzie and her husband, Brian, had been going through a challenging period. Brian had just shut down his failed business building custom race cars, and they moved back to their hometown of El Paso. They were still paying down business loans when they got the news their third child was on the way.

Brian was the first to land a new gig after the move, selling insurance for New York Life.

In her determination to get their family through this difficult transition, Lizzie did everything she could to help, at times even gathering phone numbers of people who might need life insurance and showing up at Brian's office, kids in tow, to make sure he called them.

The managers got to know Lizzie and realized she was eager to work. They asked her if she had any interest in becoming a New York Life agent, too.

She had no particular interest in insurance and didn't see herself as a sales professional. She'd been a wedding planner, had some retail and restaurant experience, and most recently had worked as an early childhood teacher for three years before taking time off to have her third child.

Selling life insurance? That would be a leap. But she had nothing to lose, so she decided to go for it.

In that situation, Lizzie could easily have been fooled by the performance paradox and dove in headfirst, making as many sales calls as possible every day. But she knew that to flourish at her new job, she had a lot of new skills to learn. She had found that to be true in her prior jobs. So, instead of jumping to prove herself from the onset and maximizing short-term income, she set out to improve herself and learn as much as she could about her new trade. She would need to learn more about personal finance and the financial products she was offering her clients—as well as about the strategies and tools her new peers found most effective.

Lizzie understood that developing skills was about more than just plunging into the work. From the start, she made time for the Learning Zone. She found out which programs were available to develop herself as a professional, and she strove to learn from the best.

"I went to every class; I never let myself create an excuse to miss one," she said. "I also promised myself I would finish one master's course and one designation course each quarter."

A few select programs were normally available only to the firm's seasoned agents; regardless, Lizzie reached out to the people in charge and asked what she needed to do to get in. Initially, they responded that she was a few years away from qualifying, but she negotiated and pushed and asked what it would take for her to qualify the following year. She made sure she stayed on their radar by going back to them periodically to check in.

Her perseverance paid off. She began to meet top mentors and coaches, and when she found out that several high achievers in the industry had a study group—a regular gathering where they learned together and supported one another—she asked to join.

Seven years after becoming an insurance agent, Lizzie Dipp Metzger became the top-performing agent in all of New York Life—among thousands. Four years after that, she was ranked by *Forbes* as the twelfth top financial security professional in the United States, and the following year she moved up to number six. The total value of her clients' policies exceeds $680 million.

Lizzie didn't achieve these results because she was a born salesperson—there's no such thing. It was her belief in her own ability to improve her skills coupled with her effective learning habits that enabled her to become a world-class financial advisor.

When you think about yourself, your team, and your organization, do you see any opportunities to break out of chronic performance and nurture better Learning Zone habits—perhaps like Lizzie's—to attain completely new levels of growth and results?

UNPACKING OUR LEARNING BAGGAGE

Why are so many of us dedicating countless precious hours to our work or our hobbies, yet still not seeing substantial progress?

Why do even superstar new hires progress so much slower than we know they're capable of?

And why is it so difficult to build organizations that truly encourage and foster growth?

The answer is that most of us, even highly trained professionals, have never been taught how to continuously grow and improve over time. We have been taught that to get better at something, we simply need to work hard. Or we've come to believe that once we are good at something—or even great at something—that's enough, we're done.

Why work on something we already excel at?

This has a devastating impact on our lives and careers. The world is ever evolving. If we don't commit to growing with it, we risk being left behind.

Just as playing as many chess games as possible is not a great strategy for getting better at the game, research shows that we don't get better at selling insurance or giving presentations just by doing these things repeatedly—unless we also experiment, solicit feedback, reflect, and implement change.

When it comes to performing skillfully, we need to stop focusing on just getting things done.

We need to adopt Learning Zone habits.

But first, many of us need to *unlearn* our assumptions about learning.

When I think back to my experiences in school, my memories of the classroom have a way of blurring together. For me, school was an endless parade of teachers lecturing us about things I didn't feel had any connection to my life—algebraic equations I didn't think I'd ever use, rocks whose properties I didn't care about, historical figures and places I didn't relate to.

The experience gave me a pretty good understanding of how to satisfy the teachers, my parents, and the system; how to memorize facts, pass tests, and progress to the next level.

But at what cost?

It got me stuck in chronic performance.

I never learned anything that seemed truly relevant to my life. Instead, I learned that the whole point of "learning" was to get a diploma so I could do other things. I carried that tragic lesson into the real world with my work in Silicon Valley. I was so focused on "doing my job" that I actually missed many valuable learning opportunities that would have allowed me to become more effective. I became trapped by the performance paradox.

Silicon Valley has a culture that places a lot of value on business lunches, which I now recognize tend to be very learning-oriented. People ask a lot of questions, pick one another's brains, and share business strategies and insights.

I always saw these business lunches as superficial networking opportunities, so I avoided them. If I had seen how much I could have learned from my peers about the work I was doing, I'm pretty sure I would have enjoyed the lunches a lot more—and gone to them.

In his book *No Rules Rules,* Netflix co-founder and former CEO Reed Hastings shares that he and other Silicon Valley executives occasionally shadow one another and debrief afterward. He understands something I didn't realize early in my career: Learning isn't something that only—or mainly—takes place in a classroom. It's something we should continue doing in our everyday work and life, no matter where we are. I wish I'd understood the connection between this kind of professional growth, innovation, and skillful execution earlier.

As I would discover, I wasn't the only one who needed some clarity about the connection between learning and performance.

Years later, when I began incorporating the two-zone framework into my workshops with executives and professionals, I was struck by how much the ideas resonated with them. Their eyes would light up when they grasped the distinction between learning and performance and when they realized just how much they'd been tripped up by the performance paradox. They could see more clearly the dynamics at play in their work and lives. The framework would generate strong insights and animated conversations, which led to clarity and better team alignment.

To get a vivid image of the two zones like my clients did, let's step out of our everyday lives and enter a realm of magic.

HOW TO BECOME A WORLD-CLASS PERFORMER

As anyone who has ever seen a Cirque du Soleil show knows—and over 375 million people around the world fall into that category— this art form requires performers with extraordinary skills. The awe-inspiring acrobatic feats executed by more than 1,000 artists from more than fifty countries couldn't happen without a well-oiled system for developing talent.

We might expect that Cirque du Soleil artists become so good because they devote a great deal of time to rehearsing their routines.

But let's pull back the curtain on the blue-and-yellow-striped Big Top.

In fact, if we were to walk into one of the training studios at Cirque du Soleil's international headquarters in Montreal, or their practice tents on the road, we'd see a lot of connections being missed and acrobats falling to mats and nets. That's because the artists don't spend much time practicing what they already know cold; rather, they work on the abilities needed for new acrobatic feats. This process allows the artists to improve, the show to evolve, and the organization to avoid the stagnation that would come if everyone spent all of their time in the Performance Zone.

Cirque du Soleil recruits many of its performers from the Olympics, bringing in athletes who have had years of effective training with top-level coaches who helped them become the best in their sport in the world. Nevertheless, when performers join Cirque du Soleil and travel to Montreal for their onboarding, they spend weeks or months working with two coaches, one acrobatic and one artistic, to learn the skills and routines needed to join a show.

Once artists leave headquarters and start performing, their daily routine often begins when they arrive at work at noon. But for most of the day, they aren't performing on a stage like they will later that night. They spend the afternoon in the Learning Zone, working on something specific like increasing the number of flips they can do in the air, or twirling one more fire baton than they could before.

There are key ways to ensure safety during this crucial period of learning—with fire batons unlit, say, until the performer feels capable of taking on that new challenge.

Think about it: While most of us are not tossing flaming rods in the air in our workplaces, we may be juggling decisions that have a significant impact on people's health, safety, or livelihoods.

Many of our choices are no less consequential simply because we're playing with numbers or words.

Yet how often do we create clear safety nets so that our teams can truly stretch our capabilities?

Performers at an innovative company like Cirque du Soleil are trained to know the difference between learning and performance. How many of us bring that same understanding to our own work and lives?

WHEN PRACTICE DOESN'T EVEN MAKE BETTER

When Melanie Brucks was a doctoral student at Stanford Graduate School of Business, she dove into the scientific literature on creativity and found something surprising: There was almost no research on whether practice and repetition can lead to more creative breakthroughs. Most people simply *assumed* they did.

Brucks teamed up with her Stanford colleague Szu-chi Huang, a professor of marketing, to investigate whether "practice makes perfect" applied when it came to brainstorming. Their research question was straightforward: If people practice brainstorming every day, will they get better at it?

The answer was a resounding no.

In fact, when they spent time brainstorming every day, they got worse.

Even more interesting, the subjects in their study *thought* they were improving. An independent panel of judges disagreed: The creativity of the ideas had decreased.

What was going on?

If you think about it, Brucks and Huang asked participants to *practice* the activity by *performing* the activity.

But what we're discovering is that when people "practice" anything by performing it—whether by setting up regular brainstorming sessions, playing lots of games of chess, or seeing lots of patients—they are not really practicing. What they're *really* doing is performing—trying to do something as best they can. It might not look like performing when there's no audience cheering you on or a manager evaluating you. It might not feel like performing when you're engaging in creative work like brainstorming.

But your brain doesn't know the difference. It's still focusing on what it knows and trying to do the best it can.

So, does practice make perfect?

No. In fact, *perfect* is one of those words I try very hard not to use because it implies there's no more room for improvement, which is the definition of a fixed mindset. Perfection can be a direction to progress toward, but not a destination, because it's unattainable.

But Brucks and Huang's study illustrates that practice doesn't even make *better*—if we "practice" by simply doing things as best we know.

True, effective practice looks very different: It involves focusing on specific subskills, trying something challenging, ensuring there are feedback loops to identify opportunities for improvement, making adjustments, and trying again. It's about paying attention to what we haven't mastered yet, grappling with something we don't yet understand or do well.

That's what it means to be in the Learning Zone.

How might a team looking to develop their brainstorming skills deliberately engage in the Learning Zone? The team members might begin by testing strategies, and then assess whether those strategies lead to richer brainstorming sessions. Research shows we can improve brainstorming effectiveness by including people of diverse backgrounds who have cross-cultural competence. Other tried-and-tested approaches include spending some time ideating in isolation before being influenced by others, focusing on quantity of ideas rather than quality, and playing games before brainstorming—having the team play a round of Wordle, for instance.

A team could easily devise a test by, say, having participants go for a brief walk in nature before their next brainstorming session and then assessing the quality of the discussion and ideas generated in the meeting.

My larger point here isn't just about how to enhance brainstorming sessions, but how to bring effective learning strategies to everything we'd like to improve. That's what's required to overcome the performance paradox.

Remember: In the Learning Zone—when our goal is to improve—we must focus on what we haven't yet mastered, which means we can't expect to execute flawlessly. Whether it is brainstorming, facilitating meetings, answering customer support calls, designing airplanes, or doing anything else, what we do in the Learning Zone is take on challenges, examine mistakes to learn from them, and determine what to adjust.

But what if you could integrate the two zones, so that you generate learning while performing what you need to accomplish?

Is that even possible?

To answer that question, bring to mind your last grocery shopping trip. You were most likely juggling more than one goal: choosing your favorite foods, fielding requests from family members, staying within your budget, and maybe searching for ingredients to try out a new recipe.

I imagine you were able to toggle between the different goals pretty effortlessly, and maybe you weren't even consciously aware of moving back and forth between budgeting goals and snacking preferences.

What if you could achieve that same elegant flow between learning and performance goals at any time?

In fact, you can.

That's what all effective teams and organizations do. It's how people improve their skills by leaps and bounds while doing high-quality work, and how companies become market leaders with sustainably higher growth and impact. We'll examine that in the next chapter.

THE ZONES ARE STATES OF MIND

It helps to remember what the zones are and what they're not.

The Learning Zone and the Performance Zone are states of mind and their related strategies. They're not places, blocks of time, or permanent states, but rather a way of thinking and acting.

So, what determines what zone you're in?

What you're paying attention to.

When you're focused on improving skills and using strategies to facilitate learning, you're in the Learning Zone. When you turn your attention to performing to the best of your ability, you're in the Performance Zone.

WORKING HARDER CAN LEAD TO STAGNATION

Here's the tricky part: Performing *can* lead to growth in the beginning stages of skill development.

When we first try something new, performance alone can appear to take us from zero skill to the most basic level of proficiency. Say you're grappling with stage fright because you've been asked to give a presentation—your first one. Even though technically you are performing by giving a talk in a room full of colleagues, you might also take note of areas to improve upon. You make a joke during your presentation, which creates a positive atmosphere in the room, so you make sure to include one the next time. People ask you to go back to a previous slide, so you learn to check for understanding. A colleague gives you some useful feedback, and you realize that being onstage doesn't have to be so scary. Your second and third presentations will surely be better than your first.

But after you become proficient, just going out onstage and speaking doesn't increase your skill level anymore. You might get stuck in chronic performance, preparing less and less over time and starting to use the same methods and jokes repeatedly. Soon enough, you stop improving. Worse, you might find that your presentations feel stale to you and to your listeners. You're doing the same thing over and over, and that's not enough to stay sharp.

That's the performance paradox in action. If we continue to limit ourselves to the Performance Zone, even if we operate at a high level, our skills and effectiveness will surely stall, and often diminish, over time.

Unless we're lucky enough to encounter a mentor who lays out the steps to improvement for us, as Venus and Serena's father did for them, we grow up without understanding the difference between the Learning Zone and the Performance Zone. We end up thinking the way to achieve and the way to improve are the same: just work hard to get it done.

Then, when our hard work leads to stagnation, we assume we've gone as far as we can. Or we conclude that the way to succeed is by working longer hours. We start associating success with constant execution, when the reality is a lot more freeing.

Regular engagement in the Learning Zone allows you to uncover and learn ways to work smarter, more efficiently, and more effectively. If you're looking to improve your speaking skills, you might watch videos of skilled speakers and compare them to videos of yourself, read books on ways to enhance your techniques, work with a coach, test something new each time you present, and solicit feedback. While it's tempting to stick to what you know—especially when you feel starved for time—engaging in the Learning Zone actually *creates* time as you learn how to improve your ability to prioritize, collaborate, and get more done in less time. This can be a playful and joyful process.

But while Learning Zone behaviors are essential to growth, we can't forget the importance of the Performance Zone.

PERFORMANCE IS NOT A FOUR-LETTER WORD

In the early days of our work evangelizing growth mindset, my colleagues and I noticed a clear trend: as people realized the power of learning, they frequently developed an aversion to performance. It seemed the pendulum had swung too far in the other direction! In the ecosphere of growth mindset advocates, *performance* was starting to be seen as a bad word. People spoke as if performance goals were inferior to learning goals and as if performance were antithetical to growth and improvement.

Too many people began seeing growth mindset as the end goal, not as just an important ingredient for transformation and increased impact.

But while learning is essential to growth, so is performance. After all, a chef can't just experiment with new recipes; she also needs to get meals plated and into servers' hands *fast* when the restaurant is at peak capacity. A baseball umpire can't just watch replays of his calls; he also needs to make the right call when the pressure is high — even if it means that tens of thousands of fans will soon be screaming for his head. A salesperson can't just read about effective sales techniques; she must convert prospects into customers.

Performance is not bad. It's necessary. It's how we get things done and how we contribute. We don't need to reject performance, but to balance and integrate it with learning so that we can expand our outcomes over time.

If we spend all of our time purely performing, we won't get better. But if we spend all of our time purely learning, we'll never get anything done.

By using the two zones, we increasingly grow our outcomes and impact.

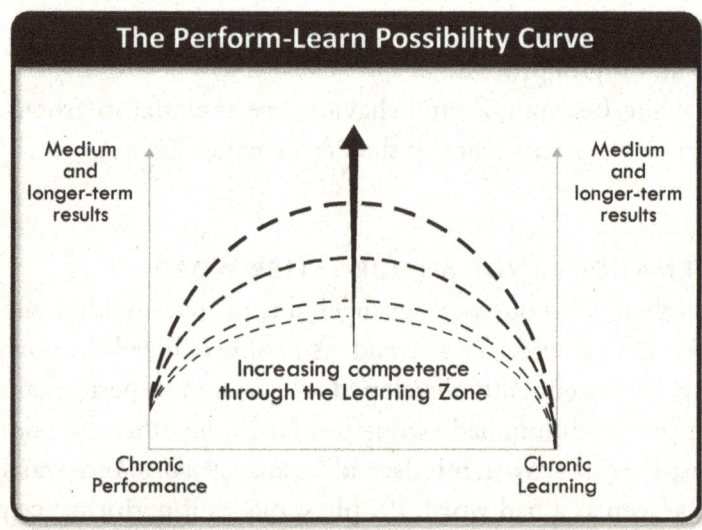

But how do we know when it's time to move from one zone into the other?

BREAKING FREE OF THE PRESENT BIAS

Imagine you're a sales rep trying to make quota for the last week of the quarter, and a big bonus hangs in the balance.

You are close, but not there yet. Should you engage in the Learning Zone that week by testing out a new strategy?

A very reasonable answer is no. It's probably not the time to rethink your sales pitch or try to break into a new market. When trying to maximize short-term performance, it makes sense to prioritize the Performance Zone.

But if you don't take a chance at the start of the next quarter to learn more about why a new product's features would matter to customers or to better understand a new target demographic, your sales are going to flatline—or worse.

The failure to prepare ourselves for ongoing change—and more broadly, to consider the future—is what behavioral economists call *present bias*. In other words, humans tend to overvalue the present and undervalue the future. Our drive to chronically perform is powered in part by our intense focus on getting things done now and reaping immediate rewards.

We treat every week as if it were a make-or-break last week of the quarter, and we assume that's what our bosses expect of us.

We see present bias play out at every level of our organizations and societies. As a Wall Street investment banking analyst, before my time in venture capital, I saw firsthand how much investors value public companies in large part based on their reported net income, or on their projected net income for the upcoming quarter or year, rather than the company's longer-term growth prospects.

The problem is, what the company earns this year or next can have very little bearing on what it will earn for its owners going forward. Imagine you owned shares in Apple back in 2007, the year it introduced the iPhone, when its net income was $3.5 billion. If you sold shares based on earnings from 2006 and 2007, rather than on the promise of future growth, you'd be leaving a lot of money on the table—after all, Apple's net income in 2022 was $100 billion.

Apple CEO Tim Cook put it this way, in a 2018 appearance on David Rubenstein's talk show, *Peer-to-Peer Conversations:* "We run Apple for the long term. It's always struck me as bizarre that there's a fixation on how many units are sold in a ninety-day period. We're making decisions that are multiyear kind of decisions."

Of course, it's hard to predict the future, which is one reason present bias holds such sway over our markets. But this pressure from analysts and investors leads many executives and senior leaders to engage in the Performance Zone as much as possible, which over time leads to decreased performance and cascades down the organization, spreading more broadly throughout the culture.

Despite the pull of the present, the world's most successful innovators and business leaders—Tim Cook among them—know that the only way to survive and thrive is to manage for the future and nurture the competencies needed to create it.

At Amazon, senior executives are pushed to "live in the future," according to founder Jeff Bezos.

"All of our senior executives operate the same way I do: They work in the future, they live in the future. None of the people who report to me should really be focused on the current quarter," he told fellow billionaire Rubenstein on *Peer-to-Peer Conversations.* "People will stop me and say, 'Congratulations on your quarter,' and I say, 'Thank you.' But what I'm really thinking is, 'That quarter was baked three years ago.' . . . You need to be [working] two or three years in advance."

It's clear that some of our greatest innovators understand the need to always be developing what comes next. But what about those of us who aren't being paid to create the future, rather to carry out our company's missions *today*?

Well, if you are seeking to grow impact, you are trying to create a future that is different from the present. Maybe it's a broader suite of products, better customer service, more streamlined operations, or more people served. If you are responsible for or part of improvements in any of those areas, you won't get there without engaging in the Learning Zone.

You can identify whether you're suffering from chronic performance by asking yourself a simple question: *What ability or quality am I currently working to develop?*

If your answer is "I don't know," you may be suffering from chronic performance.

Now ask a trusted colleague: *What ability or quality do you think I'm currently working on?*

If they can't answer that question, or if you're not regularly soliciting their feedback, you are not leveraging the power of collaborative learning.

Spending time in the Learning Zone builds our skills to better perform. But it also changes the way we think when we step back into the Performance Zone. We learn how to build in opportunities for feedback and reflection even when we're executing. In other words, we learn to integrate the two zones, which is a crucial skill we'll dive into in the next chapter.

REFLECTION QUESTIONS

- When have I engaged in the Learning Zone outside of school, and what has been the result?
- How much am I engaging in the Learning Zone in my daily work and life?
- How much are my teams and organizations engaging in the Learning Zone?
- How might my life change if I better internalize the two zones?

LOOKING FORWARD

Considering how busy I am, how might I integrate the Learning Zone into my daily life?

Chapter 3: Integrating the Learning Zone and the Performance Zone: Learning *While* Doing

BIG IDEA *We don't learn by doing, but we can learn while doing. Most of us will find our greatest opportunities not in dedicating blocks of time solely to the Learning Zone, but in changing the way we work so we regularly leap beyond the known while getting things done.*

When Simon Tisminezky was tapped to lead growth at the cosmetics subscription service Ipsy, the company was still small; all twenty employees sat together in one big room in their office in San Mateo, California. But Simon could see the company was primed for growth. It was able to retain its customers much more successfully than other subscription companies he had seen. In fact, Ipsy's churn rate—the rate at which customers canceled their service—was similar to Netflix's, which had recently gone public. That meant customers valued Ipsy's service—the company was onto something special.

But the startup had a major problem: It was growing too fast. So fast, in fact, that it didn't have enough products on hand to meet customer demand.

At the time, Ipsy provided a straightforward service: Each month, subscribers would receive a new "Glam Bag" full of makeup products, from glosses and serums to face masks and fragrances. What made the company so appealing to customers was also presenting a challenge to growth. The Glam Bags were filled with cosmetics samples from different partner companies—but those products needed to be ordered months in advance, and given Ipsy's meteoric growth, it was hard to forecast how much product would be needed.

Because they were a small startup with limited resources, they'd been wary about over-ordering. But when word of mouth about the service spread much faster than the founding team had forecasted, they found themselves facing a classic problem during the hypergrowth phase of a startup's life: more customers than product.

The team did what they could to avoid losing these eager new customers: They put new subscribers on a wait list while the manufacturing and logistics processes caught up.

But where did this leave Simon, whose main role was to further accelerate customer acquisition?

Simon didn't have the luxury of focusing solely on learning. He needed to help the company capitalize on the popularity it was enjoying. But neither could the new head of growth get stuck in the Performance Zone; after all, he had to figure out how to accelerate growth, and how to set up processes for the company to continue to grow for years to come.

Now, Simon was no stranger to managing exponential growth. As co-founder and CEO of the dating site SpeedDate, he'd helped the startup grow to twenty million users and tens of millions in annual revenue. But he was new to Ipsy and new to the world of beauty and consumer products.

How could he focus on learning and growth at the same time?

IF I ONLY HAD TIME TO LEARN . . .

During my fifteen-plus years of working with organizations and individuals committed to fostering greater growth and learning, I've heard the same initial frustrations time and again:

- I know there are areas I could improve upon, but when? I'm already working eighty-hour weeks. . . .

- If we had a bigger budget, I'd give my team more time to spend on learning, but we're all stretched too thin as it is. . . .
- If we weren't under so much pressure to hit this quarter's targets, then we could focus more on the capabilities we'll need in three or five years. But that's just not the world we live in. . . .

If you've had similar thoughts, know that you're not alone. How can we ensure that the time we commit to learning is really worth it? How can we focus on the kind of learning that actually *improves* our performance? And can a commitment to the Learning Zone actually *give us time back*?

In this chapter, we'll explore how some of the world's greatest performers move between the two zones even when the pressure is on, saving time and accelerating growth and performance in the process.

HIGH-ALTITUDE LEARNING

In the Academy Award–winning documentary *Free Solo,* we meet Alex Honnold, one of the world's best-known free solo climbers—climbers who scale unbelievable heights without the safety of a rope. To date, Honnold is the only person to have free soloed the 3,000-foot vertical rock formation in Yosemite National Park known as El Capitan.

But before attempting his free solo climb, Honnold had already climbed El Capitan about forty times—using a rope. That helped him get to know El Cap extremely well; he'd studied which hand and foot he was going to put where in which specific spots, especially in the trickiest locations. A key part of his practice involved imagining what each position would feel like if he were free soloing.

Honnold's skilled steps into the Learning Zone are lifesaving because when he is free soloing, he can't afford to make any mistakes—one error without a rope and he falls to his death. That's why he spends most of his climbing time *with* a rope. He also doesn't stay in the Performance Zone longer than he can handle—the moment he loses focus, he returns to the Learning Zone by breaking out the rope.

Now, you might be thinking:

- My life is not in danger.
- My work is unpredictable and fast-changing. At least a mountain stays in one place!
- I don't have time to practice forty attempts before doing something for real. And even if I did, my boss sure wouldn't go for it!

I understand such concerns. But in everyday work and life, integrating the two zones saves us time and increases performance. As we'll see, we don't need to scale sheer rock faces to embrace the spirit of Alex Honnold's commitment to the Learning Zone.

WHEN LEAPING IS THE ONLY OPTION

Sometimes we have no choice but to perform and learn at the same time. I was faced with one of those moments while giving a virtual keynote for Boston Consulting Group's senior partners across the world years ago.

My wife and I were living in Santa Fe, New Mexico, at the time, so my plan was to wake up at 12:35 A.M., which would give me enough time to step into the Performance Zone for the keynote that would be beamed far and wide at 1:40 A.M.

Now, I had put a lot of work into the preparations. I'd given presentations at various BCG offices before and thought deeply about how to share the work globally. During the weeks leading up to the event, I had collaborated with BCG's learning and development team to customize the session. We'd even practiced separate dry runs with the two hosts for the different time zones. We wanted to get it right because these are busy people who are constantly traveling for client meetings, so if we missed the rare opportunity when they were all together, we couldn't reschedule.

I was fully ready to step into the Performance Zone.

I woke up at just past midnight, got out of bed, turned on the light switch . . . and nothing happened. I turned on the other light switch—still nothing. I looked outside and saw that there was no power in the neighborhood.

I wouldn't be able to use my computer or lighting setup, and we had no internet service. I wasn't sure if my cellphone reception was reliable enough to use as a hotspot.

I didn't have a solution, but I knew I had a bit of time to think. For some reason, I didn't panic. Maybe it's because I was still waking up, or maybe it's because I knew BCG would be understanding. Whatever the reason, I tried to think of a creative solution while I brushed my teeth.

One thing I knew: If I could figure out a possible way to deliver the session, even if it involved risk, I would try it. I would need to leap into the Learning Zone even while performing. There was no other way.

The safe, tried, and true approach was not available. And neither was our Wi-Fi.

Santa Fe is a town of 85,000 people, where nothing is open in the middle of the night. Even so, I wondered if I could find someplace that had power and free Wi-Fi and access it from outside. But it would be dark, so the BCG partners wouldn't be able to see me presenting, which might be distracting and frustrating. I could try to present from inside my car, using the interior lighting to illuminate my face, but that would make for an awkward video, and besides, I wasn't sure I could park the car close enough to pick up anyone's Wi-Fi signal.

Then I thought of another option: I could use the car headlights. I could set up an impromptu desk in the driveway in front of our garage, line up both cars so that their headlights lit me, and use my phone as an internet hotspot. I had an external battery pack that would keep the phone functioning, and my laptop was fully charged.

I decided that was my best bet, and I went for it.

The clock was ticking before I was due to step "onstage." There was no time to rehearse. I had to learn on the fly whether my phone hotspot would give a strong enough signal. I had to learn how to give a keynote outdoors in the middle of the night, not knowing if I might be interrupted by an irritated neighbor, a foraging bear, or a curious mountain lion. And I had to figure out how to be a sound technician, lighting engineer, and speaker all at once.

In other words, even though I had to perform, I was also in the Learning Zone. Delivering a session without power was not something I knew how to do.

Right before logging in, I breathed deeply and told myself I was moving forward with the setup I felt was the best bet; now it was time to focus on doing the best I could as a speaker.

I explained to the organizers and the participants what was happening, made sure they could see and hear me, and focused on the speaking strategies that I knew would work well.

And it succeeded. The session got great reviews and the story spread within BCG, which helped them promote growth mindset within the organization.

I realized I'd learned a few things. I learned that, if needed, I can use my phone as a hotspot in Santa Fe, and I can use my car headlights to light my space.

But if the hotspot hadn't worked, I would have learned the valuable lesson of what didn't work well. Even better—having learned what can happen—I now have a battery-operated power station where I can plug in my lights if needed, and two different internet service providers with failover redundancy.

But perhaps the biggest lesson the experience reinforced for me is that it never hurts to be prepared to think creatively and take sensible risks. Because problems will happen: technical breakdowns, supply chain slowdowns, traffic jams, and every other challenge under the sun.

That doesn't mean we should always be anticipating the worst. But regular engagement in the Learning Zone ensures our continued growth and reminds us that it is always possible to stretch beyond our current capabilities, that we are never as "stuck" as it might first appear.

The Learning Zone enables growth, but it also enables a mindset shift, one that allows us to view even high-pressure performance situations as opportunities for learning. But the mindset shift is only part of the equation. Effective Learning Zone strategies are just as necessary.

THE LEARNING *BY* DOING TRAP

People often use the phrase *learning by doing* to convey their interest in becoming skilled at something by doing it. But that can easily be misinterpreted to mean that they simply *do* something and expect learning to follow. As I explained in Chapter 2, simply *doing* generates some improvement only while we are novices. Once we become proficient, it doesn't work anymore. We need to add some Learning Zone to our Performance Zone. That's why I like to call the integration of the two zones *learning while doing* rather than *learning by doing*—as a reminder not to just *do*.

John Dewey, Kurt Lewin, and David Kolb—education reformers who pioneered *experiential learning* and *learning by doing*—understood this. Their description of those concepts involved not only doing things, but also developing hypotheses, testing those hypotheses, and reflecting. The theorists usually represented the process as a cycle. There are different versions of this cycle, but they all boil down to the same basic process:

- Try something new and experience the effects.
- Reflect on your observations.
- Develop a hypothesis based on those observations.
- Plan how to test that hypothesis.
- Repeat the cycle by trying something new again.

This cycle is very different from merely *doing* because, as Dewey pointed out, "we do not learn from experience . . . we learn from reflecting on experience."

Traca Savadogo, now a speaker and relationship strategist, came up with her own version of this experiential learning cycle early in

LEARNING WHILE DOING CYCLE

try and experience something

reflect on your observations

develop a hypothesis for how things work

plan how to test that hypothesis

her career when she worked early mornings as a barista at a busy Starbucks in Seattle.

After her shifts, Traca attended college classes, and in the afternoons, she worked a second part-time job. She was also involved in student government, Model UN, and All College Council. To fit it all in, she would often start her Starbucks shifts at four in the morning.

As a sleep-deprived barista, Traca sometimes had trouble remembering orders, especially during the morning rush. She frequently had to ask her colleagues to remind her what she was supposed to be making, which was frustrating for them. She kept making mistakes, which led to waste, redos, and longer customer wait times. But she needed the job because it provided her with health insurance, not to mention regular caffeine infusions.

One day she came up with an idea: She asked her colleagues to write drink orders on the sides of the cups, rather than yell the orders over the noise of the brewing machines and customer chatter.

It worked—and not only did it solve her problem, the change also helped her coworkers better remember the orders and made the coffee shop quieter and calmer.

"We were the only store in the chain that did it," Traca told me.

But despite the success, when Traca started picking up shifts at other Starbucks locations, she encountered resistance to her suggestion.

This was not how Starbucks's employees had been told to do their jobs. Plus, writing down the orders involved an extra step that they didn't see the need for. Today, Traca would explain that the extra step helped her remember orders, but at the time she was hesitant to disclose what felt like a weakness.

Luckily, Starbucks is a learning organization. "They are always asking for feedback from their staff and customers, and they take it very seriously," she told me. Traca decided to speak up because she felt the company was building something great and she wanted to contribute. She already had data showing that the practice worked. She had experimented and gotten clear results.

She told them, "Not only is my accuracy going up, not only is the waste much better, now I can focus on the customer experience."

After continuing to improve on and refine Traca's idea over time, Starbucks now prints order information on cups globally. Regardless of whether the order is placed via the mobile app, a drive-through, a delivery partner, or in person, every cup has detailed instructions about what should go in it.

If Traca had just kept her head down and focused solely on performance, she would have continued to make the same early-morning mistakes and probably gotten fired, causing herself a lot more stress along the way.

Instead she pioneered an iconic practice that allowed her to thrive in her job, helped all other baristas, and made Starbucks locations quieter, calmer, and more efficient.

This story offers some clues about how to bring a commitment to learning even to high-pressure situations where there seemingly isn't much time to think or problem-solve.

1. **Take note of the problem.** Hint: When you notice that something isn't working, it's a great time to step into the Learning Zone.

2. **Devise a simple experiment**—a new approach to an old way of doing things. Traca paid attention to whether the "orders on the cups" strategy was working. Were customers satisfied? Were her coworkers happy with the change? Was it improving their track record for getting orders right?

3. **Ask yourself, "How might we magnify the impact?"** After getting positive results, Traca spoke up to share her discovery and suggested that other branches adopt the practice.

4. **Don't give up when you hit "know-it-all" resistance.** "That's not the way we do things here" was the refrain she heard when she first shared her idea with other branches. But her branch was experiencing a lot of success with the new practice. Why ignore a valuable lesson?

5. **Stay committed to performing.** Traca never stopped serving customers while innovating. She kept her focus on meeting customers' needs even as she asked herself, "How can we get better?"

Managers, take note: Traca Savadogo's simple, low-risk experiment is a powerful reminder of how a stubborn commitment to tradition can undercut creative solutions that improve a customer's experience. Whenever we hold too tightly to "This is the way we do things here" without considering that there may be better ways, we're effectively asking our employees to behave like robots, merely going through the motions of their jobs.

By empowering people to challenge the status quo by asking "What's not working?" or "How could things work better?" and then running small-scale experiments, we not only improve the customer experience, we empower employees to bring their own creative thinking and curiosity to their work, which increases their commitment and sense of ownership.

How is *learning while doing* different from simply *doing*? The following table teases out the difference:

	PURELY PERFORMING	LEARNING WHILE DOING
Goal	Perform	Perform & Improve
Strategies	Do the same in same way	Try new things
Plan	Only how to get it done	What to test & feedback
Sources of thoughts	Go with what I know	Solicit others' ideas
Reaction to new ideas	Implement only if quick	Consider & explore them
Reaction to mistakes	Disregard mistakes	Discuss & learn from them
Approach to feedback	Not solicit feedback	Solicit feedback
Reflection	Keep only doing tasks	At some point, reflect
An overarching approach	Stay within the known	Pursue challenging goals

Too many of us spend most of our time going through our to-dos with the sole goal of getting things done. But we have so much to gain by shifting our focus to getting things done in a way that will also lead to improvement. It's about staying curious, asking questions, trying new things, soliciting feedback, and paying attention to new information.

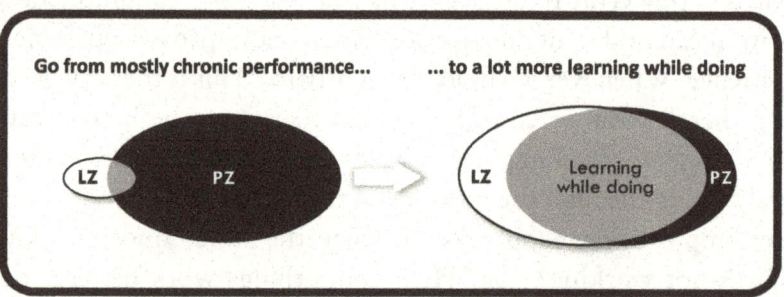

BRINGING IT ALL TOGETHER

Now that we've explored how to integrate learning and performing, let's return to Simon Tisminezky, the growth hacker we met at the beginning of the chapter, to see how he was able to help his new company achieve astronomical growth.

When Simon took to Twitter to see what people were saying about Ipsy, he saw that the company had a great product that people loved, and that customers went out of their way to share their positive experiences with others.

Still, there was room for improvement. Only 2.5 percent of customers were taking the initiative to share their love of Ipsy on social media; Simon knew that with a little prompting he could get a lot more people to share their "happy moments."

Most of the ideas they tested to promote sharing didn't work. But two worked wonders. The first was to move people up the Glam Bag wait list if they shared about Ipsy on social media. Customers could share anything they wanted; they just had to share something, such as their excitement about subscribing to the service, or a post about one of Ipsy's freely available videos.

The second key happy moment was when customers got a preview of the products they would be receiving in the Glam Bag that month. On the days Ipsy made that announcement, they had so much traffic on their website that their servers crashed. Simon created a way for customers to get the preview three days earlier if they shared Ipsy on social media. Not only did the second strategy incentivize sharing, but it also alleviated the burden on the web servers on the days of the regularly scheduled announcements.

These two strategies were so successful that at some point they were responsible for generating 60 percent of new Ipsy subscribers. Best of all, they didn't cost anything, other than the salaries of the employees working on brainstorming, testing, and analyzing the ideas.

These approaches allowed the company to grow at an extraordinary rate to $100 million in annual recurring revenue with virtually no advertising or marketing spending along the way—unheard of. This foundation enabled the company to eventually surpass a billion dollars in annual recurring revenue.

As for Ipsy's original forecasting challenges: As its practices and services matured, customer sign-ups became a lot easier to predict, even when the company was growing faster than ever before. Thanks to their commitment to learning more about their customers and to setting up systems and processes to drive growth, they became better able to forecast orders six months out. And while they had a large wait list until suppliers and inventory caught up, they were able to provide a means for the most eager new customers to get off the wait list and start enjoying the products right away.

Was Simon under pressure to turn Ipsy's early success into growth? Certainly. But his experience feels like a universal one. Who hasn't stepped into a new role or project feeling like there's so much to catch up on that they're already several months behind?

While we can always approach challenges and opportunities with an eye for what we can learn, we don't need to wait until the power goes out. We can make proactive learning a habit.

In the next chapter, we'll examine potent strategies to proactively drive our growth.

REFLECTION QUESTIONS

- Am I regularly engaging in *learning while doing,* or am I mainly spending my days just *doing*?
- Am I taking on real challenges that involve new knowledge or skills that require me to leap into the unknown?
- How might I engage in *learning while doing* every day, as an individual and with my colleagues?

LOOKING FORWARD

What skill or capability would I like to develop or further advance, and how might I go about doing so?

Chapter 4: Six Essential Learning Zone Strategies

BIG IDEA *Developing different competencies calls for different Learning Zone strategies. By periodically reflecting on how we're learning and then making adjustments, we can continue to get better at getting better.*

The performer steps off the stage to the sound of resounding cheers that continue well after she has sung her last note. If you were to ask one of the 45,000 adoring fans in the audience, they'd have told you that the show was *flawless*—no surprise that's the title of one of their idol's eighty-one *Billboard* hit songs.

But that's not how she sees it. As she told *GQ* magazine in 2013, she knows that no matter how good the show was, there is always room for improvement. That's why instead of crawling into bed after the show or hitting an after-party, she has other plans.

She goes back to the hotel room every night and before going to sleep reviews a video of the show she's just performed. She writes down critiques of herself, her dancers, her camera crew—everyone involved. The next morning, the entire troop receives pages of notes from the global superstar.

Beyoncé has been wowing millions across the globe for years, performing from the world's grandest stages. She has earned more Grammy Awards than any other artist and is the most nominated female artist in Grammy history.

Her concerts are famous for their breathtaking exhibitions of skill and creativity, a spectacle of routines that incorporate a dizzying array of moving parts, from dozens of talented dancers, singers, and musicians to remarkable light shows and dazzling costumes.

This is performance in every sense of the word.

But Beyoncé, like all skilled performers, has had to work hard in the Learning Zone to develop her abilities. As a child, she competed on the television show *Star Search* but didn't win, which she sees as a defining moment in her life, displayed at the start of her "***Flawless" music video. To overcome stage fright, she developed an alter ego that she calls Sasha Fierce.

And to this day, she continues to spend plenty of time in the Learning Zone.

"I watch my performances," she told *GQ*. "And I wish I could just enjoy them, but I see the light that was late. I see, 'Oh God, that hair did not work.' Or, 'I should never do that again.' I try to perfect myself. I want to grow, and I'm always eager for new information."

Even though she has been astoundingly successful in every aspect of her career, parlaying her talent and brand into a net worth of hundreds of millions of dollars, Beyoncé never stops learning and growing. By all accounts, after more than twenty-five years in the business, her music has deepened to become more challenging and introspective, and her performances are even more spectacular. NPR called her the most influential female musician of the twenty-first century.

So how can we all learn like Beyoncé?

In this chapter, I share six key Learning Zone strategies that are particularly powerful and that anyone can use. They range from understanding a unique kind of practice to taking a cue from a U.S. Army Apache pilot on how to turn down the volume when the stakes are nothing less than life or death.

LEARNING ZONE STRATEGY #1: PRACTICE DELIBERATELY

On August 26, 2021, the rock band Foo Fighters invited to the stage perhaps the most inexperienced drummer ever to play at the Forum in Los Angeles: eleven-year-old Nandi Bushell.

A year earlier, when she was ten, Bushell—who was born in South Africa and lives in England—had tweeted at the Foo Fighters front man, Dave Grohl, challenging him to a drum battle.

As he shared on *The Late Show with Stephen Colbert*, at first, Grohl thought the message was cute, but then a flurry of texts came in from his friends, urging him, "Dude, you need to step up."

"I thought, I'll play something simple and send it to her," he told Colbert. "One day later, she comes back with her response, and she just wipes the floor with it. This kid is, like, kicking my butt at the drums!"

For months, they went back and forth in public drum battles: Grohl would record himself playing a song and send it to Bushell as a challenge. She would learn the piece, practice, and record it, and send back a video of her expert performance, even mimicking Grohl's facial expressions. Their exchanges radiated joy, delighting millions of fans across the world during the COVID-19 pandemic.

A couple of months later, the two of them spoke over video for the first time in a Zoom call facilitated by the *New York Times*.

"I realized I'll never be as good as you," Grohl said, "so I just quit playing drums."

"Well, just practice, practice, practice," said Bushell.

While she lacked experience, she had something else that matters a lot more: *expertise*. That's what enabled her to play so masterfully that summer night at the Forum and steal the show.

As it turns out, expertise is something any of us can develop at any age—young, old, or anywhere in between.

"I play it slowly, bit by bit . . . to get it right," Bushell told the *Los Angeles Times*. "I think about, 'Am I doing this right?' . . . That's my way of working: play each section bit by bit and then eventually do the whole song in one go at full speed."

She did not simply practice—she *practiced deliberately*.

The late Anders Ericsson, the Florida State University professor who coined the term *deliberate practice*, spent much of his career studying how people become experts in their fields. He came to the conclusion that "experts are *always* made, not born." Nobody becomes an expert without having developed their expertise. And deliberate practice is one of the primary tools people use to reach the level of expert.

"Not all practice makes perfect," Ericsson, along with co-authors Michael J. Prietula and Edward T. Cokely, wrote in their article, "The Making of an Expert," published in the *Harvard Business Review* in 2007. "You need a particular kind of practice—*deliberate practice*—to develop expertise. When most people practice, they focus on the things they already know how to do. Deliberate practice is different. It entails considerable, specific, and sustained efforts to do something you *can't* do well—or even at all. Research across domains shows that it is only by working at what you can't do that you turn into the expert you want to become."

To engage in deliberate practice:

- Break down abilities into component skills.
- Get clear about what subskill you're working to improve at any given time.
- Give full concentration to a high level of challenge outside your comfort zone, just beyond what you can currently do.
- Use frequent feedback with repetition and adjustments.
- Ideally, engage the guidance of a skilled coach—activities designed for improvement are often domain-specific, and great teachers and coaches know what those activities are and can give us expert feedback.

Ericsson also conceived of another category called *purposeful practice,* which follows many of the same principles of deliberate practice, though perhaps without instruction from an experienced teacher or coach. As he explained in the *Good Life Project* podcast, "With purposeful practice . . . you can probably gain as much in two hours as you would in a couple of years just playing with friends."

Ericsson's research is sometimes erroneously simplified as the "10,000-hour rule"—but there isn't anything magical about the 10,000 number. The more performers engage in deliberate practice in an effective way, the more they improve, and the number of hours of deliberate practice it takes to become elite or world-class depends on a number of factors, including how competitive the field is.

If a tennis player spends all her time on the tennis court playing doubles with friends—in the Performance Zone, in other words—she will plateau after a certain amount of time and never improve much beyond that point. But if she is engaged in deliberate practice, a coach might place her on the court and feed her volleys of increasing difficulty, helping her correct her mistakes. By the time she gets back to a match, the mistake in her form will have been corrected.

LEARNING ZONE STRATEGY #2: LEARN BIG BY EXPERIMENTING SMALL

Olivier Perrin's colleagues were excited about their new product, a new style of yogurt that they'd created after listening to customer feedback. What more could a manager hope for than a passionate, committed team that was ready to launch big?

As he would soon discover, passion without a solid learning process can lead to derailment.

Olivier, who heads Global Product Design for General Mills, the behemoth multinational manufacturer of branded consumer foods, told me that he learned this valuable lesson early in his career.

His team initially wanted to do a small-scale experiment to test the yogurt in ten retail stores over ten weeks. However, they realized there was no way to manufacture the new offering on a small scale. The costs to do the test in ten stores would be almost the same as in a regional launch covering approximately 20 percent of the United States. They analyzed and discussed the issue and decided to go for the larger-scale launch. If things went well, then the larger initial footprint would allow them to scale faster and be further ahead of the competition.

When the product hit the shelves, the team quickly realized that although one region was performing to expectations, most were not. They were able to identify the main reason fairly quickly and came up with a solution that they could implement. But making the changes at the larger scale turned out to be difficult and time-consuming.

By the time they were able to shift at scale, most retailers had lost confidence in the product, which was taking up valuable shelf space. While disappointed, the team had no choice but to discontinue the product.

Upon reflection, Olivier and his colleagues realized that the larger-scale launch made it more challenging to achieve the main objective of the experiment: learning. While it might have seemed cost-effective to launch widely, given the high cost of producing small batches of the new product, the larger experiment turned out to be much more costly. Deadly for the project, in fact.

As Olivier's team recognized, the way they had structured their experiment was too performance-oriented; they were eager to scale before they'd learned enough, and there was no way to do another iteration quickly, which blocked their ability to continue learning. A big launch requires more time to make tweaks to packaging and marketing, more partner and customer relationships to manage, and more logistics to orchestrate.

Olivier's team is hardly the only one to be seduced by the lure of rapid scaling before sufficiently understanding the unit level.

Luke's Lobster, whose first location opened in New York in 2009, is a restaurant chain known for bringing traceable, sustainable seafood to customers across the country by working directly with fisherfolk and cutting out intermediaries. The company's growth has been remarkable, expanding in a decade from one restaurant in East Village to thirty additional locations.

As Luke Holden told Patrick McGinnis in the *FOMO Sapiens* podcast, when Luke's Lobster wanted to expand, industry veterans recommended adding restaurants in cities where Luke's already had stores, rather than expanding to new cities. That way, the company would limit its marketing and operational spend by concentrating on fewer markets.

Eager to implement the strategy, the lobster shack chain opened up many more locations. But this didn't work as planned.

It turned out that people don't tend to eat lobster like they eat hamburgers or burritos. Lobsters are more expensive, so people eat them less frequently, mainly on special occasions. Luke's customers were willing to drive farther to get lobster than they would to get tacos. Adding more restaurants created locations closer to customers, but it didn't expand the customer base proportionally to the number of locations.

Luke's Lobster concluded that a traditional clustering strategy used by many chains was not the best growth strategy for their brand. The experience also crystallized the importance of making sure to understand the customer before making decisions to develop a specific restaurant location.

Luke's Lobster could have learned those lessons more cheaply and quickly by testing their hypothesis in one market before expanding to others, which would have led to a higher return on investment for their remaining capital. But most important, they learned how to better learn. Now they invest more time and money up front to better understand neighborhood populations before building restaurants.

Experimenting at a smaller scale, with lower consequences of surprises and failures, and with ways to change and iterate quickly, tends to lead to greater learning faster. In other words, you'll be better equipped to scale *successfully* sooner.

This doesn't mean you can't test a few things at once. We first met the Peruvian education company iEduca in Chapter 1, when new CEO Douglas Franco was trying to lead the company on a path toward strong growth. When the COVID-19 pandemic started, iEduca began offering its courses online, which enabled it to start running quick and cheap experiments. Douglas was then able to encourage the executive team to start testing expansion into new markets by running one simple, standard experiment in multiple countries.

With a focus on geographic growth, they picked six countries with diverse characteristics, from large markets like the United States and Mexico to smaller ones like Panama and Bolivia. In some countries, like the United States, the results were so abysmal, they halted the experiment. In other countries, like Mexico, initial results were promising, so they continued experimenting and learning, looking for market-specific insights and optimizations. In the end, they spent less than $20,000 on all of these experiments combined. But that small investment allowed them to expand to three profitable new countries.

Experiments were so critical to iEduca's development that at some point they found themselves doing too many of them! So they set a budget for experimentation and decided to limit the number of experiments underway at any one time to fifteen. This has had the additional benefit of pushing them to get clearer about their experimentation goals and establish a three-stage process.

The first stage, Incubation, includes rough, quick experiments. If the results of a test show potential, the experiment moves to the Green stage, meriting larger investment and dedicated focus. (The Green stage was where iEduca learned that in Mexico, call centers were important.) Successful experiments then advance to the Optimization stage, moving from exploration to exploitation. In this final stage there's a greater focus on putting more money into what's working and then growing it, rather than just learning what works, though they continue to make small tweaks.

You don't even need a budget to run experiments. In my work giving keynotes and running workshops, I often run small experiments by making a slight tweak to part of the session. I don't completely overhaul things with all-new content and activities I've never used before. My customers hire me to provide an expert service, not to experiment on them with things I've never done before.

But I may add a new concept or activity that is tailored to the specific needs of the customer. Most of the time, those little tweaks go well because, over time, I have developed expert intuitions about the work I do, but sometimes people ask questions that make me realize I need to explain things in more detail or provide more examples, or allocate more time to the activity.

Chances are, you often do things you've done before, but in slightly different situations. Think through what tweaks may help in this new situation. You want to test something you think will likely enhance your performance, knowing that even if it doesn't, what you learn will better equip you for the future.

Remember:

- Clarify what you seek to learn before you scale or commit.
- Set up a small experiment to learn quickly and leanly.
- As you learn and reduce uncertainty, move from exploration to application.

LEARNING ZONE STRATEGY #3: WORK SMARTER, NOT HARDER

Tom Brady, widely considered the greatest NFL quarterback of all time, made it an ongoing practice to seek ways to preserve his health and extend his career. As a result, he became the oldest player in the NFL while still playing at an astoundingly high level. He capped off the 2021 season by winning his record-breaking seventh Super Bowl and fifth Super Bowl MVP at age forty-three. At the start of that football season, he described the method he used to find ways to improve his health and performance.

"I look at what everyone else is doing," he told Dax Shepard and Monica Padman in their podcast, *Armchair Expert*. "I'm in a locker room with every guy for twenty years. I look at everything they're doing. Everything they're taking. The way they eat. The way they talk about their body. And I'm constantly going, 'Okay, that doesn't work. That doesn't work.' But then, 'He's onto something.' And then you incorporate them into your routine. Then you go prove it."

This process started when he was in college at the University of Michigan, where his coaches extolled the value of experimentation.

"They gave me some tools—try this, look at things this way," he said. "It worked out, so I would say, 'F**k, more of that!' I'd go see our psychologist twice a week [instead of once]. I'd try that different technique throwing the ball. All right, what else can I tinker with?"

Over time, he learned the importance of working smart, not just working hard.

"Inherently we're taught that hard work is going to get you everywhere you want to go," he said. "I can work out once a day, so if I work out twice a day, I'll be better. My view of that is, if you're working harder at the wrong things, you're getting better at getting worse. If you have a good routine, a good process, I think you see the benefit."

We can always continue searching for ways to work smarter, whether individually or with others. Then we can test those ideas and reflect on what is working and what to change. We can also regularly get together with our teammates to solicit perspectives on areas of opportunity and what to try next.

Carlos Moreno Serrano considers his teammates a precious source of ideas. Based in England, Carlos leads customer success advocacy at Sonatype, a fast-growing enterprise software company with more than $100 million in annual recurring revenue.

Carlos sees the large number of new employees joining the company not just as people who need training, but as valuable sources of fresh ideas. Incoming employees have short, one-on-one meetings with all colleagues on their new team to start getting to know one another. During his meetings with newbies, Carlos always encourages them to question the way things are done, share their observations, and take the initiative to make improvements. He emboldens them to impact the operation from day one—despite Sonatype's three-month onboarding process due to the complexity of the software.

Richard Panman, a customer success teammate who had recently joined the company, proposed automating a core process that the team performed every day—an insights analysis report that includes statistics, information, and advice for customers. Over the preceding year, the team had reduced the amount of time required to create each report from two days to around seventy-five minutes, which made everyone very happy.

Still, Richard noticed that his colleagues spent a lot of time producing the reports. He examined the process and thought he might be able to fully automate it. Carlos thought that was impossible given the complexity of the sources of information, but he hoped Richard was right and didn't hesitate to encourage the newcomer to give it a try.

Richard wrote the code while he was still onboarding. Thanks to his innovation, the fully automated report now takes about one minute to create.

"He was able to get the same results without any compromises made. It completely blew our minds," Carlos told me.

Carlos nominated Richard as one of Sonatype's "values champions." At the internal company event where I spoke, they played a video of Carlos explaining how Richard exemplifies the company's core values.

"There are several values involved in this nomination; however, the one that stands out the most is *being bold*. This person just did it. Despite being new, despite still being on their onboarding, they just took the time to write the code, to do the automation. This is great, because it demonstrates that new teammates can make a big impact from day one."

Carlos's encouragement and Richard's follow-through led to something anyone covets: to work smarter over time. Here are some suggestions to help you get there.

- Make it a habit to consider what's working, what's not, and what to try differently. You can set a recurring calendar reminder to reflect on your own, or a section within a periodic meeting with your colleagues to reflect on this together.
- Identify challenges and points of frustration, and ponder how they might be turned into opportunities for improvement. For example, the number of meetings and how they are run are frequent sources of frustration and an opportunity for restructuring.
- Ask *why* you're doing what you're doing and how you might better achieve that higher-level goal. Perhaps there's a better way to achieve your end goal that is completely different from what you're currently doing.

- Deepen your expertise. Learn from articles, books, podcasts, or courses to expand your awareness of effective practices, which might inspire shifts in your strategies.
- Learn from people around you. Share your ponderings and ask others for their thoughts or feedback. More brains are smarter than one.
- Remember, there are always better ways of doing things, so take imperfection as a given and remain committed to consistent progress.

LEARNING ZONE STRATEGY #4: CREATE HABITS TO STRENGTHEN YOUR "AIR SENSE"

As the alarm went off in Shannon Polson's helmet, she knew she needed to make a decision—and quickly. She was flying an Apache helicopter mission over Bosnia, and the alarm was warning her that she and her co-pilot were in the crosshairs of the most lethal anti-aircraft system in the world.

Shannon knew that if the weapon were activated, which would take only the push of a button, she and her co-pilot would be dead.

A voice came on the radio.

"If you're nervous, return to station," the controller said, "but don't break the hard deck."

If you've seen the movie *Top Gun,* you know that "breaking the hard deck" means bringing the aircraft too close to the ground—and in the skies over Bosnia that would mean violating international rules of engagement.

"Nervous? Yeah, we were nervous," Shannon reflected. "And we had to make a decision in just a few seconds."

Shannon was an experienced pilot. In 1995, she became one of the first women in the U.S. Army to fly an Apache, one of the most advanced, formidable helicopters in the world. But in this moment, her ability to perform under pressure was truly put to the test.

So what did she do?

She reached over and turned down the alarm volume. Pilot and co-pilot continued on their mission.

Shannon told me her decision was informed by hours of briefings over days and weeks, as well as years of study, drills, deliberate practice in simulators, and countless missions. She'd also learned that provocation was more likely than actual engagement and that if they broke the hard deck, they would be breaking a rule of engagement and would likely be grounded, investigated, and possibly sent home.

In other words, the decision to continue the mission was informed by Shannon's *air sense*—the knowledge, expertise, and experience she'd developed into intuitions.

Her air sense got her through that pivotal moment. It wouldn't have been effective for her to start searching online for how to handle an antiaircraft system alarm. She was able to make a crucial decision on the fly because she was able to quickly weigh the risks and rewards and identify the most important and relevant things to focus on.

Now, few of us will find ourselves in the same life-or-death position as Shannon Polson. So, is developing our own version of air sense important? With the ubiquity of internet search engines and artificial intelligence, how much knowledge do we actually need to store in our heads?

If a direct report comes to us with complaints about a colleague, it is a lot more effective if we know how to handle the situation in the moment rather than search online. If we have developed our air sense, we may quickly take into consideration everyone's interpersonal skills, relationships, and the circumstances in order to decide how involved we should be. Our air sense informs what questions to ask and what guidance to give so if we decide to become involved in facilitating a conversation between the two colleagues, we'll know when and how to intervene.

If your multinational firm is attempting to launch in a new country, it is a lot more effective to have a deep understanding of the culture of the country you're traveling to than to read a brief memo about the place on your plane ride there. All the expertise doesn't have to reside in one person. Think about developing your team's collective air sense. How can you expand your recruitment to include candidates with deep knowledge of the language, customs, and trends of the region? What local partners can you team up with on the ground?

Integrated knowledge is useful at home, too. Alicia Ginsburgh, a friend of mine, shared a related anecdote.

"I was nine months pregnant when my water broke in the middle of the night," she told me. "My husband immediately turned over and started searching on his phone for 'woman water breaking.' I was like, I've been preparing for this for months, how about you GET UP AND HELP ME PLEASE instead of Googling right now?"

While we may shake our heads at the overzealous Googler, we have all experienced moments where we seem to lack the information we need to make the right call. My wife, Allison, likes to recall the time I started a fire in our toaster oven. I freaked out and started flapping my arms up and down like a flightless bird, not knowing what to do. She calmly walked to the toaster oven and unplugged it.

To develop your air sense, consider taking the following approaches:

TARGET AREAS FOR IMPROVEMENT

Clarify your highest-level purpose and your learning goals, and remind yourself each morning what they are. That way, over time, your purpose and goals will become top of mind as you go about your day. This will allow you to better notice information you come across that is relevant to your objectives and interests. For instance, if you remind yourself each morning to notice when you're in a fixed mindset, you'll become more adept at catching yourself and, eventually, at shifting your mindset.

FIND AND ACCESS HIGH-QUALITY SOURCES OF EXPERTISE

Subscribe to great podcasts, follow experts who regularly publish content on social media or in newsletters, or reach out to colleagues or mentors who may be up for regular meetups or working on projects together.

Develop habits to regularly access content in ways that work for you. I use an app called Pocket to save articles I'd like to read, and I keep a queue of videos I want to watch later when I have time or when I eat lunch. If someone recommends a podcast that sounds interesting, I subscribe to it on my podcast app. Sometimes while exercising on the stationary bike, I fully focus on deliberate practice to push my limits; other times, I do a less intense program so I can listen to a podcast while I exercise. The goal is not to access as much content as possible, or to get through all the content you find interesting, but to develop habits for accessing valuable knowledge regularly so that you can consistently grow your expertise and skills. The brain develops not through cramming lots of content quickly, but through steady engagement in the Learning Zone.

CONSIDER HOW YOU RESPOND TO CONFUSION OR SETBACKS

Whenever you don't know how to handle something or feel you were ineffective at solving a problem, like a conflict with a colleague or a customer question, flip to the Learning Zone. Gather feedback or ideas, or do an online search. Then, enter the new insights into one of your systems—such as daily reminders or digital flashcards— to integrate the new way of thinking into your air sense.

USE THE PEOPLE AROUND YOU AS A BRAIN TRUST

Make it a point to learn about your colleagues' strengths and areas of expertise, and even their hobbies and interests. The people in your life are a wealth of information, resources, and ideas. Likewise, share your own areas of knowledge and interest so they may call upon you when needed.

Encourage your team members and colleagues to share ideas and ask questions. If Carlos Moreno Serrano—the customer success lead from Sonatype who we met earlier—had not promoted an atmosphere of trying new ways of doing things, his new hire, Richard, might never have been emboldened to share his idea about automating the customer report.

I encourage you to develop your own approaches. You may find other methods that work better for you, such as journaling every day, or taking walks to reflect, or using a flashcard app (like the app listed in the resources web page for this book). We can always get better at using more effective strategies, which makes the journey of life more interesting and enriching.

LEARNING ZONE STRATEGY #5: DON'T BULLDOZE

As Anders Ericsson and his co-authors recounted in the *Harvard Business Review*, the violinist Nathan Milstein once became concerned when he observed the way other musicians practiced all day long, while he practiced much less. So he asked his mentor, legendary violinist Leopold Auer, how many hours he should practice. The elder responded, "It really doesn't matter how long. If you practice with your fingers, no amount is enough. If you practice with your head, two hours is plenty."

Milstein concluded that one should "practice as much as you feel you can accomplish with concentration."

Whether you're in the Learning Zone or the Performance Zone, *bulldozing*—my term for using all your time to do one thing as much as possible—may work for short periods of time, but as a long-term strategy, it's more effective to work on getting better at alternating mental and emotional states. Just like being in cheerleading mode all day, every day, would be exhausting and ineffective, so would constantly being in reflection mode, or feedback mode, or sleep mode. Ten thousand hours of cramming are very different from ten thousand hours of focus interweaved between creative activities and rest. In fact, scientists who have won the Nobel Prize are more than twenty times as likely as other scientists—and the general public—to act, dance, or engage in other performing arts as hobbies.

Many people believe that the more you engage in deliberate practice, the better you become. But in their groundbreaking 1993 study, Ericsson and colleagues Ralf Krampe and Clemens Tesch-Römer found that world-class performers limit their engagement in deliberate practice because high-quality deliberate practice requires full concentration at a level that the brain can't sustain all day.

In other words, rest is essential.

The violinists included in the study rated sleep as being highly relevant for improvement of violin performance. These elite performers napped to recover from practice and slept an average of 8.6 hours per day, compared to the 7.8 hours per day reported by less-skilled students. This finding was consistent with other studies in which elite performers judged sleep as being extremely important and were found to sleep more than the general population.

This points to the importance of finding routines that work for us. Ideally, we'd find ways to consistently get a full night's sleep. At times, you may need to temporarily go into crunch mode and sacrifice some sleep, but what is your default?

A lot of people find it helpful to establish a consistent daily cadence. For example, I like to go to bed early and wake up without an alarm. It makes me feel great and enables my mind to work well in both the Learning Zone and the Performance Zone. I've learned to find and prepare nutritious foods that I find delicious, which gives my body and mind what it needs. Most days, I don't drink coffee, but when I have to go to bed late and the next day's performance is important, I find that morning coffee provides my mind with extra stimulation that helps me perform well.

I share my rituals just as examples. Different strategies will work for different people, because we're all diverse in our preferences, situations, and pursuits. Each of us needs to find and develop the orchestra of habits that will feel harmonious.

As you reflect on your habits, consider the pace of how you work throughout the day. Some people like to set a timer when doing deep work—concentrating on just one thing for an extended period of time. When the timer goes off, they take a brief break and stretch. I do a modified version of this. I set my alarms each morning for all the points of the day when I'll need to stop what I'm doing and pay attention to my calendar for an upcoming appointment. Then, when I start a block of deep work, I write down the earliest time I'll stop the task at hand, silence all devices, and close down all sources of distraction. I use an app that plays special instrumental background music to help me focus. I usually get so engrossed in what I'm doing that I stay in a state of flow way past the original time I wrote down. Afterward, when I'm at a natural stopping point in the work, I take a break, move around, let my mind wander, or do a different kind of work or activity.

This works for me. Something else may work for you.

Periodically, we might try a new strategy, see how it works, and iterate to make sure that we're continuing to evolve. Without change, there cannot be improvement.

Jean Monnet, the French entrepreneur and diplomat who is considered one of the pioneers of the European Union, wrote in his memoir that his morning walks in nature were critical to his problem-solving. That's where he came up with ideas—though, of course, his brain had been seeded by everything he read and did the rest of the day. He couldn't have accomplished all that he did just by walking in the woods without contact with the outside world. Both solitude and stimulation were essential to his brilliance.

Since much of our behavior is nonconscious, we have to be proactive about the habits we foster.

For the great physicist Albert Einstein, music was a habit that not only offered him great joy, but also enhanced his work. There is considerable evidence that his genius was significantly enriched by his immersion in music. Einstein, an accomplished violinist, said if he had not been a scientist, he would have been a musician.

As reported by *The Conversation*, his second wife, Elsa, recalled a time when Einstein appeared to be "totally lost in thought." He would wander back and forth from his study to the piano, play a few chords, then jot down notes. At the end of two weeks, he "surfaced with a working draft of the theory of general relativity."

LEARNING ZONE STRATEGY #6: ASK WHY

To be effective and motivated learners, we need to:

- believe we *can* improve (growth mindset);
- know *how* to improve (through the Learning Zone);
- have a *why*—a reason to put in the effort to improve (this can

be through a sense of purpose, finding the activity interesting or fun, or feeling part of a strong learning community).

Those are what I call the *cornerstones of change*.

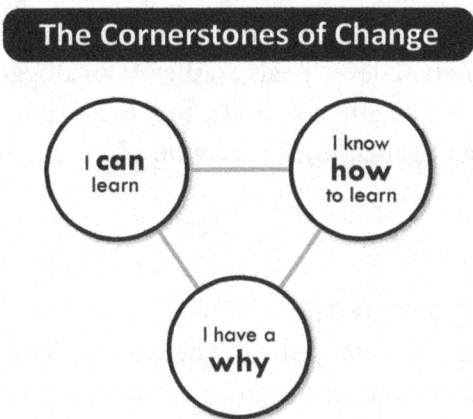

We sometimes lose sight of our *why*. Even in the Learning Zone, we sometimes get stuck asking ourselves only *how* questions. *How* can I better describe the product features? *How* can I better lead meetings? *How* can I become a better tennis player?

While *how* questions are critical, *why* questions can help us find completely different ways to achieve our higher-level objectives.

Why do I want to better describe the product features? Maybe it's to get people excited about the product. *Why* do I want to do that? Maybe it's to help them see it as a must-have. *Why*? So they can take action to get what they need. Okay, that's a more important, higher-level goal, so how can I better do that? Maybe I'd start by asking them questions about the problems they're facing rather than talking about product features.

Why do I want to better lead meetings? Maybe it's to foster more effective teams. How can I better do that? Maybe by coaching others to lead the meetings.

Why do I want to get better at playing tennis? Maybe it's so I'll have a way to blow off stress from the workday and spend time with friends who also play tennis. Maybe I can find additional ways to de-stress and enjoy time with friends while doing easygoing activities.

Just as we can make the mistake of bulldozing by doing the same activity all day, we can make the mistake of staying too focused on improving lower-level goals. Asking *why* questions gets us unstuck. We want to be the most growth-minded and persistent when it comes to our highest-level goals, rather than doggedly pursuing things that may not be effective in the first place (not to say that the things above aren't valuable, but we won't know until we ask *why* and reflect).

A UNIVERSE OF STRATEGIES

Some of these strategies may already be a part of your days, but by intentionally ritualizing them you can ensure you make a habit of consistently spending more time in the Learning Zone.

Some strategies will work for you, others won't. The key is to experiment to find what works for you and to continue to improve from there.

While I have highlighted some of the most powerful, universal Learning Zone strategies, there are many others. Some of them are domain-specific, such as practicing music scales or analyzing a chessboard position in a game between grandmasters and understanding why the grandmaster moved as she did. Other learning strategies are more general and can be applied to any domain—think experimenting, apprenticing with someone more experienced, or job-shadowing a colleague or friend.

Some Learning Zone strategies take dedicated time, such as deliberate practice, reading, or online research. Others take very little time, such as paying attention to surprises or mistakes, capturing new ideas so we don't forget them, or listening to a podcast while walking the dog.

Some strategies help us proactively drive our growth, such as taking time to identify what area needs improvement, consulting with others about how to improve, and soliciting feedback when we perform. Other strategies are about responding to surprises in a way that generates learning instead of dismay or regret. The following chart plots different Learning Zone strategies on these two dimensions.

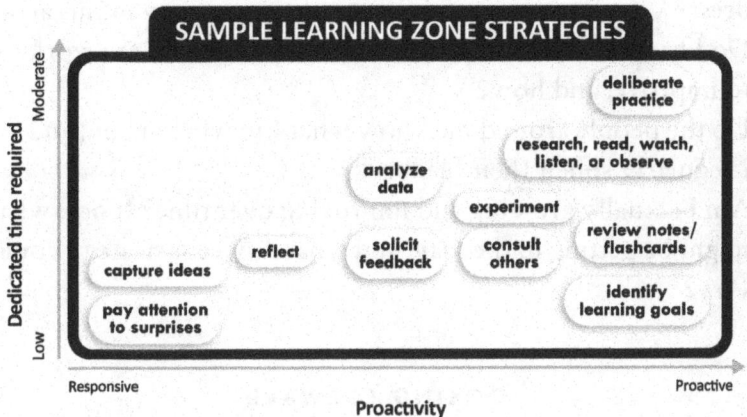

No matter what skill you're trying to improve, here is a universal formula:

1. Identify what skill you want to improve.
2. Read or listen to experts discussing how to develop that skill.
3. Try what they recommend.
4. Regularly gather feedback and reflect on how to evolve your practice. When you hit a plateau, what new exercise, experiment, or strategy could help you rise above it?

REFLECTION QUESTIONS

- What skill do I consistently want to improve but never address? Which strategies can I use to help me grow in this area?
- Do I have a way to remind myself daily of what I am working to improve, and how?
- Do the people around me know what I'm working on, and do I regularly solicit their feedback?
- Am I actually growing and improving over time? If not, what might be getting in the way, and what different strategy could I try?

LOOKING FORWARD

When and how do I go about eliciting, making the most of, or avoiding mistakes?

Chapter 5: Unleashing the Power of Mistakes

BIG IDEA *Mistakes are not universally good or bad. To improve learning and performance, we need to get clear on how and when to elicit, try to avoid, and respond to different kinds of mistakes.*

University of Texas professor Robert Duke and his colleagues set out to study the best way to improve at playing the piano. They asked advanced students to learn a passage from Dmitri Shostakovich's *Concerto No. 1* and instructed them to practice it as long as they needed, until they could play confidently at the target tempo without the metronome.

The following day, the students were asked to perform the piece. The practice sessions were closely analyzed and the performances independently ranked.

The conclusion?

The researchers discovered that the strategies the students used during practice made a lot more of a difference to the quality of their performance than "how much or how long they practiced." They also found that "the most notable differences between the practice sessions of the top-ranked pianists and the remaining participants are related to their handling of errors."

The top-ranked pianists initially made the same number of errors as the other participants; the difference was, they used strategies so they would not continue to make the same mistakes. The students identified the specific source of their error and practiced the needed adjustment repeatedly until they had corrected the issue.

As this study illustrates, mistakes—as painful as they can be—are important and powerful tools. Mistakes are fundamental to continuous improvement. They're also an essential part of innovation, which entails identifying problems that have not yet been solved and coming up with new solutions. This process requires us to closely observe the world, develop hypotheses for what might work better, and test ideas. Most of those ideas won't work, so we reflect on why, generate learning, make smarter attempts, and eventually create viable innovations.

In a fixed mindset, mistakes sting because they feel like personal flaws; we may even use our mistakes as an excuse to quit. But in a growth mindset we can examine our mistakes to learn from them and go on to develop greater competence in whatever skill the mistake relates to.

I think, on some level, many of us understand that we can learn from our mistakes and that they can make us stronger. But the reality is even more compelling: Even at a biological level, mistakes are *crucial* when it comes to changing our brains and developing our abilities.

In his podcast, Stanford neuroscientist Andrew Huberman points out that after about age twenty-five, the only ways to trigger neuroplasticity—changes in the brain's wiring that shift our thought patterns—are when something really surprises us, when something very bad happens to us, or when we make mistakes. Errors prompt our brain to sit up and pay attention: *Something new is happening here.*

Since nobody wants to actively pursue tragedies, and because it's hard to proactively elicit surprises, the most effective way to drive our own neuroplasticity is to engage in challenging activities we can't do flawlessly, and learn from the errors we make along the way.

Let's dive a little deeper into the science to understand how this works.

When we are engaged in trying to learn something new, the struggle we encounter around mistakes causes our nervous system to release a chemical called epinephrine, which increases alertness, and another called acetylcholine, which increases focus.

With these chemicals in play, our brain starts figuring out how to correct the error.

Then, when we experience some success, another chemical is released—dopamine—that allows for the plasticity, the learning, to take place. As Huberman points out, quitting in frustration and walking away from a new challenge is the worst thing we can do because that feeling of frustration is actually a signal that neuroplasticity is about to occur.

Discomfort means the brain is right on the verge of change.

If we stay with the struggle until we experience a little progress, the dopamine tells the brain that this new approach is working better than the old one. This is what starts the neural rewiring process.

If we don't try, the brain never rewires for the better.

If we quit, the brain will get better at quitting.

If we keep going, the brain will get better at persisting.

Keep that in mind the next time you feel tempted to tuck the guitar back in its case or give up on the spreadsheet formula you're grappling with.

Even if you are usually quick to throw in the towel, take heart: Huberman notes that we can actually train our brains to see the frustration as a *good thing*. We can change our mental models to appreciate and even *enjoy* the process of grappling with mistakes and the growth that comes from it.

In this chapter, we'll see how.

THE POWER OF REFLECTION

To learn and improve, we must not only make mistakes; we must pay attention to and reflect on our mistakes. Noticing a mistake should be a cue to get into our Learning Zone, observe or discuss the mistake, and explore what we can learn from it. We can ask:

- What can I learn from the mistake?
- What will I do differently going forward?
- If my mistake harmed someone, is there a way for me to repair the harm I caused?

Researchers from Michigan State University found that after making a mistake, individuals in a growth mindset paid significantly more attention to their errors and showed superior accuracy on subsequent problems compared with individuals who were in more of a fixed mindset. The researchers concluded that "awareness of and attention to mistakes are intimately involved in growth-minded individuals' ability to [learn and] rebound from mistakes."

Mistakes themselves don't lead to learning; *reflecting on mistakes* does.

How can we reflect on a mistake? Not by obsessing over it or letting ourselves be consumed by things that are beyond our control. We simply identify and make note of what we can do differently going forward.

There is always room for improvement. We will never do anything perfectly. The world is too complex for that. By accepting mistakes as a necessary part of life and learning, we don't need to get upset when we make one. We examine it, identify what to change, and move forward with greater wisdom.

There is seldom a single explanation for anything. If something goes wrong, it is usually partially because of something we did and partially because of other factors. The more we take responsibility and focus on our part—which we can change—the more we learn from our actions and improve our future results. Others will thank us for this.

Marcelo Camberos, CEO and co-founder of Beauty for All Industries, the creator of the beauty subscription brands BoxyCharm and Ipsy—which we heard a bit about in Chapter 3—points out that almost all of the major decisions that made his company successful started out as mistakes.

Take the way he spent most of his time in the early days of the company.

"I thought I had an instinctual feel for where I was spending my time, but . . . I was spending like forty percent of my time on hiring," he told me. "If I had just stopped for a second and mapped out where I was spending my time, and not necessarily trusted my instinct all the time, then I think I could have resolved that sooner."

Marcelo eventually learned it would benefit the company to hire someone with expertise in effective hiring procedures, and to delegate both the setup and the execution of hiring to that person. That's what he did when he hired Jennifer Goldfarb and made her a cofounder.

"This is my first scale startup and so I did not know what I was doing," he said. "And so I was learning every week, drinking from a fire hose." Marcelo realized that if he had paid closer attention to how he was spending his time, "it would have saved me a lot of time and a lot of consternation."

Marcelo's responses to his mistakes allowed him to identify big opportunities for improvement and implement change. He promoted mistake analysis and course correction as a cultural norm, practices that became key to the company's extraordinary success.

UNPACKING MISTAKES IN COMMUNITY

We can reflect on our mistakes on our own, but the results are even more powerful when we do so in collaboration with others.

Some medical organizations have made great strides in recent years by bringing together professionals to talk about how to reduce common errors and improve patient outcomes. Tomoe Musa directs patient safety for a provider of risk management services for large medical centers that collectively employ thousands of doctors. Her job is to help share best practices with doctors and assist them in identifying areas where they might be at risk of harming a patient. When the company's research revealed that spinal surgery was a leading area for malpractice claims, Tomoe was able to form a collaborative cadre of orthopedists and neurosurgeons to evaluate cases and together figure out what was going wrong.

"Neurosurgeons and orthopedists do not typically work together," Tomoe told me. "In some ways, they almost compete with each other for these patients."

Tomoe brought the doctors together at a restaurant—a comfortable, noncompetitive setting, outside of their hospitals, where they didn't feel the usual time pressures. The doctors had selected some of their case studies to review as a group.

"Lo and behold, everybody thinks every single case is unique, but after a while, they all start looking the same and you think, gosh, we are making the same mistakes over and over again," she said. "All of a sudden, they start to realize major areas for improvement. 'Oh my gosh, maybe we should not do surgery on people with certain injury profiles, because it doesn't help.' "

Surgeons are specialists who are expert at solving specific problems using surgery, so they tend to think of their solution as the optimal one. But that's a human tendency that is not unique to the medical profession. As the old adage goes, "If the only tool you have is a hammer, everything looks like a nail."

Similarly, as salespeople interact with customers, they may not think through or share insights that could be helpful to the marketing or product development teams. Or customer support may be so focused on solving the customer problem at hand that they may not identify how other parts of the organization could prevent a specific problem from happening in the first place.

As MIT professor Peter Senge noted in his seminal book *The Fifth Discipline*, one of the key competencies that differentiate learning organizations is *systems thinking*.

Encouraging more cross-functional communication and collaboration helps develop our ability to think more in terms of systems, so we can come up with better solutions that go beyond our silos. Some companies have created forums to communicate and collaborate not only within their walls, but also with their suppliers, customers, and partners.

Many companies use retrospectives or after-action reviews—whether within or across departments—to reflect on projects that don't go smoothly, not only to find the immediate fix for the case at hand but also to identify process improvements.

To accelerate learning, some organizations have instituted ways to elicit mistakes. Employees practice challenging situations and examine the failures generated. ClearChoice Dental Implants created a physical space for consult simulations so its patient education consultants could role-play, try different strategies, and learn from mistakes and feedback in a low-stakes setting. Even NFL teams now use virtual reality simulations to train quarterbacks. This allows them to challenge themselves and then talk about their mistakes with a coach in a situation that looks like a real game but in reality is a 360-degree video—a very low-stakes setting.

Mistakes can be a source of awe, exploration, deeper relationships, laughter, and joy in life, but we might need a mindset transformation to see them in this way.

Whether as individuals or as members of teams or organizations, we often find ourselves facing a conundrum when it comes to mistakes: We may be aware that mistakes can help us learn, but we also want to be seen as high performers who can be trusted.

This can create mixed feelings, anxiety, and a lack of clarity and alignment within ourselves and in our relationships with others. For example, we may encourage our team to take risks and make mistakes, but what happens when someone takes a risk that ends up sending key customers knocking on another firm's door?

By creating a shared language and understanding around mistakes, we can increase our performance today and pave the way for growth tomorrow. That means we must agree on when to focus on what we know and when to take risks in the service of learning.

The next section shows us how.

THE FOUR KINDS OF MISTAKES

Mistakes may be useful, but aren't some less desirable than others? And doesn't high performance—something most of us aspire to— mean making fewer mistakes? Rather than making blanket statements about mistakes being all good or all bad, it is helpful to differentiate between different kinds of mistakes and clarify which mistakes we want to pursue and how, and which mistakes we want to try to avoid.

SLOPPY MISTAKES

Your heart seizes up when you see what just happened.

You "replied all" to your entire company when you meant to write back to just your colleague Kim, with whom you were sharing a cute cat video.

One by one, the replies start rolling in.

Including one from your boss.

Congratulations! You have just made a *sloppy mistake*.

Sloppy mistakes happen when you're doing something you already know how to do, but you do it incorrectly, usually because you lose concentration or you're focused on the wrong thing. We all make sloppy mistakes occasionally because we're all human. However, when you make too many of these mistakes, especially on a task you intended to focus on, it signals an opportunity to enhance your focus, processes, environment, or habits.

I like to take most sloppy mistakes lightheartedly and laugh at them—I even keep a blog where I share them with others. My sloppy mistakes frequently come from focusing intently on one task, which results in collateral damage in the periphery. This might mean breaking the occasional glass because I am too focused on solving a work problem and not paying enough attention to my surroundings.

I'm okay with that.

We might be tempted to conclude that sloppy mistakes offer few learning opportunities; after all, we don't want to fret over every little blunder. But since even sloppy mistakes can have serious consequences, any time we make one, it makes sense to pause and reflect.

In leading team meetings, one sloppy—but significant—mistake I have made is failing to pay enough attention to the dynamics within the group, the balance of who is talking, or any interpersonal tensions. When I realized that kept happening, I had to identify what to try differently. I began taking two minutes before meetings to think about the people I was meeting with and my objectives for the meeting, and to remind myself that, as a leader, my job was to facilitate the development of an effective team, rather than focus intently on solving the problem at hand.

The next time you make a sloppy mistake, ask yourself, "Is this important to me? Do I want to change something so this doesn't happen again? If so, how can I adjust my focus to avoid making this type of mistake in the future?"

AHA-MOMENT MISTAKES

David Damberger, an engineer and social entrepreneur who was formerly one of the directors of Engineers Without Borders, has shared the powerful lessons that the organization learned when it was building systems in Africa and India.

In a TED Talk, Damberger told the story of Owen, one of the organization's staff members in Malawi, who discovered that 81 of the 113 gravity-fed water systems that the Canadian government had funded in one community were no longer working, a mere year and a half after the system had been built.

"This situation is typical," Damberger remarked. He said part of the problem is that when people donate to charities, they feel better when the money goes to something tangible, like building a well or a school, rather than to spare parts and maintenance needs.

When Owen discovered the inoperable water points, he also saw that there was an older system sitting no more than thirty feet away—this one built by the U.S. government. It, too, had broken down about a year and a half after its installation.

"How is it," Damberger wondered, "that a project that failed ten years ago was rebuilt with almost the same technology, same process, and had exactly the same failure ten years later?"

Engineers Without Borders also works with under-resourced schools in India. Some schoolchildren were spending two to three hours every day fetching water for drinking or for using the bathroom. Damberger worked with the communities to install a system that would collect rainwater from rooftops.

A year later, however, when he checked in to see how everything was going with the installations, he learned that not a single one was still operating because no maintenance schedule had been put in place.

"I had made the exact same mistake that I criticized earlier," he said. "When I thought of my friends and family back home who thought I was such a hero, I felt like an impostor."

Engineers Without Borders realized that to solve this widespread problem, the entire NGO system needed to become more transparent and accountable. A big step in that direction was to start admitting failure, discussing it, and learning from it.

"Admitting failure is actually quite hard, and I didn't tell many people about this," Damberger said. "And one of the only things that helped me feel better about this—and it's a bit of a shame to say this—was that I started to learn that other people in Engineers Without Borders had failed, too. . . . And it was only through a bunch of us talking about failure that we really got to see we're making a lot of mistakes, and we're making the same mistakes and can learn from them. And we started to innovate and change."

A decade on, Engineers Without Borders now publishes an annual failure report citing the organization's biggest failures. It also built a website called admittingfailure.org, where it invites other organizations to share their failures to help the sector learn. This helped international development professionals become more willing to share mistakes and lessons learned, and helped the sector to improve.

Aha-moment mistakes like these are those that happen when you do something as you intended, but realize it was the wrong thing to do. At that moment, you have a powerful realization—an *aha!*— a strong, new insight that expands your understanding and awareness.

You installed a rainwater harvesting system as you intended, but then realize that such projects need mechanisms for maintenance.

I have had many such aha-moment mistakes in my career. Years ago, in my keynotes and workshops, I began nudging people on the value of diversity and inclusion. Organizations were bringing me in to learn about growth mindset because they wanted to foster a culture of continuous improvement and innovation. One way to advance their higher-level goal—aside from growth mindset—was to promote diversity and inclusion, so I took opportunities to point that out.

At the time, I was participating in biweekly race and privilege working group meetings with peers. We would assign ourselves a reading or a video to watch before each discussion. One day, after one of those discussions, I was preparing the slides for a keynote when I realized that the images in my presentation reinforced the stereotypes I was trying to combat, instead of helping to break them.

It dawned on me that when I was preparing my slides, I was searching for images that would effectively communicate whatever idea I was trying to convey, without considering demographic characteristics like race or gender. The result was a set of images portraying white males as professionals and leaders, and people of color as athletes, while women were underrepresented. Because I had recently engaged in the Learning Zone with my peers—and we had examined the power of images—I was able to see my visuals with different eyes. I realized I had to *think* about race and gender while putting together my presentation images; that the visuals I chose were an opportunity to help people make different associations in their brains, to help break stereotypes and unconscious biases.

In general, learning opportunities in diversity, equity, and inclusion often stem from aha-moment mistakes. We sometimes offend or trigger other people or act in biased ways unintentionally. We can proactively learn about the experiences of people from other sociodemographic groups by reading books and articles, listening to podcasts, and consciously doing the work of becoming aware. But in addition, it helps immensely to create a safe space for others to speak up—as they have the energy to do so—when we make aha-moment mistakes so that we can learn from them and increase our self-awareness and understanding of social dynamics. It's important to then follow through with change.

Aha-moment mistakes can be hard to spot and can go unnoticed, even over a lifetime. How many leaders continue to do something that frustrates the people they lead—sometimes for years—while remaining unaware of the effect of their actions because they never solicit or otherwise receive feedback?

I used to be in the habit of emphasizing important comments my colleagues made by repeating their remarks in my own words and explaining why I thought they were significant. Eventually, through doing work in the Learning Zone to expand my awareness of common experiences of underrepresented groups, I learned that I may have been making my colleagues feel I was trying to take credit for their ideas, or implying that their voices would not be heard unless a man in a position of power repeated what they said. I could have done a better job soliciting feedback and fostering psychological safety so that others might have spoken up, and I would have learned the lesson sooner.

When those of us who are part of groups with power and advantage—as I consider myself to be—make aha-moment mistakes relating to unconscious biases, we tend to withdraw. We think the subject is too difficult and full of land mines. Thus, we disengage, with the result that we miss the opportunity to grow and effect change.

Instead, we can learn to recognize our missteps as precious aha-moment mistakes that can help us to better understand ourselves, others, and the systems we are part of, and to become more effective in advancing stronger and more equitable teams, organizations, and communities.

These aha moments can occur in a wide variety of work situations. A salesperson can't seem to close a deal—until a colleague overhears her and suggests slowing down and taking time to understand her customer's needs. A project manager realizes that her team keeps missing due dates, so she builds in a timeline confirmation step for every milestone, and makes sure to give people the opportunity to ask for more time if they need it.

The signal to pay attention and reflect comes when you are surprised by the effect of your actions. You do something expecting X, but Y happens instead. That's a cue to move into the Learning Zone and identify what is surprising and what lessons it might teach you.

Surprises are precious sources of learning, and they make life more interesting.

STRETCH MISTAKES

Whenever you're working to expand your current abilities and try something new, you're bound to make some errors along the way. These kinds of *stretch mistakes* are positive—an opportunity for growth. If you never make stretch mistakes, it means that you're never truly challenging yourself.

Dona Sarkar is a software engineer who leads the advocacy team for Microsoft's Power Platform. Previously, she worked on the development of HoloLens, a pair of holographic sunglasses, and she was head of Microsoft's Windows Insider program, which offers users prerelease updates of the operating system in exchange for feedback. While she was running the Insider program, she wanted to create stronger connections among Insiders living in the same community.

She came up with the idea to have Insider events for nonprofits: The organizations were invited to come and share a business or technology problem they were experiencing, and the Insiders would collaborate to develop solutions.

Dona decided to experiment with the Insider events over the course of three months, hosted at Microsoft stores in New York, Boston, Phoenix, and Seattle.

"First, we will learn to use our technology in a practical way. Second, the nonprofit will benefit," she explained. "Third, we will build deep community with people who live near one another."

So far, so good, right?

"It failed horribly," she told me.

The nonprofits lacked the technical acumen to maintain the solutions provided by the Insiders at the events. While they could often implement the new technology, they didn't have the resources to maintain it.

"Unless there is someone at the nonprofit dedicated to technology maintenance," Dona explained, "things fall apart really quickly."

Though the event program was a failure, this stretch mistake provided Microsoft with valuable insights that the company was able to use going forward.

"From that, I learned you cannot drop technology in and leave," Dona said. "We have to skill up the people before we introduce them to any new technology."

When you find yourself making and then repeating a stretch mistake, it's a good opportunity to explore whether you're mindlessly going through the motions or truly applying yourself to improving your abilities. If you practice throwing a Frisbee and it keeps taking a nosedive, it's time to change your technique or seek out some tips to make that Frisbee sail through the air.

Other times, your approach to learning itself may be ineffective. You might be experimenting when deliberate practice would be more effective for acquiring the desired skill. In such instances, you might ask how others have gained competence in the same or a similar area. If you're concentrating and still feeling stuck, it might be time to bring in a coach, a mentor, or another source of guidance and objective feedback.

It also could be that you've simply set your stretch goal too high. Could you aim instead for some milestone between where you are today and your ultimate goal?

Say you try to put together a conference and it fails miserably. You could, upon reflection, gather the lessons learned and try again, perhaps bringing to the team people with expertise in areas that fell short. Or you could recognize that you know too little about too many aspects of what is involved, and instead set a goal of organizing a smaller internal meeting that doesn't involve as many activities you haven't done before. That way, you can focus on learning some of the elements that will prepare you to later expand to a full conference.

You want to seek out stretch mistakes by taking on new challenges. But when you find yourself stuck and can't seem to make progress, it's time to reflect, identify a different strategy, and then adjust your approach to practicing.

When you meet your goal, it's time to identify a new area of challenge and continue stretching yourself.

HIGH-STAKES MISTAKES

As Matthew Syed points out in his book *Black Box Thinking*, in 1912, eight of fourteen U.S. Army pilots died in crashes, while early fatality rates at the army aviation schools were close to 25 percent.

Flash forward to 2019—before the skies shut down due to a global pandemic—when, out of 38.8 million flights made across the entire globe, there were only six fatal accidents (resulting in 239 fatalities out of 4.5 billion passengers).

What happened that increased safety so significantly?

In the century-plus since human beings first took to the sky, the airline industry has made impressive strides in learning how to improve safety around an activity where a simple error can mean the difference between life and death.

Which brings us to the fourth and final kind of mistake: *high-stakes mistakes*.

While mistakes can help you grow, some errors are undeniably dangerous. After all, no one wants the person in charge of security at a nuclear power plant or the captain of an aircraft to be making sloppy mistakes. Nor do you want to force employees to do a team-building activity that could lead to injury.

Luckily, you can put processes in place to try to minimize high-stakes mistakes, and over time, you can develop an intuitive understanding of when to take risks and when to play it safe.

Aside from life-threatening or potentially dangerous situations, there are many Performance Zone activities you might consider high stakes. A championship final can certainly be considered a high-stakes event for a sports team that has trained for years. Or if losing an important customer relationship could result in a significant drop in revenue, you might want to play it safe in meetings with that customer rather than experiment with risky ideas.

It is okay to see these events as performances rather than learning opportunities and to seek to minimize mistakes and maximize short-term performance. These are the moments you may want to focus on harvesting dividends from the time spent in the Learning Zone.

Even then, we can often embed low-stakes mini experiments that don't involve safety concerns within high-stakes events. For example, if you're doing a presentation with an important customer who loves classical music, you might somehow incorporate that into your presentation, and then reflect on whether it had an impact. That could mean anything from including cello music during the breaks to using classical music metaphors in the presentation itself.

The possibilities are endless when it comes to what you could test. Here are a few examples:

- Focus more on asking questions so the client can clarify the problem.
- Focus more on offering solutions.
- Focus more on stories.
- Approach the interaction more formally.
- Approach the interaction *less* formally.

In a high-stakes event, if you don't achieve your goal of winning the championship or the customer, you can reflect on the progress you've made through time, on the approaches that have and haven't helped you grow, and on what you can do to grow more effectively in the Learning Zone.

On the other hand, if you achieve your goal, win a championship, or land new business, that's great. Celebrate the achievement and how much progress you've made. Then, ask yourself the same questions to keep stretching. Continue engaging in the Learning Zone, challenging yourself, and growing your abilities.

This is what the airline industry did to make flights safer—it embarked on a relentless effort to analyze and reflect on mistakes, resulting in constant changes in equipment and procedures to improve safety. In *Black Box Thinking*, Syed describes the industry's approaches to examining mistakes. The so-called black box is the most noteworthy example of this thinking. Every aircraft contains two sturdy boxes made of durable materials like stainless steel or titanium (that are no longer black; these days they're typically bright orange to make them easier to find). One box stores information about the flight, such as airspeed and altitude. The other records conversations from the cockpit. As Syed describes, this data is then analyzed so the reason for the accident can be detected and changes made in the hopes of avoiding similar incidents in the future.

Inspired by the airline industry, some hospitals are now beginning to use black boxes in operating rooms. Bridgewater Associates, the largest hedge fund in the world, records all meetings for people to learn from. ClearChoice Dental similarly records all interactions with consenting patients so staff can learn from them. Any of us can implement similar practices. We don't have to literally record events. We can collect feedback during or after the high-stakes performance that we can examine and learn from afterward.

A friend of mine ensures he has a *feedback ally* in meetings who will observe him and make notes to share with him afterward. I often direct keynote or workshop participants to a brief survey at the end of my sessions so I can learn from their perspectives.

Dipo Aromire, formerly a sales executive at Thomson Reuters, a global provider of financial market data and infrastructure, recounted to me the aftermath of one of the biggest mistakes of his career: losing a deal with one of the company's biggest customers, which accounted for 20 percent of the revenues managed by Dipo's team. Lots of people have been fired for less significant mistakes. It began when the client indicated that they were interested in a lucrative new service.

"It was a very, very big deal for my company, but we were very, very arrogant about it," Dipo told me. "We were very complacent because we felt we've been supplying this company for fifteen years. And so that attitude carried all the way through the process, which took maybe six to nine months. In the end, we lost that deal. They took the business away from us and gave it to somebody else."

The loss was painful for the whole team, but since Dipo was the senior sales executive, he took responsibility for it. To figure out what happened, he invited the client out to lunch to debrief.

"What did we do wrong? Why did we lose?" he asked. "I wrote down about fifteen points as to what we did wrong. The big one was about just the attitude that we brought. Our mindset was wrong. . . . We felt we had it in the bag because we knew them so well."

The experience provided Dipo with life lessons he still abides by. The biggest one is to never take anything or anyone for granted just because you've known them for a long time. He even brought the lesson home and applied it to his relationship with his wife. The story wound up having a happy ending: Two years later, he won the client back, with even more business than before.

MISTAKES ARE OPPORTUNITIES TO STEP INTO THE LEARNING ZONE

Many real-life errors combine aspects of the four kinds of mistakes. Some mistakes can be high-stakes *and* at the same time aha-moment or sloppy mistakes. These are not mutually exclusive categories, but rather characteristics of mistakes to help us better reflect on situations, approaches, and implications. Better understanding mistakes helps us realize they are a temporary and necessary part of growth, so when they happen we can stay calm and learn from them.

The following Mistakes Matrix illustrates key distinctions of the four kinds of mistakes.

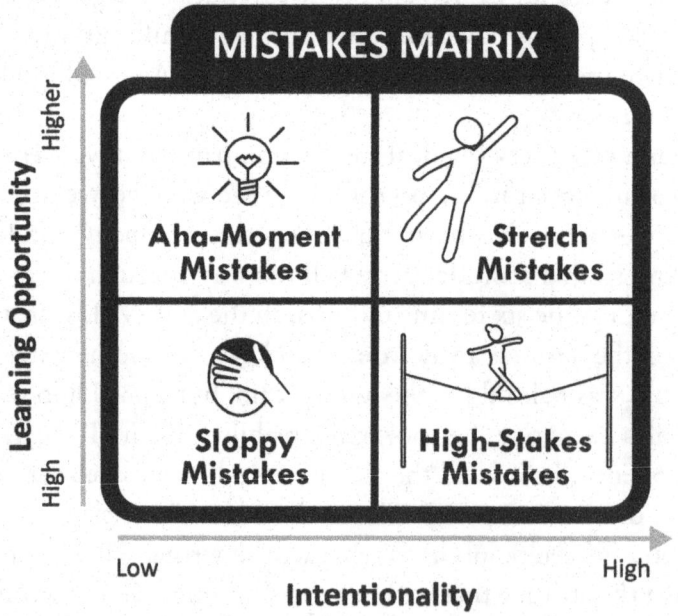

As the graphic illustrates, the aha-moment and stretch mistakes tend to be the most valuable because you can learn the most from them without significant harm. You can be the most intentional about generating stretch mistakes by taking on challenges. Stretch mistakes are those you elicit in the Learning Zone, while the other three usually happen in the Performance Zone. Aha-moment mistakes are those you come upon without planning for them, so they are low in intentionality. What you can do about aha-moment mistakes is to solicit feedback to try to uncover them, and when you notice them, treasure them and reflect on what you can learn.

When sloppy mistakes happen, you can ask yourself whether they are a cause for laughter or something to reflect on and work to avoid repeating. As for high-stakes mistakes, it is best to be intentional about trying to avoid them by shifting to your Performance Zone.

But no matter what mistake you make, you can use it as a cue to leap into your Learning Zone. This enables you to learn and grow, to better manage your emotions, and to be more resourceful and resilient.

Tomer Cohen, chief product officer at LinkedIn, incorporates an awareness of different kinds of mistakes in his guidance to the people he leads. On a whiteboard, he draws three concentric circles. The inner circle is the Performance Zone, where "you're not learning, you're doing stuff you already know." The middle circle is the Stretch Zone, where "you should feel uncomfortable, you should feel like you're stretching, and that by design you're not sure if what you're doing is going to work." And the outer circle is the Danger Zone, the area where mistakes would be costly—for example, the website crashing. He asks people to think about what percentage of time they are spending in their Stretch Zone.

"I share mine, and then I try to make sure at least a third of their time is in the Stretch Zone. And for some folks, it's forty percent and fifty percent, which is wonderful," he told me.

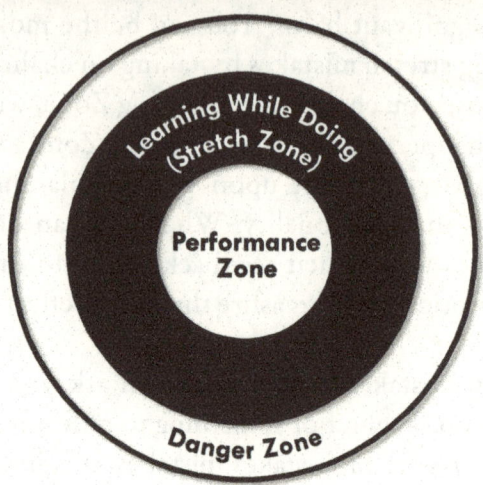

At first, it may be challenging to figure out when to reflect on mistakes. Here are some strategies:

- Reflect on your own or discuss with your team whether regular engagement in the Learning Zone is important, how you want to go about it, and implications for mistakes.
- Block out time on the calendar accordingly. Set up recurring calendar appointments and write in reminders of what you want to do and what questions you want to ask during that time.
- Incorporate reflection into recurring work processes. For example, after every keynote I give, I solicit feedback. I also spend a few minutes writing notes on what went well, what I learned, and what I might do differently going forward.
- Think through whether regular meetings could better incorporate the Learning Zone. Perhaps a weekly meeting could include a space for team members to share important lessons learned.
- If there is a fire drill that requires all hands on deck, you may skip these Learning Zone blocks to get through the crisis. But

the Learning Zone structures remain in place as a default and a regular habit.

- When you make a mistake in the Performance Zone and it's not the right time to get into the Learning Zone, make note of the issue so you can work on it later. Send yourself a quick email with the reminder, add it to your calendar or to a document you review regularly, or record a voice memo. Noticing your mistakes in the Performance Zone with the intention of working on them not only helps you learn, but it also helps you perform better in the moment by reminding you that your shortcomings are not set in stone.

WEAPONIZING MISTAKES

Beware of the potential trap of letting your perception of sloppy mistakes and high-stakes mistakes be a reason to blame and punish others for the mistakes they've made. What you see as a sloppy mistake, someone else may see as a stretch or aha-moment mistake. Weaponizing mistakes will lead others to avoid risks, hide failures, and revert to chronic performance, which will lead to stagnation.

Keep in mind that we are all human and we all make mistakes, even when we don't want to and try not to. When someone makes a mistake that angers you, remember you don't have the whole story or fully understand what they were thinking or doing. You can ask questions to understand others' perspectives, how they perceive the situation, what they are learning from it, what they plan to do differently going forward, and, of course, what you can do differently going forward.

"THE BEST DEAL I EVER MADE"

Remember Gino Barbaro, the pizzeria owner we met at the beginning of the book who was suffering from years of chronic performance?

Eager to break free of the grind, Gino was intrigued when he learned about the passive income that real estate ownership can generate.

"You've got to talk to my friend Jake," Gino's brother, Marcos, told him after he floated the idea of starting a real estate business. Jake Stenziano was a pharmaceutical salesperson who'd also been thinking about a shift into real estate.

Gino was on board.

As for Jake, he was, let's say, a bit less than enthusiastic about meeting with Gino. He'd been to the restaurant before and he wasn't so sure about Marcos's brother. Gino always seemed to be in a terrible mood, constantly grumbling about some problem or another.

Jake overcame his initial reticence about meeting his friend's grumpy brother. The two men decided to keep in touch after Jake and his wife moved to Knoxville, Tennessee, to start researching real estate investment opportunities there. Eventually, Jake and Gino decided to partner.

Before meeting Jake, Gino had a painful experience with an investment property that didn't turn out well. A friend told him about a real estate deal an acquaintance was putting together to purchase a mobile home park in Florida. Gino had exactly $172,000 in his savings account, a sum he had worked hard to acquire by putting in long hours at his restaurant. He was drawn to the idea of passive investing, putting his money to work so that it compounded over time. Without carrying out any due diligence on the property or the man running the project, Gino sunk every penny of his savings into the mobile home park. And the whole project went bust. He lost everything.

But here's the twist. Gino now calls that "the best deal I ever made" because the loss taught him that, to become an effective real estate investor, he had to also invest in his own development. Before, he thought he instinctively knew what would make for a good real estate investment, just like he thought he knew the best way to run a restaurant.

But getting hard evidence that he was wrong made him realize how much he had to learn.

After he partnered with Jake, they set out to understand how to invest effectively. It wasn't enough to simply look for properties until they found something that looked great; they also had to regularly commit to spending time in the Learning Zone. They started reading books, taking courses, and deliberately studying what constituted a good investment.

They reached out to other investors and asked for advice. They learned what type of home remodels tended to make for positive returns on investment. They developed relationships with brokers and got their perspectives on local markets. It took them two years in the Learning Zone and searching for an attractive deal before they found what eventually became their first successful investment. That provided cash and credibility to start growing from there.

The Learning Zone was so important to Jake and Gino that ongoing learning is now a core value in the companies they own and run, which include a real estate investment company, a real estate management company, and a real estate financing company. They also created a company dedicated to providing educational opportunities for others who want to become multifamily real estate investors. They call that company Jake & Gino. They have been so successful that they have amassed a portfolio of more than $225 million in assets under management, encompassing more than 1,600 units.

Gino has learned to see challenges and setbacks as opportunities. When they arise, he responds by engaging in the Learning Zone. When an economic crisis—or a pandemic—hits, he helps others view the situation not as a fire that will engulf us all, but as an opportunity to learn and reset. After all, had it not been for the challenges that the 2008 recession brought to his restaurant, he wouldn't have learned those valuable lessons that set his life in a new direction. And had it not been for his $172,000 mistake, when he lost his life savings on a bad investment, he wouldn't have discovered the power of the Learning Zone to change his trajectory.

MAKE MISTAKES WORK FOR YOU

To leverage the power of mistakes, take on challenges beyond the known and frequently solicit feedback. Challenges generate stretch mistakes, and feedback surfaces all kinds of mistakes, including precious aha moments.

When something goes wrong, ask yourself whether it could be an opportunity for transformation.

If you fear or resist mistakes, remember there is always room for improvement in everything anyone does. Mistakes are part of life and a potent source of learning. As you get into the habit of taking on challenges, soliciting feedback, and recognizing what you can learn, your feelings about mistakes will gradually shift. You will start treasuring the value they bring to your life, which will equip you to better achieve your goals.

Engage the people around you. Rather than reflecting on mistakes in your own cocoon, discuss them with others. That will foster a community where people feel more connected and can better collaborate for both learning and performing.

REFLECTION QUESTIONS

- How do I tend to respond to my mistakes and those of others? How might I influence the way my colleagues approach mistakes?
- What significant mistake have I made in the last year? How did I use it to generate valuable lessons and positive change?
- Am I taking on significant challenges that could generate stretch mistakes to learn from?

LOOKING FORWARD

What do I think growth mindset means?

Chapter 6: Six Common Misconceptions

About Learning

BIG IDEA *Platitudes and misunderstandings about growth mindset and learning abound. To overcome the performance paradox and reach new heights, we must clarify what these drivers of growth mean and how to foster them.*

I was once approached at a conference by a woman who told me that for years she had been trying to inspire others to embrace a growth mindset. But despite her best efforts, she was falling short, so she wanted ideas on how she could better inspire others.

Then, in passing, she added, "Of course, people's intelligence can't change, but hard work is critical to success, and that's what I try to get others to understand."

No wonder she was having so much trouble. This offhand comment revealed that she didn't really understand what a growth mindset was, and she didn't seem to be in one herself—at least not when it came to thinking about intelligence. She also didn't realize that hard work comes in different forms, and that hard work in the Learning Zone is what leads to growth.

This conversation reminded me of the Aesop fable "The Tortoise and the Hare," the story of a plodding tortoise who wins a race against an arrogant hare who pauses mid-race to take a nap. A lot of well-meaning educators and parents connect with the story for its message of perseverance, and many of them think that in telling the story they're promoting a growth mindset and effective learning.

But let's dig a little deeper into the fable's message. Since no character ever engages in the Learning Zone or advances their capabilities—no one gets faster or better—this narrative serves to reinforce a belief that's emblematic of a fixed mindset: Only people without innate talent need to work hard and grind it out. The innately talented, on the other hand, just need to put in minimal effort—and not get too cocky.

But we can't live our lives hoping that the hare slacks off.

And our goal shouldn't be to get further down the road without also transforming ourselves along the way.

In the last fifteen years, I've encountered many individuals, teams, and organizations that think they're much further along in developing a learning culture than they actually are. In fact, several times I have heard from people who report to senior executives that their bosses talk frequently about "growth mindset" but they don't really understand what it is or what it entails.

It has, unfortunately, become a buzzword.

I, too, have heard my fair share of myths and misconceptions about learning and growth as people get trapped by the performance paradox, and I've seen how misguided attempts at fostering growth mindset cultures can backfire. Take the experience of Anjali, who we met at the very beginning of the book. Her manager, Salma, saw Anjali as a valuable team member and wanted to support her continued growth, give her more responsibility, and grow her team. Salma would offer well-intended feedback meant to help Anjali grow, but the feedback often went hand in hand with hints that she knew Anjali was more of a "people person" than a "systems thinker." This inadvertently sent the message that there were things Anjali couldn't develop. Salma also never explained *why* she was offering feedback and didn't realize that Anjali interpreted her suggestions as a way to point out deficiencies and as a sign that Anjali was failing and her job was in jeopardy. Anjali and Salma had different ideas of what feedback is for.

Building a growth mindset culture is not as simple as just giving feedback, encouraging people to work hard, or asking them to change their mindset. It is about embarking on a never-ending journey of personal development, making it visible to others, and inviting them to join. A true growth mindset culture creates structures and rituals that support continuous learning and encourages people to apply those lessons for ever-increasing impact.

If we want to truly learn how to grow—and foster growth in our organizations—we need clarity. We need to face common misunderstandings head-on. Some of these are so prevalent and damaging I've taken a full chapter to begin dismantling them.

Misconception #1: A growth mindset is the same as positive thinking, working hard, or persevering, and it magically fosters growth.

Reality #1: A growth mindset is the belief that our abilities and qualities can change—if we engage in the Learning Zone.

People often equate growth mindset with positive thinking. I've even been asked whether growth mindset is the same as the ideas in the book *The Secret*, which claims that, by thinking positively, you will attract positive things into your life.

But it's very different. A growth mindset is not a wishing well.

Growth mindset is also not the belief that hard work is important, or that perseverance pays off, or that anything is possible. It is the belief that our abilities and qualities—including our intelligence—are not set in stone and that through continued Learning Zone effort we can grow and change. If we advocate hard work but never convey that a person can become more capable through that hard work, we're doing them a tremendous disservice.

Neither does growth mindset imply that anyone can do anything. Rather, it suggests that no one can know what a person might become able to do. As Microsoft states in its cultural principles, "potential is nurtured, not predetermined."

Growth mindset also doesn't insinuate that genes play no role. Our abilities are partly a result of nature and partly of nurture, but we tend to overestimate the former and underestimate the latter.

And the more we focus on the fact that we can change and develop, the more we benefit from the psychological effects of a growth mindset.

Research shows that when we believe we can change, we tend to view effort as positive, as something everyone can benefit from. We take on more challenges, see struggle and mistakes as part of the process, persevere in the face of setbacks, collaborate more effectively, and engage in more constructive feedback and conflict resolution. These different behaviors lead to superior results: We tend to develop more positive relationships, experience less stress and anxiety, and achieve higher performance.

Believing that humans can change is necessary for the effective behaviors to take place—but that's not where things stop.

It is our *actions* that lead to improvement, not the belief alone.

If we want to improve, we do need to put in the work. That's where our Learning Zone strategies like inquiry, deliberate practice, and feedback come in.

Growth mindset is a powerful foundation—it sets the stage for both personal and organizational transformation. But we can't stop there if we want to improve our skills or the performance of our organizations—we also need an understanding of effective strategies for improvement.

That is, if we want to improve, we need both a growth mindset and the Learning Zone, working together and reinforcing each other.

Misconception #2: The trap of the performance paradox: All this emphasis on learning and growth hinders performance.

Reality #2: Learning drives higher performance and impact—if we hold ourselves accountable.

It is so easy and common to be fooled by the performance paradox and worry that all this focus on learning will harm performance. Research tells us the opposite. People, teams, and organizations that engage in the Learning Zone attain higher performance and impact.

But that doesn't mean you're going to see immediate transformation overnight. The reality is that a focus on learning and growth can negatively impact performance in the very short term and can lead to lower accomplishments if we lose sight of what we are trying to improve or achieve.

That's why we need to hold ourselves accountable for actual improvement: Results do matter. If we are not seeing improved performance, we ask why, research possible adjustments, and try different learning strategies.

To foster accountability, some companies set measurable goals around things like customer wait time, asset utilization rates, or customer satisfaction. They track these metrics for every customer interaction and research what went wrong in the very worst instances to get to the root cause and come up with solutions. This leads them to generate innovative system changes. Then, they use the aggregate metrics to track whether they're in fact achieving the desired progress.

But beware that focusing on improving only customer and asset metrics can lead to unintentional consequences for the well-being and happiness of the workforce. At the end of the day, it's people, not machines, who determine the success of your organization. Healthy, happy employees engage in work in a deeper way that can better serve and delight customers. So don't forget to measure workplace metrics, too.

Misconception #3: All praise and encouragement is good.

Reality #3: Some forms of praise and encouragement can be helpful if not misdirected or overdone.

My friend Rajeev asked me what he could do to help his young daughter overcome her fear of taking risks. He was puzzled because he and his wife were into extreme sports such as backcountry skiing, kitesurfing, and wakeboarding—they loved a challenge. And on the rare occasions when his daughter tried something hard, she could usually do it well.

"You see?" he would say to her. "If you try, you can do it!"

Kids need positive reinforcement, right? So how could praising them after they do something well ever backfire?

But Rajeev hadn't realized that he was praising her successful *achievement,* not the act of taking the risk. His daughter remained afraid that if she tried something and failed, her dad would be disappointed.

So, she stopped trying.

Once he became aware of this dynamic, Rajeev began noticing when his daughter made courageous choices and encouraged her in those choices, regardless of whether her attempts were "successful." The act of going beyond the known and learning from it was success. His daughter's fears of disappointing her dad went away.

In a seminal study, Claudia Mueller and Carol Dweck showed the unintentional consequences of well-intended praise. They found that praising children for being smart backfired. When children were praised for their intelligence after doing something well, when asked whether they wanted to try a hard puzzle or an easy one, most of them chose the easy puzzle. On the other hand, children who had been praised for their process, their behaviors, *their choices*—things they can control—were much more likely to take on the challenge of the harder puzzle. They also performed better when faced with difficulty.

It might seem that praising children's intelligence will increase their confidence and equip them to take on greater challenges and persevere. But the opposite can happen. The lesson children can take away is that people succeed because they are smart and talented, so they often start focusing on proving themselves rather than improving, starting them down the path to chronic performance that entraps so many eager-to-please young people.

In the early days of teaching the world about growth mindset, we frequently shared this praise research. After all, we wanted parents to notice the unintended consequences of labeling their children as smart.

But we weren't clear that the key conclusion of these studies wasn't so much that we should praise effort, but that praising people for being smart, geniuses, or naturals backfires. So, people began to equate growth mindset with simply *praising effort*. This misunderstanding had consequences:

1. In concluding that it was all about praising effort, people were missing a key insight of growth mindset research: Encouraging people to work hard doesn't tend to work if the people they're encouraging believe they can't change.
2. People ended up praising others just for working hard. However, there are different types of hard work: the Learning Zone and the Performance Zone. When someone is trying hard but not making progress, they should change strategies.
3. Constant praise conditions people to do things for approval, rather than helps them develop their intrinsic interests and motivations. And we need that internal motivation; it helps us become deeper learners, gives us more agency over our actions, and fosters the resilience needed in the face of adversity.

Bottom line: Praise is not the be-all and end-all—for children or adults.

Indeed, it can be much more powerful to ask questions that prompt reflection, like: What are you working on? How are you going about it? How well is that working? What are you learning? What might you try differently?

When we ask questions and work on our own growth, we inspire a commitment to lifelong learning, and we model the way.

How much we should praise someone depends on our relationship with them, the culture we're part of, and the person's view of and need for praise. Marcelo Camberos, the CEO of Beauty for All Industries, once received feedback that he was too direct in his criticism of others without acknowledging the things they were doing well.

This made his colleagues feel he didn't care about others or notice how they were positively contributing.

This stung because Marcelo really *did* care for others and truly valued their work. He was just offering feedback the way he'd learned—from a father who didn't sugarcoat anything.

Now, Marcelo never minded his father's feedback style. He understood there was care behind the suggestions. But this blunt style didn't always work for others. Realizing this, Marcelo became much more intentional about not only sharing constructive criticism, but also explicitly telling people what they were doing well. This shift in his communication style allowed him to better support and guide people in ways that led to closer relationships, richer learning, and better performance.

In short, reflect on your language: When communicating with others, are you portraying human abilities and qualities as malleable? Or are you labeling people as smart or naturally talented? Are you using your judgments of others as carrots and sticks, or are you collaborating with them to learn and perform together?

Misconception #4: You either have a growth mindset or you don't.

Reality #4: Mindsets exist on a spectrum; they are contextual, fluid, and can change over time.

We all experience a fixed mindset from time to time: It's part of being human. If we haven't identified times when we tend to be in a fixed mindset, we haven't reflected enough.

We may be entirely willing to grow in some areas of our lives, while biases, assumptions, or hard truths are keeping us fixed in other areas. As my mentor Ron Berger, a legendary educator and one of the leaders of the EL Education network of schools, points out, "All of us have a growth mindset for particular abilities and a fixed mindset for others. I don't believe there is such a thing as a 'growth mindset person' or a 'fixed mindset person.'"

The problem is that most of the abilities we see as fixed tend to be based on incorrect assumptions. "I'm not a good writer" or "I can't do math" or "I'm not a social person" are common examples. We sometimes see these abilities as fixed when they can in fact be developed. Our misguided assumptions then become self-fulfilling prophecies because they prevent us from engaging in the Learning Zone.

Just like we can be in a growth mindset about one ability and in a fixed mindset about another, we can also be in a growth mindset about one person and in a fixed mindset about another. For example, we may see ourselves as learners and a colleague as unable to change. Our fixed mindset creates a self-fulfilling prophecy because it leads us to withhold information that could help the other person learn and grow.

That's why it's important to continually challenge our beliefs, especially anytime we catch ourselves claiming absolute certainty on any topic, or believing someone can't improve.

Mindsets are fluid. We can be triggered into a fixed mindset by challenging situations: after receiving critical feedback, when we're feeling stressed about a time crunch, or in the moments we're feeling intimidated by someone else's status or achievements. In such instances, we might find ourselves muttering, "I'm just not a team player," "I'm no good in a crisis," or "I just don't think I'm cut out for this job."

Fortunately, we can shift to a growth mindset by noticing how we're talking to ourselves—by realizing we can always change the script. If we feel frustration that we can't do something, we can remind ourselves that we just can't do it *yet*, and identify the Learning Zone strategies that can move our skills forward.

Misconception #5: Growth mindset is all about responding to setbacks and mistakes.

Reality #5: Proactive growth is a lot more powerful than staying reactive.

I welcome my mistakes because they teach me how to improve.

Sounds like a pretty powerful mindset. What could possibly be wrong with it?

While it is wise to learn from missteps, we don't need to wait for them to drive our growth. While a *reactive growth mindset*—one in which we're focused only on learning from unforeseen mistakes and setbacks—is a lot more desirable than a fixed mindset, it's not nearly as strong as a *proactive growth mindset*, the idea that *I con-*

tinuously drive my own change and evolution. We can do this by taking on challenges beyond what we know and by adopting Learning Zone habits to consistently advance our skills.

The question is, what's your default? To stay the same unless failure pushes you to do something differently? Or to drive your own constant development?

The second approach is much more powerful.

For this reason, I believe that the single most powerful habit to foster a growth mindset and cultivate the Learning Zone is to remind yourself every morning of what you're working to improve. It's what I do every day when I first turn on my computer: I remind myself where I want to focus my Learning Zone effort. This also primes a growth mindset.

Once I made the strategy a daily habit, it became automatic and effortless.

Misconception #6: We can encourage our loved ones, team members, or young people to grow, but only they can take action to achieve results.

Reality #6: If we want people to grow, we also need to cultivate environments that are conducive to growth.

As teachers, managers, parents, or leaders, it is our responsibility to promote environments that nurture growth mindsets and the Learning Zone and that support people in their development.

Learning environments prime a growth mindset. They also accelerate growth because they allow people to learn in collaboration, which is more effective than learning in isolation.

So that everyone can thrive, we also need to advance equitable systems that mitigate unconscious biases we all hold, whether about people of color, women, elders, millennials, Republicans, Democrats, or any other group.

We want to catch ourselves when we're writing someone off as having a fixed mindset, or when we're encouraging someone to work on their mindset without asking what they're interested in and how we can support them. This work is about deliberately cultivating cultures, systems, and habits that support learning for everyone.

How we can cultivate such cultures, systems, and habits in teams and organizations will be the focus of Part Two.

MOVING FORWARD WITH CLARITY

Understanding that we can change equips us to examine *how* to do so. The more we apply these effective strategies, the more deeply we understand our malleability. It's a self-reinforcing cycle with compounding results.

So, in your quest to improve, remember to cultivate a growth mindset—the belief that people can change—and the Learning Zone—the mental state and behaviors that actually lead to change and growth.

If we miss either, we get stuck. By embracing both, we can embark on a journey to shape ourselves and develop powers we never imagined. How to do that is the subject of the next chapter.

REFLECTION QUESTIONS

- What situations tend to trigger me into a fixed mindset? How could I work on developing the ability to catch myself in real time? (Awareness is the first step.)
- What abilities and qualities do I value in myself and in colleagues, friends, and loved ones? Do I believe these abilities are innate or that they can be developed?
- Am I asking questions to prompt reflection and engagement in the Learning Zone?

LOOKING FORWARD

What do I need to develop in myself to excel in the two zones?

Chapter 7: The Growth Propeller: Five Key Elements

That Drive Growth

BIG IDEA *To become a master learner and performer, work on developing your identity, purpose, beliefs, habits, and community. These elements work together like a propeller, equipping you to move confidently toward your boldest ambitions.*

Lizzie Dipp Metzger, the newbie insurance agent and financial planner we met in Chapter 2, had always been interested in working to make the world a better place.

But selling life insurance?

She hadn't seen that as her life's calling; what's more, she dreaded calling people to try to sell them something. But she soon began hearing stories from her new colleagues about how their work had made a big difference in the lives of some of their clients. She cherished those stories as motivation.

One day, Lizzie found herself in a conversation about financial planning with Emilio, the father of one of her daughter's closest friends. He was considering getting life insurance, and he welcomed further dialogue. Lizzie wrote a reminder to call him back to continue the conversation, but she kept putting it off. She didn't want to appear "salesy" to family friends.

At some point, calling Emilio was the *only* reminder left in her task list, yet she still couldn't bring herself to make the call.

A few months later, she got the news that Emilio, only in his mid-forties, had died suddenly, leaving behind a wife and children—and a lot of financial uncertainty, as the family had relied on his income.

Lizzie was devastated. She called Emilio's widow, who was also her friend, to offer her condolences and to apologize that she hadn't called sooner. She learned that the couple had decided to engage Lizzie in financial planning and to purchase a life insurance policy from her but had been busy and hadn't followed up. They thought they had plenty of time.

This was a turning point for Lizzie. It taught her not to delay life insurance (which can be secured quickly before putting a full financial plan in place) and it solidified her sense of purpose. Since then, she hasn't let her dread of appearing pushy stop her from making phone calls. She knows most of her sales calls will result in rejection, but others will change lives for generations to come.

Lizzie has continued to learn more about her clients and the impact she can have on them. Though typically talkative, she has learned to pause, ask questions, and listen, especially during the early stages when she is getting to know people.

Initially, in those conversations she felt pressure to show that she knew her stuff. But over time, she learned—in part from more experienced peers—that to best serve clients, she needed to learn about their needs first.

In other words, she needed to engage in the Learning Zone.

But it was a strong sense of *purpose* that gave her the energy and direction needed for the time she spent in both zones. This sense of purpose, combined with her strong identity as a learner, served as a foundation around which she built the beliefs, habits, and community that enabled her to succeed.

In this chapter, we'll understand how committed learners like Lizzie Dipp Metzger drive their own growth by exploring a framework I call the growth propeller—the five elements that enable us to overcome the performance paradox and achieve our aspirations.

HOW DO I STAY COMMITTED TO LEARNING AND GROWTH?

How can we consistently engage in the Learning Zone and get things done in the Performance Zone? How do we avoid spending weeks, even months, in the Learning Zone but not making as much progress as we'd like? How do we stay motivated and effective?

The answer is to develop a strong *growth propeller,* which encompasses the five key elements needed to excel in the two zones.

Picture an airplane propeller with three blades. At the center of the propeller—the hub—are our identity and purpose, which provide the core energy and direction that drive our efforts. The three blades are named for the elements that propel us forward: our beliefs, our habits, and our community, which determine how effectively and harmoniously we engage in the zones.

Let's explore each of these elements more deeply.

IDENTITY

When Linda Rabbitt's husband became emotionally and physically abusive, she left him to protect herself and her children, as she recounted to Mahan Tavakoli on his podcast, *Partnering Leadership.* Her ex soon took all of their assets offshore, leaving the stay-at-home mom and her children with nothing. As she and her daughters were forced to move into a friend's cramped apartment, she felt like a failure. It was the lowest point in Linda's life.

Committed to proving herself and providing for her daughters, she went to work as an executive assistant at KPMG, one of the Big Four global accounting firms. She didn't know anything about accounting or executive support, but she knew she could learn.

Linda worked hard at KPMG and gained the respect of her boss. But her goal was to become an executive, something that would be difficult to accomplish at KPMG without an accounting degree.

As Linda was thinking about her future, a woman she knew through the local Chamber of Commerce approached her with a unique opportunity: She was going to start the first woman-owned construction company and she was looking for a partner. Linda expressed interest, and the two women partnered.

When she told her boss she was starting a construction company, he said, "What do you know about construction?"

"Absolutely nothing, but I can learn," she responded.

Over the years, Linda encountered many challenges—and eventually had to break ties with her original partner—but her identity as a learner helped her to ultimately become the founder and owner of Rand Construction, the largest woman-founded, woman-owned commercial construction company in the United States.

While her identity as a learner has remained steady throughout her career, it has also evolved in other ways. She now thinks of herself as a business leader, philanthropist, mentor, and advisor, which wasn't true early in her career.

You can think of yourself as having multiple identities (such as mother, runner, and artist) or one integrated identity with multiple aspects. What's important when it comes to overcoming the performance paradox is that your various identities, or aspects of your single identity, are all consistent with being a learner—someone who evolves and grows over time. Various scholars and theorists have called this *learning identity,* including Stanton Wortham and Alice and David Kolb.

Pay attention to your language and the labels you place on yourself and others. When you call someone a "born leader" or think of yourself that way, you inadvertently send the message that leadership is a fixed trait, and no one needs to work at it. Similarly, labeling yourself an extrovert may prevent you from engaging in potentially helpful activities such as introspection, mindfulness, or attentive listening. Identifying yourself too rigidly as an introvert may inhibit you from seeking ways to connect and collaborate with others, which is key to growth and high performance.

This view of identity as malleable and changing is not the same as having no sense of self. Even as Linda Rabbitt embraced her identity as a learner who evolves, she remained grounded in values she learned from her immigrant parents—the importance of being disciplined, continuously improving, persevering, forging community, making a difference, and living life fully. But had she identified too rigidly as a stay-at-home mom, she might not have developed the aspirations to grow into a pathfinding business leader. Later, had she identified too inflexibly as a chief executive, she might not have decided to focus more on mentoring and supporting others.

As the renowned psychiatrist Thomas Szasz said, "The self is not something one finds, it is something one creates."

PURPOSE

As a young girl, Meirav Oren spent a lot of time pretending to be sick so she could skip school and join her father, a general contractor, at job sites where she could hang out with construction workers.

But she discovered she liked school when she got to college, where she had more control over her time and course selections. She could focus her studies on the subjects that interested her, leading her to pursue both an MBA and a law degree.

She went on to work for Intel, where some of her favorite projects involved Intel's philanthropic endeavors. Meirav was able to spend significant time engaged in two of her greatest joys: learning and giving back.

Several years later, her brother, while working as a project manager at a construction site, lost one of his workers when he fell from a scaffolding. Meirav was profoundly affected by the tragedy and by her brother's distress over it. In the aftermath, she founded Versatile, a technology company that helps make construction workers' lives safer and projects more efficient. Versatile provides a device that, when hooked between cranes and their loads, scans the job site and uses artificial intelligence to help coordinate the work and flag any hazards. The efficacy of the product has helped the fast-growing company rapidly expand its customer base and raise more than $100 million.

Meirav's interest in making an impact had always steered her to meaningful work opportunities throughout her career. But her brother's struggle, combined with her emotional ties to her childhood days at her father's construction sites, opened her eyes to her new purpose: making construction sites safer and more efficient.

Rather than think about *finding* your purpose, which reflects more of a fixed mindset—as it implies purpose is predetermined—it is more helpful to think about *developing* it. Paul O'Keefe, Carol Dweck, and Greg Walton found that people who use this approach are more effective at expanding their interests and are more resilient when faced with challenges.

So how do you go about developing your purpose? At first, simply explore, tinker, and try things out, while at the same time developing your knowledge and skills through the Learning Zone. In going beyond the known, you're breaking out of the performance paradox, and in the process, you're evolving.

Some of your explorations may not ignite a fire within you. That's okay. Others will. Go deeper into exploring what you might enjoy in the long term, rather than pursuing something that feels like a permanent chore.

Not everyone has the same privilege to choose their pursuits—and luck is always part of the journey—but by noticing things that sound interesting and taking chances, you're more likely to wind up doing something you love. When you see your interests as changeable rather than as fixed, you are more active in your search and better able to achieve your goals.

Developing purpose is also about seeing with new eyes. Think about why your work and your interests matter to you. How do they contribute to other people's lives?

Now that we've examined the hub of the growth propeller—your identity and purpose, which give you a solid foundation for your efforts in the Learning Zone and the Performance Zone—it's time to move to the blades, which determine your effectiveness in the two zones.

BELIEFS

A year and a half after starting her career as an insurance agent and financial advisor, Lizzie Dipp Metzger was at a New York Life event in New Orleans when she was invited to an oyster bar by a group of seasoned agents, members of the company's prestigious Chairman's Council, a recognition given to the top 6 to 8 percent of agents in New York Life for their sales excellence.

They immediately hit it off, and during dinner, one of her colleagues told her, "You should become a Chairman's Council agent this year so that we can all hang out more."

By breaking bread with these highly successful agents, Lizzie realized they weren't fundamentally different from her. She could become one of them. She took their encouragement to heart, and when she got home, she wrote on a Post-it Note: "I will be a consistent Chairman's Council agent starting the 2012 Council year." She kept the note on her desk as motivation to do what she needed to do, such as getting through those dreaded sales calls.

She kept that promise to herself, making Chairman's Council in 2012 and, as of this writing, every year after, for eleven consecutive years and running.

"I've never looked back. It's all about your beliefs," she said to Chairman's Council members in a keynote address I attended. "When we free ourselves from our own confinements, we have limitless possibilities."

As Lizzie points out, beliefs are critical, not because they work like magic, but because they make it possible for us to behave differently. Instead of being stuck in chronic performance, Lizzie does the hard work in the Learning Zone to figure out how to achieve a new goal every year, and she builds the habits needed to get it done.

"Looking back at that pivotal moment in New Orleans, you might say it was simply a series of lucky circumstances, being in the right oyster bar at the right time," she says. "But because I had been preparing and studying, when those fantastic agents entered into my life, I was ready to run with them."

Many beliefs affect the way we behave. The performance paradox itself is rooted in the mistaken belief that the best way to succeed is to perform as much as possible. By replacing that with another belief—that combining performing with learning enables us to perform much better—we can begin to overcome the paradox.

In particular, our beliefs about *competence*, *agency*, and *transparency* can support or undermine our growth and performance in any area. We can take a look at each of those beliefs—is it propelling us forward or holding us back?

Let's start with our beliefs around *competence*—the ability to do something well.

When Linda Rabbitt's boss asked what she knew about construction, and she responded, "Absolutely nothing, but I can learn," she was demonstrating that while she didn't yet possess understanding of the industry, she *did* believe in her competence *as a learner*. This gave her the confidence to leave her job and start a new company. She knew she could figure things out along the way, and grow in the process.

Consider this the next time you encounter a new challenge at work or in your personal life: You may have never managed a large team, renovated your bathroom, or trained a dog before, but you *have* learned many new skills over the course of your life. What has worked, and what hasn't? What experts can you bring in either to get the work done—if you want to divide and conquer—or to support you as you build up your competence in this new area, if it's something you want to learn?

By focusing on developing our competence as learners through the many strategies described in this book, we can lean in to the uncertainty of the new.

Next, *agency* is, as University of Pennsylvania professor Angela Duckworth describes it, "the conviction that you shape your own future." It is the belief that you navigate life by taking actions, whether big or small, to chart your path and influence the systems around you. It's the opposite of feeling like a helpless victim.

Alex Stephany, a London-based technology entrepreneur, was in between ventures, meeting with many people to explore what he would do next. As he moved across the city, he got to know an unhoused man named Lucas at his local underground train station. He would regularly bring Lucas a cup of coffee or a bite to eat, and they would chat.

A few months in, Lucas disappeared for some time. After he re-appeared, Alex learned that Lucas had suffered a heart attack and had been in the hospital. He looked ten years older and beat up by life. Alex realized that bringing Lucas food hadn't really been helping. In fact, Lucas's situation and outlook had only deteriorated.

Faced with Alex's situation, many of us might feel helpless and, not knowing what to do, simply move on with our lives. But Alex had a core belief in his own agency. He asked himself what Lucas really needed. The answer was not coffee and food, but rather the resources and support to learn valuable skills so that he could get a job. Alex dove into his Learning Zone, meeting with other un-housed people and their advocates in government agencies and nonprofit organizations.

Eventually, Alex founded Beam, a crowdsourcing platform that links people in need with those who want to help them turn their lives around. Through the app, anyone can donate and send mes-sages of support. Beam partners with nonprofits to assist clients who are ready to develop the skills to start a career. As of this writ-ing, the organization has enabled more than 1,400 people to turn their lives around.

Every effective learner and performer who effects change—who makes anything happen—has a sense of agency. Without it, people tend to remain paralyzed.

One strategy for fostering agency is to focus on progress rather than on perfection. We cannot snap our fingers to create a perfect world, but we can put in consistent Learning Zone and Performance Zone efforts to make the world better.

Finally, let's consider our beliefs about *transparency*—the sharing of our thoughts and feelings with others. The greatest achievers know that transparency fuels learning and performing and enables others to better collaborate with us and support us.

Many years after becoming the CEO of Rand Construction, Linda Rabbitt regularly met with five other CEOs in the construction industry. One day, one of the CEOs said, "You know, Linda, with all due respect, your talk about being an underdog almost sounds disingenuous at this point. You are so successful. Like, you have to change your talk tracks: You're not really the underdog anymore."

Reflecting on that moment, Linda says, "That was such an act of friendship to tell me that, because I am not inauthentic, but I was sounding that way. But that had been what had motivated me for so long, that we were the underdog."

Linda realized she wasn't a newcomer anymore, and that she had to embrace a new identity that better matched her current reality. But first, she had to be transparent about how she saw herself, and the other leader had to be transparent about how Linda was coming across. When we view transparency as a means to greater learning and effectiveness, we end up having more open and honest conversations, which leads to improved learning and performance, and closer relationships.

Often, whether in our partnerships, friendships, or workplaces, we tend to withhold our frustrations, impressions, or ideas for fear of coming across as ignorant or difficult.

But by sharing our inner selves and working through conflict, we come to better understand people and find more harmonious ways to interact.

Of course, I don't mean we should share everything that passes through our minds. We need to exercise judgment and inhibit some of our impulses. Before sharing anything that feels potentially charged, take a moment to ask yourself whether it would help the other person or team better achieve shared goals. Then ask yourself how best to deliver the information.

For instance, you can:

- ask whether the person wants feedback;
- state *why* you're sharing the information (because you care about the person/team, you're sharing your impressions in case they're useful);
- focus on objective, observable behaviors and their effect on you, rather than making assumptions about someone's intentions or feelings, which are easy to get wrong.

To reflect on your beliefs, ask yourself:

- To what extent do I see myself as a learner who is in a lifelong process of becoming?
- What circumstances in my life do I tend to take as fixed that I might actually be able to influence?
- How might becoming more transparent lead others to more effectively collaborate with me for learning and for performance?

HABITS

Now let's examine the second blade of the growth propeller: habits.

Throughout this book, we've discussed a variety of Learning Zone strategies, but unless we incorporate them into our routine, we won't benefit from them.

By habituating these actions, we program ourselves for growth. We can separate habits into three categories.

1. *Proactive habits* are those we put in place to develop a particular skill or body of knowledge. Expert performers don't just

wait for setbacks or challenges to feed their learning journeys. They are always proactively working to stretch beyond their current capabilities.

Linda Rabbitt follows a habit of daily reading. "I read or I listen to podcasts, or TED Talks or whatever, and whenever there's something that particularly strikes me, I send it to people who I think could benefit from it. So, every morning, from like six-thirty to maybe seven-thirty, I'm reading. I wasn't schooled in business, but I have been a student of business, and I've read everything I can read about succession planning and so forth."

2. *Responsive habits* are triggered by events around us. While we want to be proactive learners, we also need to learn from setbacks, missteps, surprises, and feedback.

During a busy period for Rand Construction, the leadership team was under significant pressure and ended up assigning a relatively new staff member as a project manager with a client. But the new hire wasn't quite ready to properly represent Rand on the job. He reacted defensively to client criticism, which led to an unhappy client.

How did Linda respond?

"I called the client and said, 'I'm really embarrassed, we're better than this. I want to hear from your perspective what we did wrong, so that we can all learn from this.' And the client said, 'You know, everyone makes mistakes. Here's what we hate the most, when we give people feedback, and they get defensive. Thank you for not getting defensive.'"

Responsive habits are about how you take action when you make a mistake, receive feedback, are surprised by something, or encounter a challenging situation. You can reflect on how you tend to respond; identify the events that trigger undesirable behaviors; choose your desired response; and establish a habit to remind yourself of how you want to respond when a particular situation arises.

3. Finally, *stem habits* are stable habits that ensure our constant evolution. While proactive habits change from time to time as we build different skills, stem habits largely do not. These include habits like setting your learning intentions at the start of each week, month, or year, and reviewing them every morning; journaling; or attending a regular gathering to learn with others.

One stem habit I treasure is reminding myself every morning, when I first turn on my computer, what habit I am working to develop or change. I open the same document every morning, which includes reminders to myself. This stable habit fuels my constant evolution and primes a growth mindset and the Learning Zone on a daily basis.

Ask yourself:

- Am I proactively doing something in the Learning Zone daily or weekly to improve in whatever it is I want to get better at?
- Am I regularly soliciting feedback to constantly generate information for my ongoing growth?
- Do I have a stem habit that sets me up to continuously drive my own evolution?

COMMUNITY

Each of us is capable of learning on our own. But we can learn faster and accomplish more in any area if we have access to others who can give us feedback and help us to think, get things done, access resources, and connect with new allies. That's why *community* is the third blade of the growth propeller.

The people around you also deeply influence the other components of your growth propeller—your beliefs, habits, identity, and purpose.

To build an effective community, think about who you want to develop close relationships with, and foster *trust, belonging,* and *collaboration* with them. You can develop trust by transparently sharing some of your thoughts and feelings, gradually going deeper as people share more of themselves in turn. You can cultivate belonging—the feeling that your community is your home—by building trust, identifying common goals, and valuing others for what they bring to your relationship and common pursuits. You can foster collaboration by soliciting and offering help, so that interdependently you can learn and accomplish more. We discuss these important concepts in more depth in subsequent chapters. Part Two of this book is all about building strong communities, teams, and organizations.

As you reflect on your relationships, beware of the stereotypes you hold that may be preventing you from reaching out to people who are unlike you. Diversity brings strength, creativity, and collective intelligence. We want to build communities that recognize the strengths of diversity, in which people of any background feel valued and safe.

As you get to know people and work with them in the two zones, you further advance trust, belonging, and collaboration, which in turn strengthens your ability to engage with them in the two zones. It's a self-reinforcing cycle.

Ask yourself:

- Are my existing relationships serving me well, or would I better grow and perform by surrounding myself with different relationships?
- How can I make this community feel more like home for myself and others?

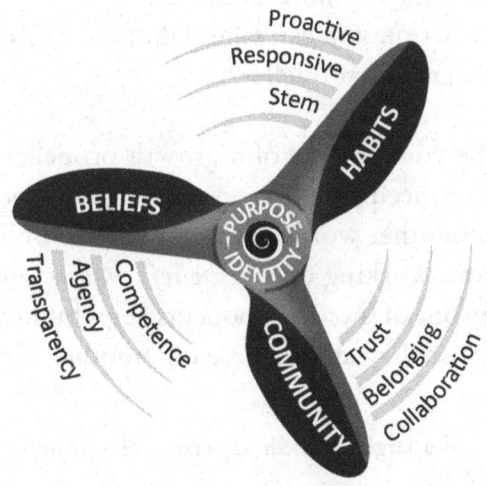

DESIGNING YOUR GROWTH PROPELLER

Now that you have examined the components of a strong growth
propeller, I recommend sketching a vision for yours. What would
you like key aspects of your identity, purpose, beliefs, habits, and
community to become?[1]

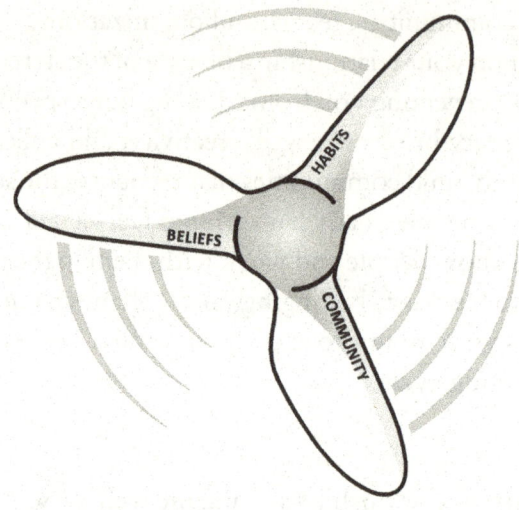

Spend some time reflecting on what you've discovered.

- What parts of your propeller are strongest?
- What parts could use more attention?
- What is one action you can take right now to strengthen one
  area of your growth propeller?

Note that the components of a growth propeller are intercon-
nected; hence, we need to work on them simultaneously, not one
after the other. In other words, we don't have to build our *identity*
or *purpose* before working on our *beliefs, habits,* and *community.*
Working on any one of these components helps build and strengthen
the others, because they all reinforce one another.

[1] You can download a larger, worksheet version of this image at briceno.com/
paradox/resources/.

When the parts of our propeller are aligned, we feel "together," or rooted, which makes us feel more confident and better equipped to navigate life and work.

As Linda Rabbitt puts it, "At the end of the day, you get to be whoever you want to be. And you get to decide how you want to comport yourself, who you want your friends to be, how you want to live your life, how you want to be thought of as you retire. And we all get to make those choices."

You can think through the components of your growth propeller as they relate to any area of your life, be it play, mindfulness, health, rest, joy, or anything else. If you want a thought, emotion, or behavior to gain more presence in your life, work to strengthen your growth propeller accordingly.

For now, after reflecting on your growth propeller, identify what you want to work on for the next month or two, and set a calendar reminder to reflect on how you're doing and what steps to work on from there. Better yet, make that a recurring calendar reminder.

REFLECTION QUESTIONS

- When I reflect on how I want to develop, which of the five elements of my growth propeller feel stronger and weaker? Which are in more need of deliberate work in the Learning Zone?
- Have I developed effective proactive, responsive, and stem Learning Zone habits to continue developing my knowledge and skills? How might I further progress as a skilled learner?
- Am I an active agent of change within my scope of influence?
- Have I reached out to connect and collaborate with other learners?

LOOKING FORWARD

What might a learning organization look like?

Part Two:
Overcoming the Performance Paradox
in Teams and Organizations

Chapter 8: Pillars of a Learning Organization

BIG IDEA *The strongest organizations are learning organizations. Their structures and systems make the development of people the everyday default, which makes them agile, resilient, and impactful.*

When Satya Nadella was promoted to CEO of Microsoft in 2014, the company had a know-it-all culture. Microsoft hired capable people, but new employees soon learned that the way to earn promotions was to be the smartest person in the room and to help their team be the best, relative to other teams in the organization. As Nadella describes in his book, *Hit Refresh*, at times the company felt like a confederation of fiefdoms. The workplace culture discouraged people from being curious, continuing to develop their knowledge and skills, and collaborating to learn and get things done.

A lack of attention to development gave employees the sense that leadership regarded human abilities as largely fixed. This can lead people to avoid taking risks, to withhold information, and, at times, even to sabotage their coworkers. As a result, despite being the largest software company in the world, Microsoft missed giant opportunities cycle after cycle in internet search, mobile operating systems, social media, and cloud technology. Google, Apple, Facebook, and Amazon zipped past them in these new categories.

Microsoft had been fooled by the performance paradox. Stuck in chronic performance, employees largely continued to do things as best as they knew how, without truly challenging themselves in uncharted territory. I've seen this in many companies, and you probably have, too.

While nobody wants to create or work in such a culture, we get into self-reinforcing bad habits because:

- We have learned in our schools, communities, media, and workplaces that we're supposed to know how to do our job and focus on getting things done, and that when things get hard, the solution is to work harder.
- We have gotten used to coming up with to-do lists that fill up our time, rather than taking the time to identify what's most important and how to become more effective at it. It's not just individuals who have gotten used to this, but also our teams and organizations.
- We have internalized the widespread societal assumption that high performance is rooted in competition rather than collaboration. This leads us to work independently and withhold information rather than work together to grow our competencies and collective outcomes.
- Our human bias to overvalue the present and undervalue the future, coupled with reinforcing structures (such as Wall Street's focus on the next quarter's earnings), lead us to forgo investments in the Learning Zone that would yield great performance dividends later on.
- We don't notice the opportunity to work differently because we keep our blinders on, doing too much of our work the way we're used to, purely in the Performance Zone, rather than learning while doing.

In Part Two, we examine how Microsoft and many other organizations have broken out of the performance paradox by setting up structures and rituals that make engaging in the two zones the everyday default.

The objective is not for you to implement everything other organizations do, but to understand what it takes to improve performance and identify a small subset of strategies to work on. Keep in mind that all approaches shared are founded on two principles. First, always portray human abilities and qualities as malleable. Second, put in place the habits, structures, and tools that support both the Learning Zone and the Performance Zone.

In this chapter, we will specifically examine organization-wide structures that enable teams and people to embrace the two zones. These structures are necessary to transform know-it-all cultures into learning organizations — places where people better align, communicate, collaborate, deepen their understanding of customers, innovate, adapt, and remain resilient to drive change and achieve outstanding results.

To avoid missing more opportunities in emerging sectors such as artificial intelligence, mixed reality, quantum computing, and beyond, Nadella — in partnership with Chief People Officer Kathleen Hogan and others — needed to inspire and lead a cultural transformation. Microsoft's 100,000-plus employees had to develop different beliefs, habits, and communities centered on asking more questions, ideating more frequently, collaborating across departments, taking more risks, and pushing boundaries. To overcome the performance paradox, they needed to think beyond flawless execution and embrace the two zones.

MY OWN MISSTEPS AS AN ORGANIZATIONAL LEADER

In 2007, I graduated from the Stanford Graduate School of Business with a mission.

I wanted to take everything I was learning from Carol Dweck's research on mindset and help people put these life-changing ideas into practice. And so I co-founded a company called Mindset Works to help schools cultivate lifelong learning beliefs and behaviors in staff and students, impacting parents and communities in the process.

In our earliest days, we were very clear that we wanted to practice what we preached. That meant building a *growth mindset culture* that looked very different from the way so many organizations operated.

Since we were the team pioneering this new kind of organization, we wanted to model it in the strongest way possible. We were inspired by companies like Patagonia and Zappos, known for building cultures that are wholly unique and connected to their missions.

Headquartered on the Southern California coast, Patagonia is all about the outdoors. When the surf is up, employees are free to leave the office and hit the waves—the company even posts the surf report to keep everyone informed about surf conditions.

While Patagonia has built a unique culture around its passion for nature and outdoor recreation, Zappos has focused deeply on customer service: The company hires for personality and encourages its employees to truly connect with customers, even if that means staying on the phone much longer than a typical customer service call. As reported by *Business Insider,* one Zappos representative famously clocked a record-breaking ten-plus-hour call with a customer!

"Sometimes people just need to call and talk," explained the member of the Zappos Customer Loyalty Team. "We don't judge, we just want to help."

What could these organizations teach us about building a culture that was wholly our own? They had developed cultures that made a strong statement about what they stood for. As a result, they attracted employees who were passionate about the purpose and who pioneered the cause as ambassadors.

We wanted to do the same. We would be extreme when it came to the development of people.

What could possibly go wrong?

A MISGUIDED APPROACH

At the time, very few people had heard of growth mindset. When we spoke with prospective customers, they were intrigued, but they already had a long list of priorities, and growth mindset wasn't on it.

We were okay with that. We saw our work to effect change as a marathon, not a sprint. Considering our mission a lifelong endeavor, we didn't raise any money—investors can be impatient. We decided to bootstrap.

As a way to establish our unique culture of extreme development, I spent considerable time in that first year teaching myself to code so that, with co-founder Steve Goldband's guidance, we could develop our website and enable our preexisting CD-based program to live online. It made for a nice origin story and it fit our nonexistent budget.

Rather than recruit highly experienced people, we would seek a passion for learning and for our mission. We thought that by building the strongest growth mindset culture on the planet, our people would develop their skills at an unprecedented rate, including me as a first-time CEO.

One day, I went to the local Supercuts to get a haircut. Seated in the chair next to me was a recent UC Berkeley grad who was telling his hairstylist what he was looking for in a job. He was seeking something with meaning, something that could change people's lives.

When I overheard him add that he had experience working with youth, I heard passion for the type of work we were doing. And so, after we were both done with our haircuts, I introduced myself, told him about our venture, and asked him to lunch. He later told me that he really didn't know what to make of this stranger approaching him out of nowhere. But, luckily for me, he agreed to the lunch.

Not only did Cole Turay become our first hire, but he and I constituted our whole team for our second year of existence, and we worked together for five years as our team expanded. We stuck to the same hiring philosophy—a passion for learning and contribution—though we did branch out beyond recruiting at Supercuts.

We began finding schools and educators who right away understood the power of growth mindset and signed up for our services, and we made the mistake of taking on as many as we could. We grew rapidly for several years, but eventually we plateaued. Beyond the early adopters, we were failing to persuade prospective customers to make growth mindset a high priority, and our team struggled to navigate school district politics and decision-making processes.

We knew little about sales. We also struggled to work together effectively. Following our strategy to seek only passion, we had built a remote-only organization with staff living all over the United States and across three continents. But we had underestimated the challenges this structure brought to developing relationships and to collaborating, especially during those pre-COVID times when the world wasn't used to it yet.

We had also discounted something important: Learning and improvement, while crucial, take time.

The truth was that passion for our work and for learning wasn't enough to build a company: The preexisting skills job candidates possessed were also very important. We had hired great people with a ton of potential, but we had limited time and resources to support their development. No matter how much we cared about growth and learning, as a cash-poor organization, all too often we had to just focus on getting things *done*. We had been fooled by the performance paradox.

We made a mistake that billionaire venture capitalist Marc Andreessen sees all the time. "I think the archetype myth of the twenty-two-year-old founder has been blown completely out of proportion. . . . I think skill acquisition, literally the acquisition of skills and how to do things, is just dramatically underrated," he said to Stanford engineering students at an event shared on the *a16z Podcast*. "People are overvaluing the value of just jumping into the deep end of the pool, because the reality is that people who jump into the deep end of the pool drown."

We were floundering in the deep end, with too few and inexperienced staff members to serve too many customers with too few resources. This left us in perpetual crisis management mode. Eventually, we applied for a grant, which allowed us to hire more people and develop more robust programs. That way, we gained greater capacity and time for engaging in the Learning Zone rather than needing to be in chronic performance all the time.

Mindset Works eventually did grow, through word of mouth, to serve thousands of schools. We also seeded an ecosystem that made growth mindset a common term and desired approach in many schools throughout the world. But in retrospect, we could have gotten there a lot faster if we had a clearer understanding of what it takes to improve and perform. I learned that having a growth mindset, while necessary, is not enough. And passion and a desire to learn, on their own, are insufficient: Organizational structures that support work in both the Learning Zone and the Performance Zone are crucial.

After five years with us, Cole moved to Salesforce, where he could access more resources and structures to develop his sales skills. He is now a successful sales leader.

As for me, I evolved my understanding and approaches to leadership. When I seek to hire anyone these days, in addition to authentic passion, I also look for domain competence and learning competence: someone who has the specific skills needed to hit the ground running relatively quickly and then grow from there.

In my work over the years since, I've seen many companies of all sizes fall into the same trap we did, but I've also seen great companies with powerful structures for effective growth. In this chapter, I share many of them. Remember that the idea is not for you to implement all of these, but to develop a vision of what learning organizations look like and identify next steps in your journey.

WHAT A LEARNING ORGANIZATION TRULY LOOKS LIKE

When Kevin Mosher joined ClearChoice Dental Implant Centers as CEO, he noticed that 5 to 10 percent of the company's centers were selling their dental procedures much more effectively than the rest of the company.

He called Andy Kimball, a former colleague, and asked him to come on as a consultant to study what those centers were doing differently.

Andy dove into the Learning Zone, observing and asking questions, curious to discover what might account for the difference.

He found that most of the company's salespeople were using the *spray and pray* sales technique. "They would spray information about our procedures at a patient and pray that something met a need," he told me. They were pushing the treatments and the effectiveness of the doctors, without listening to what was really going on in the patients' lives.

Meanwhile, the outstanding salespeople were doing a lot more listening than talking. They didn't see themselves just as salespeople, but also as *problem-solvers*. It had become part of their identity.

Andy, who eventually joined ClearChoice as its chief performance officer, observed that the top sales staff were able to draw out the patients' stories and learn that some were carrying a great deal of shame about what they perceived as their imperfect teeth. "They were trying to also learn from their patients the vision they had for how their life would be with the smile of their dreams. What would be the happy ending for their dental story?"

The company trained all of its salespeople and doctors to learn from those successful practices and set up systems to continue learning. ClearChoice installed video cameras in every consult room. Each week, sales staff and doctors select a skill to work on related to patient communications, and with patient consent, they record the interactions. Between consults, the professionals review a brief segment of the video and consider how they came across or how they could have better answered a question. They rapidly alternate between the Performance Zone (time with patients) and the Learning Zone (the video reviews). Staff can also share videos with a coach or colleagues to solicit feedback, although the videos cannot be seen by others without permission and can be used only for developmental purposes, not for job evaluation. In weekly meetings, people share with peers the things they are working to improve. Since the company began this practice, the highest performers are those who most frequently review and analyze their own videos.

Andy Kimball explained why video is such an essential tool. "Normally when you hear feedback, you can dismiss it. You can say, 'Well, those people obviously don't like me or they don't know me or they don't see me in the consult room.' But when you see yourself on video, there's nothing to dismiss. The video is the great leveler. Video always tells the truth."

ClearChoice staff regularly receive feedback from a variety of sources to help them continue to grow their skills. As a result, the company has flourished, surpassing a core market share of more than 50 percent.

At ClearChoice, videos are used to provide three elements needed for developing a skill. First, they provide a successful model to emulate. From the time employees join the organization, videos of skilled practitioners are used to discuss effective practices, but also to show that even the most skilled practitioners can further improve. Second, videos are used as an opportunity to practice in the Learning Zone. Salespeople participate in recorded training sessions in which they role-play with their coaches, and then the group analyzes the videos together. And third, doctors and sales staff watch their own and one another's daily interactions with patients on video to reflect and provide feedback. The result is a set of solid structures to engage in the Learning Zone, with the clear goal of improving in the Performance Zone.

When ClearChoice first introduced videos as learning tools, about a quarter of the sales force showed a true passion for learning and watched their videos religiously. About 60 percent would watch the videos because they knew they were supposed to, but they didn't have that same level of fire in their belly; the final 15 to 20 percent had a serious aversion to watching themselves on video.

"In this business, when you're trying to train large populations, it's all about skewing the normal curve," Andy said. "We don't get everybody. But if we can get that normal curve to move to the right, where instead of twenty-five percent of the people that have a passion for learning, now we have thirty percent or forty percent, that makes a big difference."

Watching videos is not the only way ClearChoice employees learn. Among my favorites is a collaborative game in which a staff member flips a card and reads a description of a patient case. Each of the other players shares how they would respond, and the group discusses the ideas. Then, the person who initially read the card gives it to whoever provided her favorite approach. The person with the most cards at the end wins the game.

There are also systems for employees to access learning resources to progress on their personal mastery paths, and they earn badges and financial rewards when they reach certain levels. People toward the middle of a learning progression must coach or mentor someone earlier in their development in order to advance—by, for example, observing a performance or watching a consult video and providing feedback. This fosters collaborative learning.

ClearChoice is a learning organization: Everyone comes to work every day in part to grow and is offered the resources, opportunities, and relationships to do so. As Andy said, "It's all about driving passion for learning and then giving the passionate learners the tools they need to satisfy their passion."

As a result of its systems for continuous learning, ClearChoice continues to beat its own records. For the first seventeen years of the company's existence, no salesperson had ever collected more than a million dollars in a single month. Then one of them did, so the company started a million dollar club to celebrate those who reach that milestone. Within the next year, seven other salespeople hit the same milestone.

When the company held an event to celebrate, and the eight club members shared best practices with others, someone asked what they did when they had a bad day, week, or month. Every one of them responded that they turn to reviewing their videos.

In other words, for high achievers, struggle is a cue to jump into the Learning Zone.

We've seen many other examples of that in this book, and we'll see more. When he lost a major sales opportunity, Dipo Aromire scheduled a lunch with the customer to learn what his team had done wrong. When Traca Savadogo struggled to keep up with orders at Starbucks, she experimented with new ideas. When a project went sour, Linda Rabbitt called the client to ask for feedback. When Luke's Lobster's new restaurants achieved disappointing results, leaders gathered data and identified how to plan openings differently going forward. Using struggle as a cue to leap into the Learning Zone is the norm in learning organizations.

FROM KNOW-IT-ALL CULTURES TO LEARNING CULTURES

A group of researchers led by Elizabeth Canning and Mary Murphy set out to explore whether organizations can be considered to have a mindset. They surveyed more than 500 employees at seven Fortune 1000 companies and found that employees at each of the companies generally agreed with one another about whether their company viewed talent as fixed or malleable. Companies like Clear-Choice that make the Learning Zone a vital aspect of operations are perceived by their staff to endorse a growth mindset. Organizations that are all about selection and evaluation aimed at weeding out the incapable and keeping the gifted, without dedication to people's continued growth, are perceived to endorse a fixed mindset.

Canning, Murphy, and their colleagues found that employees who believed their organizations supported a growth mindset also reported higher levels of collaboration, innovation, integrity, trust, and commitment in their workplaces. At those companies, employees were more willing to work interdependently, leap into the unknown, and be honest with themselves and others.

That is, these organizations were more likely to have learning cultures as opposed to know-it-all cultures. When organizations emphasize people's development, employees can more easily build strong growth propellers that allow them to excel in the two zones.

The path to becoming a learning organization involves a combination of top-down and bottom-up efforts. Any of us can start from where we sit. Rather than get frustrated if some people are hesitant, we can connect where there is strong interest and build from there. Focus on what you can most control—starting with your own behavior—and keep pushing the boundaries of what you might be able to influence.

In the rest of this chapter, we will examine additional structures used by learning organizations to foster growth. While this chapter discusses organization-wide structures, many of these strategies can be implemented at the team or even individual level.

CLARIFY YOUR GUIDING LANGUAGE

When Jake and Gino began their real estate company, neither of them thought that having a mission statement or core values was important. Gino's family restaurant had never had anything like that, and Jake's previous company had a mission and core values printed on posters on the walls, but nobody referred to them, and they didn't affect how any of the employees behaved.

But after reading books and attending workshops about business best practices, the two came to understand why being intentional about building culture is critical to success.

Really, it is about designing and cultivating strong growth propellers.

Their company's mission is to "create communities that empower people to become the best version of themselves." Its core values are *growth mindset, make it happen, people first, unwavering ethics,* and *extreme ownership*. They name each core value and identify what behaviors each value entails and why it matters. Jake and Gino refer to the core values regularly and point out when people model or deviate from them, as do others. Staff live by them every day.

This can be done at any scale. One of the companies I serve, Procter & Gamble, ensures that all of its 100,000-plus employees are intimately familiar with what the company calls its PVPs—Purpose, Values, and Principles. In the course of daily work, people throughout the company regularly refer to the PVPs. When someone is not living the PVPs, it is a serious issue that needs to be addressed. This creates a safe environment for those who embrace the principles, which is something anyone can do.

Our statements of mission, core values, and key behaviors should not be exhaustive. Instead, they should be simple, memorable, and focused on the most important desired attributes. This is necessary so that everyone in the organization can easily remember and refer to them daily when giving and receiving feedback, or when they notice the presence or absence of desired behaviors. If people can't recall what the key principles are—which is common in organizations that pick too many—the frameworks in practice don't help guide people's behavior.

With clear, organization-wide guiding language, leaders and individual contributors have more tools at their disposal to advance the desired culture.

DITCH PERFORMANCE-ONLY EVALUATION SYSTEMS

Many organizations have performance management processes through which managers evaluate and share feedback with their direct reports and touch base on career progression. But, fooled by the performance paradox, these yearly rituals most often focus solely on performance rather than also on learning.

The companies I've worked with that are achieving the most success in fostering the two zones have changed their performance management systems to:

- **Get rid of forced rankings where employees are graded based on their relative performance against one another.** In a high-functioning learning culture, all staff can thrive. By collaborating in both zones rather than competing, employees can grow and achieve more. We can encourage that by assessing people based on standards rather than against one another.
- **Include learning goals, not just performance goals.** Ask employees to reflect on how successful they were in developing the skills they set out to grow during the last cycle, what they will set out to learn this coming cycle, and what strategies they'll use. Encouraging them to share this information with their colleagues further cultivates a learning culture and generates more useful peer feedback and support.
- **Foster more frequent, development-oriented conversations.** Rather than a yearly performance conversation, these companies ensure at least a quarterly development conversation, with encouragement and templates for more frequent dialogue.

Ask yourself the following questions to identify opportunities to improve the performance management and support systems in your organization. If your organization's systems have some holes, consider how you can fill them for yourself or for your team, and how you might influence the enterprise:

- When people set goals, do they set only performance goals, or do they also identify what skills they want to improve and how they will go about it?
- Do people reflect on and discuss learning and improvement and what to adjust going forward?
- Are people evaluated relative to others or based on their own effectiveness?
- Are performance goals just individual or also team-based? (Team performance goals can promote collaboration, for both performance and learning.)
- Are there structures beyond the formal evaluative process for people to learn and receive regular feedback?

SET UP SYSTEMS FOR HOW TO LEARN

An organization needs structures and systems to support skill and capability development. These will vary based on the organization's needs.

Dona Sarkar, the software engineer who leads the advocacy team for Microsoft's Power Platform, has noticed that Microsoft's training regimen changed dramatically in recent years after Satya Nadella became CEO.

"Our training used to be 'tech thing, tech thing, tech thing.' Now, when I look at my training schedule, it includes things like 'ethical AI,'" she told me. "If you are building AI and you are not thinking about how it impacts people in South Africa, for example, you are doing it wrong. So, ethical AI is a major mandatory training for every single person in the company."

Other mandatory trainings at Microsoft include building inclusive teams, examining privilege, and communicating across differences. Many other optional trainings and resources are provided for those who want to dive deeper.

Notice that such structures for training and professional development are being used to build not only domain-specific skills, but also the shared identity, purpose, beliefs, and habits that make for strong growth propellers.

"We have people from every generation playing a role: Gen Z, Millennials, Gen X, and Boomers talking about different communication styles across the decades and generations," Dona said. "There were a set of people who were super shocked. They were like, 'What? What are we talking about these at work for? They do not belong in the workplace.' And honestly, for those who didn't come to understand the reason, the answer was, then this might not be the company for you. Because it really, really is a company that values bringing your whole self to work and making it a safe place for everyone to bring their whole selves to work."

In the interest of contributing more broadly, Microsoft has made many of its learning resources on diversity and inclusion publicly available to anyone for free at its Microsoft Inclusion Journey website.

Liquidnet is another company that has many structures to support learning. One is very simple but powerful: All full-time employees are eligible for a $2,500 yearly stipend for pursuing professional development and continuing education opportunities. This benefit doesn't end with the completion of a training; employees are expected to share what they learned with their colleagues. "Continuous learning is baked into the organization's DNA," said Jeff Schwartzman, the company's global head of learning. "It's part of our normal business processes. As an example, someone returns from a seminar and tells their colleagues, 'I took this great program on strategic thinking. I learned about five different types of strategic thinking and how to apply them to different situations.' If it stops there, that's great. The team has benefited from this learning. Sometimes, it even goes further. A colleague will then say, 'That's pretty interesting. I'm going to sign up for that seminar, or I am going to try what I just learned from my colleague and share my experience.' For us, learning should be contagious."

At Telenor, one of the largest mobile telecommunications companies in the world, every employee is given forty hours of paid work time per year to devote to learning, in or outside their workplace. To advance its culture, the company once challenged its staff to break the Guinness World Record for the most people to complete an online personal development lesson within twenty-four hours—a feat they achieved. For the challenge, they chose a course on growth mindset. I had the honor of being part of a broadcast video that invited staff members to participate in the challenge, which the company used as an opportunity to deepen their people's understanding of learning and growth.

New York Life has numerous initiatives to help employees grow and develop skills. One, called the Internal Mobility Program, provides employees with counseling and workshops on topics like career planning, résumé writing, and effective interviewing.

The company also encourages all agents to join a "study group," a group of peers who regularly meet to support and learn from one another, like the one Lizzie Dipp Metzger joined. Unsurprisingly, agents who participate in study groups are much more likely to attain higher performance. From agent surveys, New York Life estimates that 58 percent of its most successful agents participate in study groups, whereas only 7 percent of its least successful agents do. From conversations I've had with many of NYL's high-

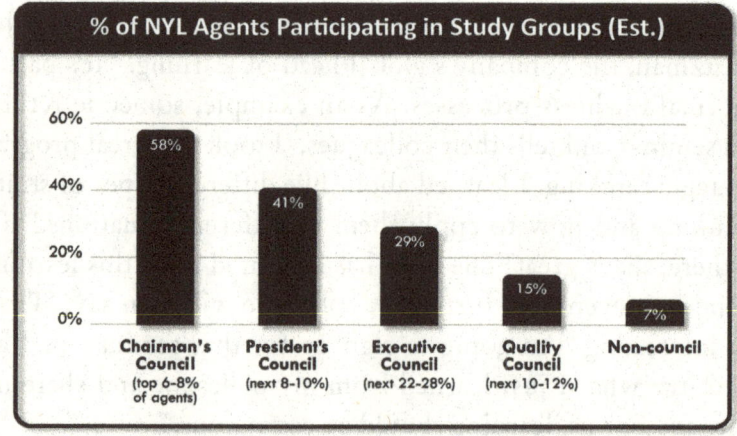

% of NYL Agents Participating in Study Groups (Est.)

performing agents, I believe that those who don't engage in study groups do regularly engage in other Learning Zone strategies.

This relationship between the Learning Zone and performance has also been shown in research. Sabine Sonnentag and Barbara Kleine found that the best insurance agents engage in learning at least once a week. They read to expand their knowledge, consult with colleagues or domain experts, try out new strategies, run mental simulations, ask for feedback, and reflect.

It's just like we saw earlier in this chapter with ClearChoice Dental—the more salespeople review videos to learn from them, the higher their results. The pattern holds across companies and industries. It shows that the Learning Zone does not detract from high performance; it enables it.

Organization-wide tools and structures can support any of the Learning Zone strategies we have examined so far in the book—experimentation, mid-action reviews, and feedback, to name a few. When senior leaders make these structures and tools available rather than relying on managers and employees to develop these habits on their own, it becomes easier for everyone to regularly engage in the Learning Zone.

Any of us can put in place resources and programs that help colleagues learn about growth mindset and other foundational beliefs, habits, and principles, or point people to excellent resources that are already available. It can be as simple as giving each person a yearly budget for learning programs they want to attend, like Liquidnet does, or providing guidance and spaces for employees to learn from one another, like New York Life does. And if our main sphere of influence is the team level rather than an entire organization, we can align with our close colleagues to implement any of these approaches.

When creating initiatives to support development, we need to consider who these programs and resources are open to. Everyone should have access to resources for further development, from the most junior to the most senior staff members. If we choose to designate some programs for only employees assessed to have "high potential," similar programs should be available to others, and we should take care not to forever mark people as either high potential or not.

Consider these questions:

- What is the most important skill for you, your team, or your organization to get great at?
- What Learning Zone strategies would drive development in that skill or capability? What structures can support the use of those strategies?
- Who might be a sponsor or ally to help strengthen Learning Zone structures?

SET UP STRUCTURES FOR RISK-TAKING AND EXPERIMENTATION

Large technology companies like IBM or Google have research and development teams whose job is to explore uncharted territory: to expand the boundaries of science, invent new technologies, and turn them into products. These structures have led to many of the inventions most of us now can't live without, from personal computers and smartphones to medical imaging machines and wireless connectivity.

Multinational professional services company Deloitte launched Deloitte Ventures as a resource for any employee to access innovation strategies, tools, and communities. Global textile manufacturer Coats created Innovation Hubs, dedicated spaces with specialized equipment for employees to ideate and prototype new product ideas together with customers and suppliers. Microsoft implemented massive hackathons for any employee to recruit a team and collaboratively ideate, prototype, test, and evolve any new ideas they want to work on.

But do we need high-tech or massive R&D budgets to stretch our capabilities or innovate?

Certainly not! At the team level, when Brad Willoughby, Oracle

Cloud Infrastructure director, was leading the Major Incident Management organization, he instituted small experiments as a way of promoting a culture of intelligent risk-taking. Each quarter, everyone in his team did an experiment of their choosing and presented findings to their peers. What he cared about was participation, intelligent risk-taking, and sharing lessons learned.

Using this procedure, the team made many process improvements, like ending a recurring daily communication task that was time-consuming and mentally draining, and—they hypothesized—not generating useful information. Thanks to their experiment to eliminate the task—which didn't result in complaints from the people receiving the reports—the team members discovered that they had more power to influence their environment than they realized. Most important, they fostered a culture of intelligent risk-taking.

As you think about ways to foster experimentation, consider:

- What times and spaces can serve as low-stakes islands for people to take risks to learn, without causing significant harm?
- How can you bring diverse people together, perhaps across functions or organizations, to widen the range of ideas, perspectives, and know-how?
- How can you set up structures that guide and remind people that the purpose of experimentation is learning?

SCALE BEST PRACTICES

There's no reason why quarterly small experiments—or any other Learning Zone structure—couldn't be instituted at the department- or organization-wide level. That can help advance culture, community, identity, beliefs, and habits. But beware of mandating too much. The Microsoft hackathons, New York Life study groups, and Deloitte Ventures programs are optional, which is wise.

We need to balance scaling structures and processes that work—which also makes it easier for people to take action—with not extinguishing people's ability to choose what works best for them and to try other approaches that might work better. One way is to make programs easily accessible but optional.

Consider those tensions when you're designing organization-wide structures to promote a learning culture and habits, such as:

- innovation rituals like hackathons or quarterly small experiments;
- ways to tap external expertise, such as access to LinkedIn Learning, external speaker events, or trade association resources;
- tools for people to test new ideas with small groups before launching big;
- structures for analyzing mistakes and failures, transforming processes that led to them, and sharing lessons learned.

RECRUIT, HIRE, AND ONBOARD FOR GROWTH

Recruiting, hiring, and onboarding can help us not only select people who are already effective learners, but also ignite their further transformations.

Incoming employees are going through a life transition, which is an opportunity for change. That can include parts of their identity, beliefs, and habits.

During transitions, people know they need to make changes to adapt to the new context. They are highly attentive to how people in the new sphere behave and what they value, so that they can act accordingly in order to be accepted and thrive.

That's an opportunity.

For this reason, a lot of growth mindset research interventions are done during times of transition, such as when people start a new school, grade, university, or program.

We want to put in place systems that make clear statements to potential recruits about what our organization stands for, such as learning, taking risks, discussing failures, soliciting feedback, and changing as the default. We want people who are attracted to those philosophies to energetically engage in the recruiting process, and those who are fearful of them to seek other places better suited to them. And we want those who join to learn more about how to live those values every day in collaboration with others.

Not only does this clear messaging help attract the people with the strongest growth propellers, but it also gives those people greater clarity and confidence to engage in the desired behaviors off the bat, rather than being more tentative and feeling that they need to learn more about the culture before taking risks.

At ClearChoice, the onboarding of a new salesperson starts with a series of learning missions they complete during their "Observation Week." One of their first missions is a scavenger hunt to learn about the organizational structure, interview key colleagues, and draw what they learn on a piece of paper. Then they study the form salespeople have to fill out for each customer interaction and sit in on consultations with customers to observe and coach a more experienced salesperson as they apply the form in real life. Coaching is viewed as a learning process. "No one learns more than the coach," remarked Andy Kimball.

Once they finish those steps, new hires travel to company headquarters in Denver to debrief on what they've learned, study the company's values and principles, watch videos of actual consultations to assess effective and ineffective practices, and, finally, practice in high-fidelity role-plays.

"The goal is not to teach them a script. We don't believe in scripts. We believe in teaching them concepts and principles for success. Then we offer them a structure, a best-practice sequence in which to apply those principles," Andy explains. "What we want them to do is to find their own voice. We practice for them to remember the steps, then we practice for them to weave their own voice into those steps. It's kind of like practicing for a play: You first have to remember the words, then you have to make it your own, and you can improvise once you really understand what you're trying to accomplish."

In the process, newbies come to see clearly that learning doesn't stop at onboarding.

PROMOTE BELONGING, TRUST, AND COLLABORATION

On the growth propeller, belonging, trust, and collaboration are key elements of the *community* blade. Clearly, onboarding processes that build those elements set people and teams up for success, and we can continue to reinforce them going forward.

Accenture onboards more than 150,000 new employees across the world every year, in the same space, called One Accenture Park. It's a virtual campus located within the "Nth floor," Accenture's metaverse. For a fully immersive experience, new employees wear a virtual reality headset that effectively teleports them into the space. They can move around, meet other new hires from all over the world, and speak with them. Just like in a real room, they hear the people they're speaking with loud and clear, and others nearby at a lower volume in the background. After the formal program begins, they are teleported to replicas of real spaces, such as Accenture's innovation lab in San Francisco. This allows new employees to learn about Accenture and to feel welcome and connected with others. The virtual space remains available going forward, for people to gather for work meetings or just to socialize.

Of course, there are also low-tech ways to promote belonging, trust, and collaboration. Many organizations bring people together via inexpensive video conferencing services or in person.

Dale Carnegie & Associates long-time CEO, Peter Handal, fostered trust and belonging by frequently reminding everyone in meetings and communications that the company had several assigned ethics officers that anyone could contact about ethical issues, including any type of harassment. Handal regularly gave everyone the mobile phone number of the outside counsel that they could reach if they weren't comfortable bringing up an issue with an in-house ethics officer. Not only did this give people a sense of agency and transparency if any ethical or harassment issue arose, but it also gave everyone the sense that they were valued and protected.

When setting out to promote belonging, trust, and collaboration, it pays to invest in the Learning Zone to become more aware of dynamics that often affect underrepresented populations. For instance, when almost everyone in a group belongs to a particular demographic, people in the majority group may not consciously discriminate or treat anyone differently, so they may disregard sociodemographic characteristics like race or gender and view them as nonissues. But people in the underrepresented groups tend to notice that they are the only ones in a room. They wonder why, and they may be wary of taking risks that could reinforce negative stereotypes about their group. Stanford professor of psychology Claude Steele coined this phenomenon *stereotype threat*. As he describes in his book *Whistling Vivaldi,* this negatively affects people's performance, and a growth mindset helps mitigate it.

When we have a diverse workforce and foster a sense of belonging, not only do we avoid stereotype threat's drag on performance, but we also increase the group's intelligence, because as more people speak up, we are able to tap into a greater variety of knowledge and perspectives that make for more informed and creative ideas. This strengthens our collective effectiveness in any situation, but especially when we seek to serve a diverse customer base. It supports both the Learning Zone and the Performance Zone.

SET UP STRUCTURES TO PROMOTE DIVERSITY AND INCLUSION

During their first year at the Stanford Graduate School of Business, Eugene Baah and Patrick Kann roomed together. Early in the year, the two went out to dinner in the neighborhood. They ordered at the counter, paying separately, each with their credit card, but only Eugene was asked for identification. It was clear to both of them that the reason was race—Eugene is a dark-skinned Black man, while Patrick looks white.

Patrick was shocked by the cashier's behavior, but he was also surprised that Eugene didn't seem fazed. Patrick, who is from Brazil, was confused. He saw Eugene as a polished, Princeton-graduated

Stanford classmate with a sophisticated British accent. Why was Eugene discriminated against and not him? By the time they sat down to wait for their food, Patrick had processed his thoughts enough to express his astonishment to Eugene at what had just occurred. Eugene explained that this sort of thing happened to him all the time. Patrick asked what they should do—whether they should ask to speak with a manager. Eugene told him, "Patrick, here's what I'd like you to do. One day, you will start your own company. I want you to make sure that the people you hire don't act like that."

It was a life-changing moment. A decade later, Patrick cofounded Papaya, the bill payment mobile app. His co-founder, Jason Meltzer, another white man, also cared about equity, and they set out to build a diverse and inclusive workplace.

And yet, two years after Patrick and Jason founded Papaya, they looked around and realized that they had compiled a team of half a dozen white men. They had made the mistake of becoming so solely focused on researching customer needs, building prototypes, and testing assumptions, that they had overlooked setting up structures to foster the diverse and inclusive workforce they sought. They learned from their mistake and began putting systems in place, and they have achieved great progress ever since. Today, about 60 percent of their staff comes from underrepresented groups, which they consider a great source of strength for their organization.

The company shies away from hiring quotas, believing it can do a better job at increasing diversity by instituting processes to attract more diverse pools of candidates. For instance, Papaya is now very careful in how it writes job postings.

"We know that, on average, underrepresented job seekers are less likely to apply to a job if they don't meet all the requirements," Patrick points out. "So, we remove anything that is 'good to have' and just include the must-haves. And we challenge ourselves about things like, do they need five years? Could it be four, could it be three? We always challenge ourselves on putting in things that are strictly necessary."

They also clearly state Papaya's values regarding diversity and inclusion at the top of each posting. This encourages the self-selection of people who resonate with the values, and it also attracts people from underrepresented groups. On one occasion, when Patrick was interviewing a person of color, he asked her why she wanted to work at Papaya. Without missing a beat, she recited from memory part of Papaya's values statement from the top of the job posting: "Flexibility, communication, and a willingness to learn are of the highest importance. Papaya believes that diversity helps build an inclusive culture where all team members can grow, contribute, and feel valued. If you agree, we'd love to hear from you!"

Once candidates come into headquarters for an interview, they see an office that Patrick describes as "boring." The idea is to remove any decorations or items that might send a subtle message to candidates that they don't belong.

"We don't have Ping-Pong tables because they could discourage people who do not like Ping-Pong," he told me. "Anything that could be associated with some sort of demographic, we will remove that. So, it's a boring office on purpose."

Employees can personalize their space, but common space is unadorned.

If the candidate is being interviewed by a panel, Papaya makes sure that the panel includes employees who represent a variety of demographics. Papaya also isn't shy about hiring a great candidate right away, even if the position the candidate will fill won't be opening up for another six months or a year.

At first, Papaya operated like many fast-moving startups, without formalities like hierarchical titles or yearly performance reviews. But Papaya discovered that performance reviews can be highly valuable for underrepresented staff members, providing an idea of where they stand and what they need to do to advance to the next level. The company also discovered the importance of titles.

"It's the common thing at startups to say, 'It's not about titles, it's about attitude, it's about impact to the company,'" Patrick said. "But the reality is that if you are an underrepresented professional, you can be more affected by unconscious bias. Like if you are a director versus a manager, how you are heard is different. So, we have learned that actually, titles are very important in terms of inclusion."

Papaya's diversity and inclusion gains have come as a result of its leaders continuing to engage in the Learning Zone in pursuit of the goals they care about. And they do so not only to help particular people, but to improve the company's systems for the benefit of all present and future staff and the organization as a whole. Their approach has helped Papaya develop a great service, raise more than $65 million in funding, and expand its customer base to hundreds of thousands of organizations and many millions of users.

When leaders don't continue to engage in the Learning Zone to question their assumptions and discover more effective approaches, the seemingly strong cultures of their organizations can be a major obstacle to progress and growth.

Environmental activist and social entrepreneur Angelou Ezeilo, who is African American, founded a nonprofit called Greening Youth Foundation to educate young people of color about the vital importance of being stewards of the environment and to expose them to the vast array of careers in the environmental world.

As Ezeilo wrote in her book *Engage, Connect, Protect,* when federal agencies recruited from GYF's pool of applicants, they focused their review on information that was relevant to the skills needed for the job. So that's the information GYF was accustomed to providing, as government agencies made up its first client base.

But when Ezeilo began approaching private companies, she noticed they worked differently.

"They wanted so much more. . . . What are their personal interests? What are their hobbies?" she wrote. "We were stunned, trying to figure out what these companies were looking for. Why did they care about all these intangibles? What we eventually realized is that they were thinking about their corporate culture."

Ezeilo and her team recognized that the companies were trying to assess which of the GYF applicants might be a good "fit." But when companies don't examine whether their idea of "fit" is exclusionary, as Papaya did, it's easy for them to end up with a homogenous workforce. It has contributed to the environmental movement being largely white.

The hiring processes of the companies with which Ezeilo was engaging were in direct conflict with their new goal of diversifying their workforce.

Ezeilo points out that promoting belonging isn't just a racial issue. Even inside her foundation, whose staff is all Black, there were some challenging moments, such as when she tried to incorporate wellness practices like meditation and yoga into the company culture. One of her employees complained that he was uncomfortable being alone with his thoughts because he was going through some personal difficulties.

"I had never considered anything like that," she wrote. "I'm constantly growing as I deal with my staff. But these are important moments, demonstrating the value of diversity and being considerate of many different viewpoints. Diversity pushes us all to be empathetic. And just as importantly, to be flexible."

This means identifying what is truly essential and gathering a team of people from all walks of life who share that passion and approach.

As these stories illustrate, the journey for strengthening belonging, trust, and collaboration—especially when it comes to fostering diversity, equity, and inclusion—involves a lot of aha moments. When these surprises arise, we must reflect on them to extract their precious insights.

We can also proactively engage in a learning journey to read about or listen to what people in underrepresented groups tend to experience and what experts have found out. Then we can interrogate any of our organizational systems, such as reporting structures, compositions of teams, and who collaborates with whom. Some questions to consider:

- How might I learn whether everyone feels a sense of belonging?

- Where might we be excluding people from important conversations, and where might we be overwhelming people with too much information or too many meetings?
- Does everyone feel supported in pursuing stretch areas of interest?
- Might I sometimes hold lower expectations for some groups of people, and how might that affect my interactions with them and how much they grow as a result?
- Who gets to interact with customers? Who *doesn't* get to—and is that preventing them from learning directly from the people we serve?
- Are there job rotations and other cross-divisional structures to promote systems thinking, multidisciplinary collaboration, and an organization-wide identity?

CONDUCT PULSE SURVEYS

Through engaging in open and honest conversations as we collaborate, we may gain a good sense of the strength of our culture and the extent to which people are embracing Learning Zone behaviors. But we shouldn't stop there.

Conducting regular *pulse surveys* generates more objective data, giving everyone an equal voice and helping us uncover blind spots and biased perceptions in our interactions. It allows us to act based on data rather than on assumptions. Make it a habit to measure the experiences of the whole workforce by asking them to what extent they agree with statements such as:

- This company cares for and supports my development.
- My supervisor encourages me to take smart risks and acknowledges they may not work out as planned.
- When people make mistakes or take a risk and fail, colleagues respond by extracting lessons learned rather than placing blame.
- My peers solicit feedback frequently and learn from it rather than get defensive.

- Senior leaders solicit feedback, indicate what they're working to improve, and share their mistakes and lessons learned.

Consider also asking for open-ended feedback so that employees can share ideas that may not be on your radar.

MANY ROUTES TO A LEARNING ORGANIZATION

In building a learning organization, keep in mind that a workforce of engaged and thriving employees isn't the only benefit. A high-functioning learning organization will also induce better performance and result in a meatier bottom line.

Microsoft truly transformed its culture, and results followed. In the eight years after Satya Nadella became CEO, revenues more than doubled. Net income more than tripled. The stock price increased more than 700 percent. For a global behemoth that was almost four decades old when Nadella took charge, that's remarkable. It is the result of identifying key principles of success, aligning around them, and working to change all structures and behaviors accordingly.

When assessing your company policies on your path to a learning culture, keep in mind that any one policy or structure can inadvertently promote a fixed mindset, a growth mindset, or neither. We want to avoid structures that can be interpreted as implying that abilities are fixed, such as evaluation systems that simply compare people to one another and thereby suggest that talent is zero-sum.

We also want to have many clear ways to support the Learning Zone in everyday routines, so it is evident that the development of people, teams, and the organization is a core priority and supported in real ways.

This does not mean we should seek to put in place a ton of new structures overnight. We can start where we are, invite people to experiment, and improve from there, focused on what we can most influence. We can encourage testing and iteration as well as the idea that a great culture is ever evolving.

With a picture of what learning organizations can look like as the end goal, let's dive into ways to foster learning teams—a crucial building block.

REFLECTION QUESTIONS

- Does everyone in my organization feel a sense of belonging? What structures might need modification to become more inclusive?
- Do we have routines in place for everyone to regularly identify learning goals and how to pursue them, assess progress, and identify desired adjustments?
- What structures and systems could better support the learning habits my colleagues and I want to build and promote, and which structures might be getting in the way?

LOOKING FORWARD

How might I inspire my team to embrace the two zones?

Chapter 9: Getting Teams in the Zones

BIG IDEA *Powerful norms, principles, and techniques can equip any team to embrace the two zones. You can draw inspiration from design thinking and adapt its techniques to build a distinctive learning culture.*

When I started my graduate studies at Stanford, the university was launching the Hasso Plattner Institute of Design. The "d.school," as it is called, was initially housed in a temporary modular trailer set up on campus. After eighteen months, it moved to another department's floor—still without its own space. True to the school's philosophy, it was prototyping itself as it launched its initial classes and programs, some of which I participated in. The leadership and students were learning while doing, which was delightful to observe and experience.

A classmate of mine, Razmig Hovaghimian, took a course called Design for Extreme Affordability, nicknamed "Extreme." He was assigned to a group with three other students, all strangers, and they were presented with a challenge.

In their first twenty-eight days of life, more than three million babies die every year. A significant reason, especially for babies born premature, is hypothermia, which, if the baby survives, can also cause lifelong health issues such as cognitive impairment, early-onset diabetes, and liver disease. To prevent hypothermia, premature babies are put in incubators that keep them warm. However, these devices are very costly—around $20,000—and are unavailable in many parts of the world.

The Extreme program challenges students to come up with solutions that cost 1 percent of currently available alternatives. This meant that the student team needed to design an incubator that cost no more than $200 to produce. Additionally, all designs needed to be small enough to carry via backpack or bicycle.

The students dove into the Learning Zone to get smart about the problem. As Tom and David Kelley describe in their book, *Creative Confidence*, the students sent one of their teammates, Linus Liang, to Nepal to meet medical practitioners, parents, and others affected by the issue. He was surprised to find unused incubators in hospitals. Some had been donated, but there wasn't always a skilled technician available to operate the machines or to perform the regular maintenance they required. Some incubators were in a state of disrepair.

Linus learned that 90 percent of the babies dying from hypothermia were born in rural villages, far from hospitals. The villages often lacked skilled technicians, funds to purchase expensive machines, or, in some cases, reliable electricity. He also learned that 85 percent of babies were born at home.

The students set out to design a device that worked without electricity and that was inexpensive, portable, safe, and easy for a mother or midwife to operate at home.

By the end of the two-quarter course, the team had designed a prototype, similar to a sleeping bag, that could provide heat at the required constant temperature of 98.6 degrees Fahrenheit for up to four hours. It was easy to use and portable, and could quickly be rewarmed (and sanitized) by placing one of its components inside a pot of boiling water for a few minutes. The students would later receive a patent for their invention.

The incubator could be made for $25.

The students took the course because they wanted to learn about design and work on projects where they could make an impact. But after learning about a serious need and coming up with an idea that could save millions of lives, they felt called to pursue it after graduation. The students formed a nonprofit, which they called Embrace, to develop a viable product and bring it to the world.

They decided initially to focus on India, a large market where more than two million premature babies are born each year, mostly in villages. They could manufacture the devices there and later expand to neighboring Nepal and Bangladesh.

The team moved to Bangalore. They designed a device that could be manufactured cheaply and was reusable, yet durable—no easy task. The group also had to make the device safe, intuitive, culturally sensitive, and conducive to enabling mother-child interactions, following the "kangaroo care" practice endorsed by the World Health Organization.

Aside from designing the incubator, the team needed to figure out how to persuade elders and midwives in rural villages to trust them enough to place fragile newborns in this new device. Through interviews, the team found that they needed to convince village doctors, whom they learned sought guidance from town and city physicians. The team figured out ways to work through the line of influence, and eventually conducted clinical trials that showed the device was as effective as a traditional incubator.

As of this writing, Embrace has saved more than 350,000 lives across twenty countries in Africa, Asia, and Latin America, and has done so at less than 1 percent of the cost of an inaccessible alternative.

Embrace is just one of the organizations that have come out of the Extreme program. Two other classmates of mine, Sam Goldman and Ned Tozun, took the same course the prior year, when it focused on Myanmar. Like the Embrace team, they didn't know each other before taking the class. Through the course, they identified a huge need for affordable lighting and power, designed a solar-powered system, and started d.light, a company whose name pays tribute to the d.school. Over time, they developed a suite of products ranging from lanterns to full home systems, as well as local support, financing solutions, and partnerships with phone, radio, and TV manufacturers. They have now sold more than twenty-five million products to low-income, off-grid families that previously didn't have access to reliable power, devices, or financing. They have impacted the lives of more than 140 million people across seventy countries. In the process, they are helping the world transition from kerosene—which emits greenhouse gases and can cause burns and fires—to solar.

What powerful process enables a group of strangers to dive into a challenge they know nothing about, become a learning team, and rock the two zones to innovate in a way that impacts so many lives?

The foundational principles and techniques taught at the d.school—called *design thinking* or *human-centered design*—foster learning teams. This problem-solving approach was pioneered by the design firm IDEO—whose founder David Kelley was also a key founder of the d.school—and is now used by thousands of organizations throughout the world. Design thinking can equip any team to overcome the performance paradox and has led to breakthrough innovations from leading companies, including Airbnb, Apple, GE HealthCare, Google, IBM, Intuit, Microsoft, Netflix, Nike, Procter & Gamble, Uber, and many others.

The good news is that anyone can learn design thinking techniques and philosophies and use them to ignite learning in their teams so that they act with resourcefulness and imagination, all while making life and work more fulfilling and "d.lightful" along the way.

Design thinking is just an example. There are many other philosophies, norms, and processes you can use to foster learning teams. These can be inspired by other leaders or organizations we meet in this book, or you can make up your own, as many of the people we are meeting have done. We have already seen many such examples—"be bold," "extreme ownership," "learn big by experimenting small," "work smarter, not harder," "change is our default," "video always tells the truth," and "progress rather than perfection"—and we'll see many more.

But if you're not sure where to start, design thinking provides an established, cohesive set of simple principles, norms, and techniques that anyone can draw from, and it benefits from a worldwide community that can help facilitate learning and practice. It can be used to complement other principles and techniques you draw from.

Going through the design thinking process together helps you form a community with shared identity, purpose, beliefs, and habits to thrive in the two zones.

A beautiful aspect of the design thinking process is that it's flexible. You can adjust it to fit your needs, and you can apply some of the principles to different aspects of your work to cultivate and support a culture of learning and high performance.

Consider the following steps, principles, and techniques, inspired from design thinking, for cultivating a learning team. I was introduced to these concepts and exercises during my time at Stanford. Great books to learn more about design thinking are d.school executive director Sarah Stein Greenberg's *Creative Acts for Curious People* and the Kelley brothers' *Creative Confidence*.

As always, the goal is not for you to do every one of these things, but to consider which techniques could be of use. Also remember that all techniques are grounded in two core principles: portray abilities and qualities as malleable, and set up structures and habits for the two zones.

GATHER PEOPLE FROM DIFFERENT DISCIPLINES AND BACKGROUNDS AROUND A COMMON PURPOSE

Design thinking encourages the gathering of a multidisciplinary and diverse team. The Design for Extreme Affordability program is open to students from all Stanford schools, and the faculty carefully crafts each team. The Embrace team included two students from the engineering school (Rahul Panicker, electrical engineering, and Linus Liang, computer science) and two from the business school (Jane Chen, who came from the world of philanthropy, and my friend Razmig, who came from management consulting and international development).

People from different backgrounds and specializations tend to offer different knowledge and ways of thinking, which generates a smarter and more innovative collective. In the case of Embrace, none of the team members had any background in neonatology or medical devices. But even people who have no specific knowledge of the challenge being tackled can see things through different lenses and tap into ideas from different contexts. Some of the ideas generated might initially be naive or problematic, but they may still serve as seeds that sprout feasible solutions.

Your team should have a common purpose. At a hospitality company, it could be to ensure a hotel is meeting the needs of guests living with disabilities. The team could focus on creating accessible pathways through the property, identifying potential disability needs, and rebuilding the website to be more accessible for those with impairments. Some of your team members may be more or less motivated, but you can foster cohesiveness by reminding people of the higher purpose of the work and how it impacts lives. Going through the design thinking process builds purpose and cohesion, because team members discover human needs and experience insights, and in the process they deepen their connections with one another.

Having a strong shared purpose—an emotional tie to our work—and strategies for how to realize it bonds us to one another and gives us the energy to put in the mental and physical effort required in both zones.

AGREE ON ONE OR MORE FACILITATORS

If you're going through the design thinking process, it can be helpful to have one or more facilitators who are familiar with it to craft the process for your team, to guide it along the way, and to propose norms and foster team alignment.

The process moves through stages, which generally alternate between divergent thinking and convergent thinking—between expanding possibilities (creating options) and narrowing them (making choices). Team members must be clear on what stage they are in, as each entails different thoughts and behaviors.

Divergent thinking is like hitting the gas, while convergent thinking is like hitting the brakes. You don't want to be hitting the gas and brakes at the same time.

Divergent thinking is when we seek to expand possibilities. We explore, research the unknown, and add ideas. Sample norms for this stage:

- Bring a beginner's mind. Focus on what you don't know rather than what you do know.
- Observe, ask open-ended and follow-up questions, and seek to uncover new insights.
- Encourage wild ideas and go for quantity, not quality.
- Defer judgment. Welcome ideas without evaluating them— and don't evaluate your own contributions.
- Get silly and energetic, and have fun.

After a divergent thinking stage comes a convergent thinking stage, which is about making choices. We take the explosion of observations, insights, and ideas generated in the previous stage and we slow down, engage our reasoning, consider what may hold the greatest promise, and identify the guiding question, hypothesis, or idea we will test. Sample norms for a convergent thinking stage include:

- Write down all the observations, new insights, and questions that have emerged, one by one, vocalizing them in a shared space.
- Discuss your insights as a team, thinking together in order to go deeper.
- Identify a guiding question, central need, or point of view.

Norms like these create clarity and alignment so members can more confidently behave in ways that will help the team succeed. Any of us can use these norms—or ones like them—to build learning teams.

An overarching philosophy of design thinking, which also helps foster a growth mindset and the Learning Zone, is to trust the process. That is, don't evaluate design thinking until you have completed the process. Once people have gone through a cycle, they are often amazed by the end at what they and their teammates were able to learn, invent, and accomplish. Once they have experienced this magic, it is easier going forward to leap into the Learning Zone in other contexts.

ESTABLISH TRUST

Aside from developing trust in the process, it's essential to develop trust among teammates. Effective collaboration, in both the Learning and Performance Zones, requires it. Without trust, people tend to become guarded and risk averse.

You can build trust as you work together, but it's often helpful to spend a bit of time up front getting to know one another. Each person can share their intentions, what draws them to this work, and what they hope to gain from it and contribute. By having these conversations, you also set a foundation to further strengthen trust as you work together, because in making the implicit explicit, it becomes easier for others to interpret your words and actions in the ways you intend, leaving less room for misunderstanding.

EXPLORE, GET PROXIMAL, AND EXAMINE CLOSELY

After the team agrees on a population or user to focus on, the design thinking process generally starts with research. This can include more traditional investigation such as online research or expert interviews, but ideally it also involves human-centered empathy work. That means getting out of the office and into the space inhabited by the people you seek to serve, observing them in their natural settings going about their daily routines. You can also interview them with open-ended, probing questions. Engage in exploratory inquiry without preconceived notions, trying to get in their shoes and identify their unrecognized needs.

The research process falls under the category of divergent thinking because we are seeking to expand our awareness. We get rid of previously held assumptions, venture into the unknown, and notice what we've never noticed before. When we do this as a team, it requires collaboration to prepare good questions, secure users, put them at ease, and make close observations. It's an emotional, shared experience of discovery and of generating insights for the task at hand that also brings us closer together as a team. This is true of all aspects of design thinking.

We tend to overestimate how much we understand the people we seek to serve, in part because of the *false consensus bias:* the natural human tendency to think that others think like us. But there's no replacement for getting close to the people we seek to serve in their own setting.

It's one of the things Satya Nadella started doing once he became Microsoft's CEO: devoting parts of his executive team retreats to customer visits. Initially, "there was more than a little eye-rolling and groaning," he writes in *Hit Refresh*. But then his colleagues saw the value. "The executives listened. They learned together. They made new connections with one another. They put down those proverbial guns and discovered new ways Microsoft could fulfill its mission in the world. They experienced the power of having a diverse, cross-company team solving customers' problems together."

By observing and discovering together, we gain insights and nurture a culture of exploration, collaboration, and growth.

IDENTIFY A GUIDING QUESTION OR NEED

After exploring and researching, we pause and take time to share our observations and insights. We also come up with a guiding question, need, or point of view.

We're moving into the realm of convergent thinking.

Sharing insights expands our awareness. We voice what we have seen with new eyes, hear about what others saw, and build on one another's observations and wonderings. We are collaborating to synthesize what we've observed, to narrow down on the user and need, and to co-create a guiding question or point of view that will direct our next steps.

A number of techniques can help us synthesize and define.

HAVE ONE CONVERSATION AT A TIME

Engage your teammates in an inclusive and collaborative conversation instead of splitting into side conversations, with different people speaking simultaneously. After someone shares something, they write it on a sticky note and place it on a poster or wall where everyone can see.

You can split that wall into quadrants including, for example: Said, Did, Thought, and Felt. This prompts teammates to capture more observations.

Include anything that surprised you while you engaged in close observation of your end user: new insights, pain points, opportunities, needs. Teammates might write down observations like "Feels she's doing it on her own"; "Wants more direct contact with her colleagues"; "Feels scattered because her supplier is unreliable"; "Has symbols of her ethnicity throughout her space"; "Brightened with a big smile when we asked about the accordion."

While any of these design thinking steps can be done in less structured ways, clear norms support learning, performance, and the development of culture. For example, establishing the norm that two people shouldn't talk at the same time ensures that everyone hears everyone else and is on the same page for the next steps. It also tends to mitigate unconscious biases and foster inclusion.

CATEGORIZE INTO THEMES

Look for patterns. Move the sticky notes around to create clusters that relate to one another. As themes emerge, you will see connections that lead to additional insights and areas of opportunity.

IDENTIFY A USER

Design thinking is human-centered. This means that the whole process is focused on the needs of a specific person, avatar, or target population.

The Embrace team had to decide whether to focus on the needs of babies, parents, or nonprofit workers—and specifically which ones. They decided to focus on "desperate parents in a remote village, without resources to access a major hospital."

A restaurant chain might decide to use design thinking to discover the unmet needs of families on a tight budget, single professionals in a rush to get back to work, or kitchen staff under workplace and personal stress. A shipping company might focus on the needs of senders, recipients, or drivers. A hospital might focus on the needs of patients getting knee surgery, their families, or the nursing staff.

IDENTIFY A NEED

The Design for Extreme Affordability program teaches students to develop a "laser-sharp focus on the essential needs of the user," says course professor James Patell.

Articulate the need you're seeking to solve. It should address a specific problem and shouldn't be too broad or too focused on a specific solution, thereby leaving room for creative freedom while being clear on the goal. Ironically, having some constraints—such as having a specific purpose—helps people generate more creative ideas.

The Embrace team identified the parents' need "to give their dying premature baby a surviving chance."

CRAFT A "HOW MIGHT WE?" GUIDING QUESTION

A "How might we?" question is an articulation of what the team seeks to pursue—what need it seeks to meet and for whom. This inspires the team to focus on solutions rather than obstacles, and to think creatively.

The Embrace team landed at: "How might we give desperate parents in a remote village, without resources to access a major hospital, the means to give their dying premature baby a surviving chance?"

Stating a clear need in a concrete and human-centered way inspires us to leap into the Learning Zone to find innovative solutions.

Here are other examples:

- How might we enable our hotel guests living with disabilities to feel welcomed and safe while making check-in easy, accessible, and efficient?
- How might we provide a transportation experience in which isolated people can connect with others, and those who need to focus can get their work done?
- How might we help our colleagues working remotely to maintain a sense of camaraderie and connection with those working in the office?

"How might we?" questions provide focus, direction, and inspiration, and guide subsequent stages in the process.

IDEATE WITH "YES, AND"

With clear focus, we are ready to generate an explosion of creative ideas: a divergent thinking stage.

During ideation, the team generally stands up, with each person holding a stack of sticky notes. Setting a timer for, say, five to twenty minutes, they generate as many ideas as possible. Each person voices their ideas, one at a time, projecting so everyone can hear them. As one person writes an idea down and places it on the wall, someone else has already started stating their idea—ideally building on what they just heard—and writing it down. The team is going for volume, listening to others, and using that as inspiration to generate further. It's fast. Laughter erupts.

As you ideate together, don't evaluate the ideas. Instead, embrace the improv comedy technique of "Yes, and." That is, take what was said as a given and, if possible, build on it. If someone says, "We could build a bridge with paper clips," don't say, "No, that wouldn't work." Say, "Yes, and we could link the paper clips and magnetize them!"

Embrace came up with many ideas for solutions to its "How might we?" question, including a tent, hot water bottles, heat bulbs, a box, a sleeping bag, a heated blanket, and many others.

Ideation is rapid, energetic, and fun, and all about leaping into the unknown—the Learning Zone—with colleagues.

Sample norms that guide ideation are:

- Go for quantity. At this stage, you're looking to come up with *many* ideas, not good ideas.
- Defer judgment. Whether an idea is sound is irrelevant; remember, you're looking for quantity.
- Encourage wild ideas. Wild ideas are precious because they can lead to things you wouldn't have thought of otherwise, and because they bring energy and fun to the activity, which increases creativity and brings the team closer together. Go for extremes. Ponder questions like, "What would be the most expensive way to do this? The cheapest? The fastest? The slowest? The ugliest? The most beautiful? The heaviest? The lightest?" Going for extremes helped Embrace come up with the foundation for a $25 incubator.
- Tell yourself, "Yes, and." When someone shares an idea, think, "Yes, and," and then add something to it. Don't reject any idea; rather, embrace it and use it as fuel.
- Go fast, but one at a time. Avoid speaking when others are speaking. You want to listen to one another. This generates a shared experience and shared understanding as you work together throughout the project.

IDENTIFY POSSIBLE SOLUTIONS

After the explosion of options during the ideation stage, we move to a convergent thinking stage in which we think through the ideas we generated. You can use many of the previous techniques when synthesizing observations, such as moving sticky notes into theme-based clusters.

Point out ideas that intrigued you and thoughts they evoked. Feel free to add additional ideas as you think together.

In this stage, you identify possible viable answers to your "How might we?" question so you can prototype and test them in order to learn more.

PROTOTYPE

Create one or more quick *low-resolution* prototypes to test. You're looking to build something rough, not precise or fully functional. The objective is not to come up with a finished product, but to test some hypotheses on what might work so you can learn and generate additional insights. Ideally, you want to come up with something visual or physical that the user can hold or interact with, but a prototype might be as simple as rough sketches, or a crude model made of folded cardboard and a Sharpie. Consider acting out the situation with the people you're designing for. The idea is to try to replicate how the experience would work and what it would feel like, so you can get their feedback.

TEST

The goal of testing is not to validate what we have come up with, but to generate feedback we can learn from. End users interact with our prototype and we observe how they react. Afterward, we debrief on what we observed, revise our hypotheses accordingly, and identify next steps.

ITERATE (AGAIN AND AGAIN!)

Design thinking is iterative, but that doesn't mean that you need to go back to the initial research stage after testing. Perhaps your test suggested that your core idea might have merit but a key assumption needs to be revised. You might go back to prototype a revised version. Or the test might reveal new ground for possibilities you want to explore through another ideation session. Or it might uncover new insights that lead you to conduct empathy research work with a different stakeholder group or perhaps ask different questions.

STAY OPTIMISTIC

Throughout the process, we want to experience joy, enthusiasm, and optimism—grounded in the belief that our actions can lead us to success. These positive emotions help us notice new insights and possibilities and aid us in generating creative solutions, particularly when we are working with others.

If you're not used to generating positive emotions in yourself, it may take some practice. But this is something you can learn to do authentically. Design thinking often leads to valuable solutions, which is a reason to feel optimistic.

Even if the process doesn't lead us to a solution to implement, we will learn from it. This is yet another reason to remain enthusiastic and optimistic. These activities lead to progress, because even if our prototypes don't work, they generate useful lessons about why they didn't. The process will make us smarter, deepen our relationships, and help us develop ourselves as a learning team.

DEBRIEF ON THE PROCESS

As a team, debrief on how the process went. What went well? What didn't go as well? How can the team improve? Speaking in turns, what do people appreciate about what each person brought to the team, and what can they work on to become even more helpful? How can others support them? This seeds the Learning Zone habit of discussing how to continuously evolve as a team.

PICK, CHOOSE, AND ADAPT

Although it has principles, design thinking is not a rigid process. The steps I laid out in this chapter are meant to inspire you, not box you in.

To help build a learning team, you can mix and match or adjust any of these principles and techniques for your team, based on your needs, and use them to complement other structures and routines you set in place. If you've never gone through the steps in this chapter, consider searching for a local design thinking workshop so you can experience it firsthand.

Remember that design thinking is just one example of the power of principles, norms, and techniques. We have seen many other examples in prior chapters, and we'll encounter a lot more of them, such as *radical transparency, launch and learn, start with care,* and many others. You can create your own concoction for your unique culture.

As long as your team is working together to learn and co-create, with a mindset of discovery and trying new ideas—and with norms and processes toward that end—you have a building block for a learning culture.

REFLECTION QUESTIONS

- Does my team have effective norms, strategies, and habits to rock the two zones?
- How might I help take our practices to the next level?
- Am I eliciting feedback to ensure our norms and techniques work for everyone on my team?

LOOKING FORWARD

How might I help build a more cohesive team?

Chapter 10: The Collaboration Superpower:

How to Forge Mighty Teams

BIG IDEA *To truly form a learning team, members need to apply the Learning Zone not only to the tasks at hand, but also to their relationships. By building trust, psychological safety, and transparency, we can collaborate more effectively when learning and performing.*

Growing up in Miami, Willy Foote fell in love with the Latin American cultures that surrounded him. Soon after graduating from Yale, Willy went to Wall Street, where he specialized in Latin America corporate finance. But the life of a Wall Street banker wasn't satisfying to him. He wanted more.

Willy moved to Mexico. There, he began to learn about the difficulties farmers and small businesses face in securing financing. Willy had grown up watching his father, who was president of the University of Miami for two decades, extend his influence far beyond the university to become a force for good in the community. Willy wanted to become a force for good, too, and decided that this could be his opportunity.

In Mexico, he saw that farmers were often in a bind. They needed money to buy raw materials such as seed and fertilizer to grow their crops of avocados, bananas, or lettuce. But they often lacked the money needed early in the season, and lenders were traditionally uninterested in making tiny loans to small farms in these regions. Willy thought there had to be ways to aggregate small businesses into larger collectives and create win-wins for everyone.

With his Wall Street mindset in one pocket and his family principles in the other, Willy founded a nonprofit called Root Capital, which provided credit, financial advice, training, and access to markets. Today, the nonprofit has provided more than $1.8 billion in loans to nearly 800 agricultural businesses in Africa, Asia, and Latin America. Those businesses have, in turn, paid nearly $5 billion directly to 2.3 million farming families. It has helped these farmers—particularly women—build profitable livelihoods.

Through Root Capital, Willy also founded the Council on Smallholder Agricultural Finance (CSAF), an alliance of lending institutions that share the goal of building a market for small- and medium-sized agriculture businesses in developing countries. The sixteen institutions in CSAF are ostensibly competitors, but they come together to share learning and develop industry standards. Willy calls the alliance a "chamber of commerce" for organizations in the same lending space. It is a remarkable example of learning teams collaborating for the greater good.

We live in a world that venerates competition—the opposite of collaboration. It is taken for granted that the way organizations succeed is by competing against one another, even within mission-driven nonprofit sectors. It reinforces the performance paradox and fools us into chronic performance.

You would think a nonprofit that cares about its mission would want to collaborate with other organizations that have the same mission, pooling resources, sharing lessons, and helping one another. Yet, the fight for seemingly limited funding, staff, and beneficiaries often leads organizations to withhold information from others in an attempt to become the hero. They put their institution before the mission. The same views are even more pronounced in for-profit sectors and in our collective psyche.

But, as we'll explore in this chapter, to be able to tackle the greatest challenges and achieve the greatest impact, we have to collaborate. In fact, our ability to collaborate is what has enabled humans to survive as a species, and to transform ourselves and our environments.

Collaboration drives better learning and better performance. More brains can think in different ways, contribute information from different vantage points, combine diverse areas of expertise, and engage in more systems thinking rather than just siloed problem-solving.

Satya Nadella at Microsoft realized and prioritized this. He and his colleagues identified One Microsoft as one of their five cultural attributes—along with Growth Mindset—for encouraging everyone to think of themselves as part of the larger whole and to collaborate across departments. He also guided people to look for ways to build alliances beyond Microsoft, even with their traditional rivals, as Willy Foote did.

The year after becoming CEO, Nadella gave a keynote at Salesforce's annual Dreamforce conference that shocked everyone when he pulled out . . . an iPhone!

On the giant screen, he showed a close-up of his biggest rival's product, complete with all of the Microsoft applications on its screen. The two companies had never before integrated to such an extent.

In *Hit Refresh,* Nadella writes, "Today one of my top priorities is to make sure that our billion customers, no matter which phone or platform they choose to use, have their needs met so that we continue to grow. To do that, sometimes we have to bury the hatchet with old rivals, pursue surprising new partnerships, and revive long-standing relationships."

Microsoft has now developed significant partnerships with its traditional rivals, including Adobe, Amazon, Apple, Google, Facebook, and Red Hat.

Might there be value in starting to think about some of your "competitors" more as *mission allies*?

I want to be clear that I'm not saying competition has no value, and neither is Nadella. A competitive spirit can help all parties remain accountable for putting their best foot forward in both the Learning Zone and the Performance Zone, pushing one another higher. But a sole focus on competition misses the valuable opportunities that can come from cooperation. It can also generate performance anxiety, narrow our vision, let the performance paradox trap us in chronic performance, and lead us to miss out on opportunities or strategies our competitors may not be pursuing.

Within organizations, competition is much more destructive than helpful. It's fine to compete against our own past personal best, but competing against our colleagues is a recipe for keeping one another underwater. Yet, too often, people feel competitive with their colleagues, compelled to work without them, or worse. So, how do we build collaborative learning teams to achieve greater long-term performance? How do we incentivize collaboration despite the societal tendency to reward, from childhood, individual achievement?

To realize their effective collaboration, Root Capital and the other alliance members have had to develop trust and a shared purpose. Whether spurred by survival, growth, contribution, or anything else, people and teams collaborate most effectively and learn the most from one another when they develop trust and shared goals. This happens when we coalesce around a mission, assume good intentions, set clear expectations, follow through on our commitments, and collaborate to develop domain and learning competence, resources, and effectiveness.

Whether within organizations or between them, learning teams change the world.

With that in mind, let's explore the foundations of a great learning team.

LEARNING TEAM FOUNDATION #1: ESTABLISH TRUST, RELATIONSHIPS, AND PURPOSE

If your business or team has yet to develop collaborative learning habits, don't despair. It's never too late. And it starts with a step the Embrace team missed, which initially led them into trouble.

Of the design thinking–inspired principles and practices I described in the preceding chapter, the only one you won't find in many design thinking guides is *establish trust,* but facilitators often add it to the process. I've participated in several design thinking cycles at the d.school in which the team has spent some time up front getting to know one another and building trust.

But when my friend Razmig Hovaghimian and his classmates took the Design for Extreme Affordability course, there was no explicit process for the students to form relationships. It was assumed that, even though they had been assigned to groups without ever having met one another, the students would form bonds *by doing* the collaborative work. But it didn't work out that way.

"Honestly, we didn't really know each other yet," Razmig told me, referring to the time period right after the six-month course had ended and the team members had decided to found Embrace. "We had one class, it was all work, work, work. There wasn't really interpersonal getting to know each other, where we found out about why we chose to be here, what drives us, or even the casual stuff like family members, this and that. It was a bit of a challenge, because we're like, 'Okay, who's the person I'm working with?'"

The design thinking process—which focused only on the task at hand—had left them with a strong sense of purpose, but without a sense of belonging or clear team norms beyond the tasks.

Conflict emerged. Some team members were bothered by others' communication styles, or lack thereof. A team member would start a conversation with someone outside the group about a collaboration, or present the idea without telling teammates, which felt like putting personal advancement before the team and the mission. Yet, most teammates kept quiet instead of sharing important concerns. They hadn't agreed on norms like transparency, or identified the things that were important to them.

Each of the Embrace founders felt that the societal need they had discovered and the solution they had created was so important that they had to go after it, but they knew they couldn't do so if team dynamics remained as tense as they were. So, they decided to put effort into trying to resolve their conflicts and truly forge a cohesive team.

In one instance, they decided to all climb a tree and not come down until everyone had shared what they were feeling. This was a Learning Zone activity focused on uncovering teammates' thoughts and feelings and how each person was affecting others. There were long periods of silence and awkwardness, but there were also moments of laughter and camaraderie. It was dark out, and when other students would walk past the tree and hear voices but not see anyone, it made for a comical scene.

On another occasion, they spent a weekend in a rented house several hours away from campus where the team members had an opportunity to share their thoughts and feelings. Finally, they were starting to better understand one another. They worked through conflict and decided that, going forward, they had to have full transparency and agree to give others the benefit of the doubt. They also decided on roles and responsibilities, and elected Jane Chen CEO.

Looking back, the founders of Embrace now realize that had they spent some time up front getting to know one another and establishing norms, it would have helped them avoid some pitfalls and allowed them to better work through missteps so that resentment wouldn't keep building until it blew up. They could have shared their backgrounds, interests, philosophies, and goals, and worked to align on principles.

My mentor Chip Conley was a seasoned hotel executive when he was recruited by Airbnb to serve as the CEO's mentor and be a part of the executive leadership team. As he describes in his book *Wisdom @ Work,* he realized shortly after joining that the leadership group had great potential but was not optimizing as a team.

"They had irregular meetings," he told me. "They did not have an alignment to strategic initiatives that everybody agreed upon."

The solution?

They started engaging in the Learning Zone in team-building meetings.

"We went through a really rigorous process of offsite retreats once a month, and then a minimum of once a quarter an overnight retreat, two or three nights somewhere," he said.

It was a big commitment, Chip pointed out. To spend time with their team, people had to take time away from their regular tasks, not to mention their families and lives, for several days each quarter. But it was a priceless investment that helped them create a culture of learning that would outperform other companies in the long run.

In *Wisdom @ Work*, Chip explains that the leadership team needed to get to a point where the members were comfortable openly debating issues as a group, to avoid competing factions forming outside of the meetings.

"We learned just how valuable it was to debate, decide, commit, and align, even and especially when our differences—whether in age, background, or personality type—might have slowed us down," Chip wrote.

They also collaborated on crafting language aimed at guiding and inspiring. They brainstormed compelling words or phrases that later became the Airbnb mission: "to create a world where anyone can belong anywhere." It provides them with a shared sense of purpose.

But what if your company doesn't have the budget for regular offsites or some of your teammates don't feel safe climbing trees? Or what if you're simply looking for other ways to build camaraderie and set the stage to learn and grow together?

Cindy Eckert, CEO of Sprout Pharmaceuticals, started a ritual of colleagues regularly having lunch together and talking about what Sprout could learn from other businesses, which she described in *The Tim Ferriss Show* podcast. They even took field trips to observe and gain ideas. They visited sites like Pike Place Market and Beecher's Handmade Cheese shop in Seattle to figure out what those businesses do exceptionally and how they invite people into the experience. In the process, they also learned about one another's likes and dislikes—and built relationships.

Creating opportunities to connect and learn together not only advances people's knowledge and skills, but also conditions people to regularly engage in the Learning Zone, and to do so collaboratively. It develops team culture while building competence. Cindy Eckert was fostering a shared team identity of being students of great businesses. It's an inclusive identity, because anyone can embrace it. Group activities like Eckert's lunch ritual also deepen a sense of belonging and trust among participants.

To foster a sense of belonging and elevate the purpose of the collective:

- Spend time as a team getting to know one another. Share what brings you to this work, what you hope to gain from it and to bring to the group, and how you aspire to work together.
- Identify your common purpose and values. These might be established for you by senior leaders. If so, unpack what they mean and what behaviors they entail. Agree to point out to one another when you see those behaviors and when you see opportunities for improvement. Ask whether everyone is on board or has any concerns.
- Identify the team goals and strategies. To achieve your ambitions, how will you distribute responsibilities and collaborate within and beyond your team?
- Avoid symbols of belonging that could be exclusionary, such as sports fandom, late-night parties, or luxurious trips, which could lead future colleagues to feel excluded. Cultivate belonging through things a diverse workforce can choose and enjoy, such as purpose, values, and inclusive rituals.

When people are first getting to know one another, or even if they have known one another for some time, conversations can stay superficial and not feel very meaningful. This gets in the way of developing deeper relationships, engaging in transparency, and unleashing more powerful collaboration in the two zones. For this reason, I created a game called Bonding Stories that you can play with your teammates and others. Whether you're just getting to know people or already know them well, it helps build trust and deepen relationships. You can find the game at briceno.com/paradox/resources/.

LEARNING TEAM FOUNDATION #2: EMPOWER PEOPLE TO
INITIATE CHANGE

What happens when employees have a ton of suggestions for how their team or company can improve but there's no process for putting their ideas into action?

This is exactly what a team at General Mills faced before Jenny Radenberg introduced collaborative learning habits. Whenever people would suggest better ways of doing things, they often felt like no one was listening because they didn't see their suggestions go anywhere.

Too many leaders and organizations inadvertently squash employees' interest in engaging in the Learning Zone when employees generate new ideas and no one listens or when people get reprimanded for not doing things the way they're told.

When Harvard Business School professor Ethan Bernstein studied the second-biggest phone factory in the world, situated in China, he found that managers were trained to follow established procedures and ensure that their employees followed best practices. In partnership with the company's executives, Bernstein placed three of his students on the factory floor, posing as ordinary employees, and instructed them to report their observations. They noticed that employees had plenty of ideas for improvement but often didn't voice them for fear of being reprimanded, or only implemented their ideas when a supervisor wasn't looking.

To set up an experiment, Bernstein put up a big curtain between the control group and the treatment group so that they wouldn't be influenced by each other. When the curtain went up, one of the employees said, "Wouldn't it be nice if they hung up curtains all around the line, so we can be completely closed off? We could be so much more productive." Bernstein loved the idea. He scratched his original experimental design and decided to test putting up more curtains in the treatment group so managers couldn't see what employees were doing. The result? The employees now felt safe to implement their own ideas. After just one week, their hourly production of defect-free units went up by 10 to 15 percent, depending on the shift. Being out of managers' sight enabled employees to engage in "productive deviance, localized experimentation, distraction avoidance, and continuous improvement."

This is not to say that managers are detrimental. Managers who embrace the two zones add value.

Jenny Radenberg—whose team felt that leaders didn't listen to or follow up on suggestions—instituted monthly meetings at General Mills where team members could provide feedback and discuss best practices. Jenny ensured that she always closed the loop by explaining decisions once suggestions had been considered.

The team saw a dramatic change in how it operated after instituting the meetings and follow-through. With team input, decisions on issues like how to transition the manufacturing line from one product flavor to another—called changeovers—were made with an eye for saving the company money and being more efficient.

So, what else did they discuss in the meetings?

"I love data," Jenny told me. "We were pulling up metrics to say, 'These were our changeover times against the target. You guys did that!' And it was kind of this pride point, month over month. Then, every time we had a changeover, they're like, 'Okay, what's the target—in three hours?' I'm like, 'If you can do it in two, I'll make cupcakes.' And they're like, 'Okay, well, what would it take to get to that?'"

When team performance data trends are put in front of people, it can motivate them to collaborate to reach new heights. The team members are competing not against another team but against their own personal best, which is both fun and motivating.

"They are the people that drive those metrics," Radenberg said. "So, if I'm not informing them of it, how do I expect them to deliver on it? . . . They really took pride in these numbers and their ability to impact them. And when things did go wrong, they took responsibility. . . . It was not leadership's metric. It was their metric that they were proud of and they wanted to deliver."

We need to ensure that people feel that engaging in the Learning Zone can lead to real change. Leaders need to give their staff true agency so that their effort in the two zones reaps real rewards. Employees will have different opinions on issues, some of which may be in conflict, but when they feel heard and understand how a decision was made, they're more likely to continue thinking about how to improve and contribute.

LEARNING TEAM FOUNDATION #3: PROMOTE RADICAL TRANSPARENCY

Bridgewater Associates, the largest hedge fund in the world, records all of its meetings and makes the recordings available to everyone in the company. The recordings become a tool for anyone to listen to and reflect on what they did well or could improve upon, for people to give feedback on parts of the conversation that were helpful or problematic, and for those not in the room to slip into the Learning Zone and learn from discussions they weren't a part of. The company even created a group that highlights the most instructive parts of key meetings and makes them available to any employee, as a way to spread the lessons and effective practices so that more people and teams benefit from them.

This reflects a principle that Bridgewater's founder, Ray Dalio, calls "radical transparency." As *Business Insider* reported, employees spend at least an hour every week reviewing meeting recordings and reflecting on what they observed. They learn principles like question your superiors, admit your weaknesses, and do not hide from criticism. The philosophies are documented in Dalio's series of books, Principles.

Dalio encourages employees to engage in radical transparency and feedback by pointing out and celebrating the behaviors when they take place. In his TED Talk, he did just that, sharing an email he once received from an employee that started with, "Ray, you deserve a D– for your performance today in the meeting. . . . You did not prepare at all because there is no way you could have been that disorganized." That's what radical transparency looks like, explained Dalio.

People who seek jobs at Bridgewater know that constant learning permeates the company. That is part of what attracts them to it, because they have growth propellers that are aligned with the organization's culture.

We all can learn from the company's practice of radical transparency.

Transparency, an element of the growth propeller, involves sharing our improvement objectives along with our concerns, questions, feedback, mistakes, and lessons learned.

Being transparent doesn't always feel easy. Sometimes people believe that sharing information could harm them, so they feel vulnerable. Other times, they may rationally know that sharing is good, but still emotionally fear it. As we begin to cultivate learning cultures, we can expect some discomfort as people adjust to sharing openly and experiencing their colleagues' reactions.

Early in my career, I responded defensively to feedback, often rationalizing excuses instead of really listening to what others were saying. Through Carol Dweck's research, I came to understand that my behavior was getting in the way of my goals. I gradually developed a very different understanding of feedback, which shifted my emotional responses to it.

But even after that, for a long time I struggled to give honest feedback to others. Over the years, I've pushed myself to go beyond my comfort zone to give the gift of feedback. The more I've done it, the more I've experienced the power of doing so, which has helped me become a lot more confident and effective at radical transparency. If you're not there yet, I encourage you to keep pushing yourself and stretching your comfort zone.

Over time, as we get used to sharing transparently and see others respond in a constructive way — or when we resolve conflict when they don't — we can get to the point of sharing transparently without feeling vulnerable. That's when we know we have created an environment of psychological safety.

Let's explore that concept more deeply.

LEARNING TEAM FOUNDATION #4: CREATE A CULTURE OF PSYCHOLOGICAL SAFETY

When I worked in venture capital as the most junior investment professional in my firm, fear kept me from being transparent.

I often didn't have a strong conviction about whether an investment opportunity was attractive. But I kept my doubts to myself.

I was afraid of being judged incompetent or insecure.

I was in the mode of *fake it till you make it*. I didn't share the uncertainties and questions that would have given others the opportunity to help me. My behavior distorted our conversations and decisions and promoted a culture of pretending.

But here's what's interesting: I don't recall anyone ever telling me that I *had* to have strong convictions after each pitch. I learned that from observing the people around me. But my colleagues had decades more experience than I did, so why did I feel I had to behave like them and pretend to know what they knew?

I made up a story in my mind about what the people around me valued, based on what I saw them do. But it is very possible that they wouldn't have expected someone just starting out in the profession to form strong convictions from the outset.

So, my fear was self-generated. And that fear made for a weak growth propeller. It hurt the team and hurt me.

It turns out that this fear is a common and major hindrance to the effectiveness of teams—sometimes not because people create fear, but because they don't do enough to create clarity and safety.

As a first-year doctoral student, Amy Edmondson, who is now a renowned professor at Harvard Business School, joined a research team to examine error rates in hospitals. Logically, she hypothesized that more effective patient care teams made fewer errors. But, as she describes in her book *The Fearless Organization*, she was surprised to find the opposite: The error rates appeared to be higher in what a validated survey instrument deemed higher-performing teams.

She could have published her interesting findings—giving in to performance pressures to publish—but instead she dove deeper into her Learning Zone and sought to find out what was happening.

She engaged Andy Molinsky—at the time a research assistant who, by design, didn't know anything about her preliminary findings or hypotheses—to look into differences in how the teams operated. Combining Molinsky's observations with the data, Edmondson discovered that while the higher-performing teams didn't make more errors, they did report them more often. That's why her study had initially found a counterintuitive relationship between mistakes and performance.

Members of the higher-performing teams felt able to talk about mistakes. They discussed them openly to learn from them and to identify ways to catch and prevent them.

Edmondson went on to study the concept of *psychological safety,* which she defined as the shared belief held by members of a team that the team is safe for interpersonal risk-taking. Later, in numerous studies, she and other researchers found a strong relationship between cultures of high psychological safety and high performance. Google found the same thing when it studied its teams: psychological safety was the number-one driver of team effectiveness.

Psychological safety drives performance because transparency is a necessary ingredient for effective collaboration, both in the Learning Zone and in the Performance Zone. If transparency feels perilous, the team suffers.

"When psychological safety is high, candor no longer feels risky," Edmondson and her colleague Henrik Bresman wrote in a working paper. "Offering ideas, sharing doubts, asking questions all become easier."

But what do we do when we are trying to build a team with high-functioning growth propellers—which foster psychological safety—within a company whose culture is rife with fear?

First, we should know that it can be done. Most companies are filled with teams that have widely varying cultures with regard to transparency, risk-taking, and acceptance of failure. If we feel our organization is like an ocean filled with sharks, we can create safety islands by aligning with close colleagues on how we want to work and by developing trust. This strengthens our ability to learn and perform. This is what Traca Savadogo did with her team at Starbucks even when employees at other locations were resistant to change. Then, she used the benefits achieved by her team's innovation to influence the rest of the company.

Edmondson and Bresman suggest that teams can promote psychological safety by using *framing* and *inquiry*.

Framing is about clearly communicating so that people interpret a situation or behavior in a desired way, most notably as one that calls for candor and learning. It involves making our implicit assumptions explicit so that we can all align around them.

During my time in venture capital, my colleagues never told me I needed to express a strong conviction after every startup pitch. While they didn't generate my fear, they also didn't create clarity and a sense of safety, despite being very nice people. They did not clearly communicate how they wanted people to behave. That was left to each person's interpretation. So, I made up my own story.

Might your teammates think you want them to always do things as best as they know how, minimizing mistakes, grinding away in chronic performance? Is it possible they worry that if they share an uncertainty or try something that doesn't work, you'll think a little less of them? Ask yourself, when was the last time a member of your team chose to admit making a mistake? If you can't remember, you may need to work on creating psychological safety.

While you might not be doing anything to generate fear, are you doing enough to generate *safety*? Are you encouraging one another to take risks and engage in the Learning Zone?

Creating psychological safety involves actively making the implicit explicit—being deliberate about stating our principles and desired behaviors. It's about clearly identifying norms, discussing them, writing them down, and regularly referring back to them. It's about celebrating when someone exemplifies them, and pointing out when someone behaves contrary to them.

When someone exemplifies the norms, we might say:

- "I'm very proud of how the team tackled this project. I think it showed our value of 'Embrace the Adventure.' We took on the big challenge, persevered when the system shut down,

and tried different strategies until we found something that worked. That's what it looks like to Embrace the Adventure!"
- "Even though the project didn't work out at the end, that's what it looks like to 'Embrace the Adventure.' If we keep taking smart risks like that, we'll find new solutions."

When someone behaves contrary to the norms, we might say:

- "Rishi, I care about you and our team, so I need to share something with you. I think the way you behaved in that meeting went against our core value of Humility. Anna and Abdul were trying to share their thoughts but were not able to get a word in. As I saw it, you interrupted them and didn't let them finish, and you kept making statements rather than asking questions to understand what they were thinking. That's how it came across to me. How did you see it?"
- "Tom, I'm concerned it seems you withheld sharing that the project failed to produce the desired results, which goes against our core value of Honesty. Are you on board with that core value? Is there something I am doing—or that others are doing—that is making you nervous about being honest? Or is something else getting in the way?"

Inquiry is about explicitly asking members to contribute their thoughts—to be transparent—by, perhaps, using questions like the following (suggested by Bresman and Edmondson):

- What do you want to accomplish?
- What are you up against?
- What are you worried about?
- What do you bring to the table?

Edmondson's work, Google's data, and Traca Savadogo's story demonstrate that regardless of the culture of your organization, you can create psychological safety within your team.

LEARNING TEAM FOUNDATION #5: ENCOURAGE PEOPLE TO SOLICIT FEEDBACK FREQUENTLY AND BROADLY

While psychological safety is necessary for fostering a culture of growth, it is not sufficient. People can feel safe and yet not see a reason to engage in learning—or they may not know how. For example, a lot of people are unsure of how to go about providing and receiving feedback, an essential Learning Zone strategy in collaborative work.

When people set out to promote feedback in their teams, they often start by encouraging employees to give feedback. That's not a bad thing, but it tends to be an uphill battle. Many people haven't yet developed an understanding of what feedback is— communication anyone can benefit from in order to learn what others are thinking—and why it's helpful. Or, they may fear that their teammates don't see feedback the same way and may react defensively. A more effective way to start the journey is to focus on encouraging everyone to *solicit* feedback instead, with leaders modeling the way.

When we develop habits of soliciting feedback frequently and broadly—from various people, not just one or two—we make it a lot easier for others to give us feedback. This also makes us feel less vulnerable because we are initiating the process, thus reinforcing our sense of confidence and agency.

Many people feel critical feedback is negative feedback. But critical feedback is the most powerful source of information for growth, so how can it be negative? Those who learn to love critical feedback develop themselves at a much faster pace than others. By using the term "negative feedback," you may be clogging the feedback faucets. Consider shifting your language. People who excel view both *critical* and *reinforcing* feedback as positive and powerful.

When you *give* feedback—as my Stanford business school professors David Bradford and Carole Robin explain in their book, *Connect*—it is best to avoid making assumptions about other people's thoughts, feelings, or intentions, because when you do you are often wrong, and you might make the other person feel misunderstood or even attacked.

Instead, when giving feedback, focus on sharing what is on your mind or in your emotions (which you do know) and comment on behaviors anyone can observe and how they affect you.

Especially in the initial phases of building culture and common understanding, we sometimes need to be gentle or adjust our approach to meet the other person where they are. While someone might logically understand the importance of feedback, they still may react with fear or anger. The brain takes time to rewire.

So, early on when giving feedback, we might need to explicitly remind people of our intentions and use careful framing. But as the neuropsychologist Donald Hebb famously said, neurons that fire together wire together—meaning repetition builds and reinforces new thought patterns, enabling people to gradually shift their mental models and responses, as I and many others have done.

The dialogue might sound like this:

"Sam, I was disappointed because I feel this work doesn't meet our high standards. I'll point out where I saw issues, but first let me tell you why I'm sharing this. I have really appreciated when others have shared with me that my work hasn't come across as high quality and how I can make it better, and that has really helped me improve, which is something I continue to work on. I know you can develop your ability to create high-quality reports, so I want to share some opportunities I see to get there. Do you want to hear them, and is now a good time?" Then, if they're ready, consider starting by asking them if they see some opportunities for improvement.

Keep in mind that different cultures and countries might have different communication norms. Feedback that is considered too direct in Japan or in some regions of Brazil may be considered too indirect in Israel or the Netherlands.

When we prompt people to frequently solicit feedback, they can slide into the driver's seat. They feel agency, self-esteem, and status in the conversation they initiate.

For each of us, frequently soliciting feedback—with a genuine interest in learning from it—is the fastest route to changing our own neural wiring.

ANYONE CAN PROMOTE A LEARNING TEAM

What if you're not the leader of an organization or even a team leader? Can you still bring collaborative Learning Zone behaviors into the office?

Absolutely!

Start by asking yourself: Am I in a fixed mindset or a growth mindset about my ability to lead and influence others? If I don't yet feel confident about my ability to grow my influence, how might I develop those skills?

And who might be able to support me in my journey to lead a learning culture, from wherever I sit?

Often, we have more influence than we think, and we can always learn how to get better at impacting our environment. Culture results from the beliefs and habits of *everyone* within a community.

Sure, we don't know how others will react when we take risks to lead as a visible learner. But we can start by taking small risks, such as by soliciting feedback on something we think we did okay but could do better, by sharing with a colleague that we're a little nervous before making a presentation, or by asking someone what they think about an issue and disclosing that we're looking for others' ideas.

When we take small risks, others tend to reciprocate in kind, especially if we have framed our intentions. Then, we can take slightly larger risks, like sharing what we're working to improve, or asking for suggestions about a challenge we're grappling with. On the other hand, if colleagues remain guarded and opaque, we can go back to having conversations about the culture we want to create, check whether we all have the same intentions, and unpack what behaviors that entails.

As we get started on our journey toward developing a learning team, it's usually a good idea to first share our suggestions privately with those in leadership roles and ask for their reactions and feedback. This creates a safer Learning Zone for us and for them—a lower-stakes island that doesn't put leaders on the spot in front of the whole team.

It also gives us an opportunity to fully explain what we mean, learn from others' perspectives, address any questions, get buy-in, and align before introducing learning strategies to the wider group.

Once we've introduced our ideas to our teammates, some will enthusiastically embrace the effort. Rather than worry about bringing everyone on board from day one, it generally works well to focus on the people who get excited. This tends to be the vast majority, because growth mindset and the Learning Zone resonate widely when people learn about them.

Continue to engage with those who are excited about these ideas. Learn with them. Share what is working and what is not, and identify next steps together. As the circle of partners starts seeing results, share and celebrate them more widely, inviting others to join in.

If some people don't engage in learning behaviors, we can get curious about the reason. Perhaps they are in a fixed mindset and believe that people can't change, or they may not care about the shared purpose or about progressing in that skill. Or they may not feel supported, know how to improve, or have the resources.

Each of these reasons calls for different responses. We can remain curious. We can share what we're observing and get their perspectives. We can point out the shared team goal of fostering a learning culture and ask whether they are on board with the intention. We can ask how they see things, what's getting in the way, and how we can support them. We can give and receive feedback, and together come up with next steps.

If they're not on board with the intention, or if after some iterations they are still not engaged in the behaviors or making actual improvement, you can consider parting ways. Building a team and organization is partly about fit. If some team members are not interested in developing learning habits while the majority are, part ways with detractors and empower the majority to continue building the organization they desire.

Conversely, if you're trying different approaches and failing to influence your team to cultivate a learning culture, you can consider switching teams or organizations. If this work moves you, I encourage you to be deliberate about finding an organization, team, and teammates who value what you value and want to regularly engage in growth. So many people are waking up to the transformative power of the two zones and will share your enthusiasm.

You might also consider searching for ways to build learning communities outside of your immediate team, either within your organization or outside of it. Whichever route you choose, remember that there is so much you can do to influence and lead even if you don't have any formal authority.

In the next chapter, we begin to explore additional strategies for how to do just that.

REFLECTION QUESTIONS

- How do the people around me help or hinder me in my efforts to regularly engage in effective Learning Zone strategies?
- What assumptions might just be in my head?
- How might I build relationships and advance a culture of learning in my team?
- Does my team have a strong sense of purpose? If not, how might we get there?

LOOKING FORWARD

Regardless of my role, how could I lead my team to better engage in the two zones?

Chapter 11: Leading for Growth

BIG IDEA *To learn and perform at high levels, people need leaders who care about them and who provide clear guidance on when and how to engage in the two zones.*

When Mike Stevenson was a young man, he met someone who would transform his understanding of leadership—and his life.

Mike, now a public speaker based in his native Scotland, was a bricklayer's assistant in the 1960s, moving from site to site in London. At one particular site, he was welcomed by the foreman, a military veteran from Wales with a broken nose.

Right away, Mike could tell there was something different about him.

"Normally, you get to the site and they tell you, 'This is the length of the wall we want, this is the height, and we want it done by Thursday morning, otherwise we will take money off your costs,'" he recalled. "But he took me aside, put his arm around me, and said, 'Welcome, Michael. Before you start, I want to show you something.' He showed me the plans and he said, 'This is the palace you are building.'"

It was actually a pub they were building, but the way the foreman presented it transformed Mike's mindset.

"I suddenly felt, 'Wow! I am actually doing something extraordinary. I am going to create something that is going to be a legacy, that will stand for years to come.'"

That's what framing can do—depicting a situation or concept in words that lead others to see it in a new way.

"I felt a surge of confidence," Mike told me. "He was fantastic. I used to get to work early every morning; I would be the last to leave at night."

One day, the foreman gave Mike the job of locking up that evening, which meant he would be responsible for securing tens of thousands of dollars' worth of equipment. This sign of respect and confidence elevated his self-esteem.

"That was the moment that I grew about four feet in height because he trusted me," Mike said.

The foreman understood that trust is a two-way street. To foster it in a relationship, we need to extend trust to others—that's the definition of leading with trust.

"And when he saw something that I could do better, that is how he would say it: 'You can do that even better, a bit faster. You can get it. Here are a few tricks that I can show you.' He never belittled you. He never berated you for making a mistake. He just guided you into a way of doing it better. That was the first experience of leadership, real leadership, that I ever had, and I grew as a person working on that site. My confidence soared.

"This guy was always calm, always consistent, and his body language was always very open," Mike said. "He made full eye contact as well, and he talked respectfully to everyone. . . . He was nurturing. . . . He taught me more than anyone else in my entire life, honestly."

Construction sites pose a challenge that is becoming increasingly relevant in many industries in the age of the gig economy: How do we foster community within teams that are temporary—project-based—even when composed of independent contractors?

Mike's foreman grasped how important it was to get everyone at the site working together harmoniously, even though this team would be together for only a short time. That's a challenge. Members had different responsibilities, represented a variety of racial and ethnic groups, and spoke different languages.

"You have bricklayers, you got plasterers, you got plumbers—it was a whole load of people at the building site. And to coordinate those people to talk to each other, work together, and cooperate is a huge task because building sites are often shambolic," Mike said.

"Without that kind of leadership, they go over costs. The plasterers plaster the wall and the electrician comes in and knocks it out to put the plugs in. All of these things, they notoriously go over costs, and they notoriously go over deadlines. In our case, we were finished before the deadline and there were fewer reworks to do when the site was complete. The costs were under budget. That was leadership. I felt so excited every day, and so proud of what I was doing."

When Mike would meet friends at a pub after work and they asked him what he was doing, he would tell them, "I am building a palace."

The striking structure still stands more than half a century later. Whenever Mike is in London, he makes sure to drive by to admire it.

A NEW ERA OF LEADERSHIP

While forms of management and leadership have existed for thousands of years, management theory was born in the Industrial Revolution, a period in which the main challenge was mass production: making products available to lots of people cheaply. Organizations hired the few people who had learned about the subject to lead the charge. The approach was command and control: Managers would design systems and tell people what to do.

That's how the concept of management came to be defined. We still hold many tired assumptions about managing people as if they are cogs in a factory. "This is the length of the wall we want, this is the height, and we want it done by Thursday."

But these days, repetitive tasks are increasingly automated, the economy comprises more service sectors, and the pace of change has greatly accelerated. The management challenge has shifted from producing a cookie-cutter black Model T automobile as cheaply as possible to becoming human-centric: identifying unmet needs, driving innovation, and personalizing service. Machines on their own are not great at those things, and neither are people when they are treated like machines.

Too often, leaders—and sometimes workers, too—hold an implicit assumption that employees are not equipped to think independently and make decisions, so they need to be micromanaged, like the employees in the phone factory who weren't allowed to deviate from their detailed instructions. This belief often creates a self-fulfilling prophecy.

If only a few people in an organization are doing the thinking—those most removed from the customers or from the work being done—then the organization will have significantly less cognitive power to identify customer needs, drive innovation, personalize service, and solve problems. Organizations need to nurture their collective intelligence.

To build teams and companies that crush the performance paradox and deliver results while continuing to reach new heights of success, we need to shift our beliefs—our mindsets—about people, management, and leadership. We need to go from command and control to painting a vision, inspiring purpose, fostering well-being, empowering employees to take initiative, and supporting their development—like Mike Stevenson's foreman did on that London job site. Successful leaders cultivate the environment to sustain both the Learning Zone and the Performance Zone, and they join in. They ensure there is fertile soil for human cognition to flourish, and they inspire their colleagues to support one another, keep one another accountable, and drive toward a common, ambitious goal.

WHO CAN DO THIS

As leadership scholar Warren Bennis wrote, "The most dangerous leadership myth is that leaders are born. . . . That's nonsense. In fact, the opposite is true. Leaders are made rather than born."

Nobody is born a leader, command and control or otherwise. We learn our assumptions from our parents, schools, media, and workplaces.

We can now learn something different.

Regardless of formal title, anyone can learn to become an inspiring leader who develops positive relationships and advances a culture of learning and high performance through the two zones.

This chapter and the next will show you how.

A POWERFUL SHIFT

When David Tashjian was moved into leadership positions at Comcast, he had a track record of success. But there was one major problem: David had been trapped by the performance paradox and was coming across as a bully.

During meetings, his powerful personality dominated the group, leaving little space to hear from others who weren't as forceful.

"I can remember sitting in meetings, thinking, 'Why are we still talking about this? I know the right thing to do. Can we just move on?'" he told me.

The pressure he felt to perform—manifested as tunnel vision for the task at hand and disinterest in others' ideas—had left colleagues worried that if he kept getting promoted, the company would pay a high price in diminished employee engagement, teamwork, and development.

After spending a year in the vice president role, he had his performance review with his boss, the president of the division, who was one of David's mentors. What David heard devastated him.

"He said, 'Hey, there's no question you're an accomplished leader. But the way you get things done, and this notion of a bit of a bull in a china shop, it might be a fatal flaw,'" David recounted. "I was furious. I thought, I get great results. This is BS. It's not true. I'm not all these things."

Looking back, David realizes that his leadership style was driven by his own insecurities. He was afraid to reveal his vulnerabilities; he failed to show transparency when dealing with those in his charge.

He was what many call a "bad boss."

Bad bosses are a major reason people leave their jobs. There are others, too: family reasons, wanting a higher salary, or feeling unchallenged, underappreciated, uninspired, or burnt out. But many of these reasons can be influenced significantly by bosses.

Who among us has not experienced an ineffective leader creating toxicity within a team? Or a supervisor who gives feedback in a way that leaves team members demoralized and voiceless? Or a leader who talks about the importance of taking risks only to penalize team members when those risks don't yield the hoped-for results?

For more than twenty years, Gallup has conducted extensive surveys measuring employee engagement. These have shown that managers account for at least 70 percent of the variance in employee engagement scores, and that only about one-third of Americans are engaged in their jobs. One in two employees has left a job to get away from a bad manager at some point in their careers. Checking out is even easier to do when working remotely. Unsurprisingly, this has a dramatic impact on company performance.

The impact of a "bad manager" affects people outside of the workplace, too, as employees bring their work misery home with them, compounding their stress and hurting their relationships and overall well-being.

In recent years, employees have become increasingly disillusioned about the value and merit of work in their lives. This has led to massive shifts in where, when, and how people work, and even whether they will work at all.

Leaders at any level need to create the relationships, environment, structures, and support systems that will enable employees to get excited about what they do and engage with others in both learning and performing. In many cases, this will require managers to use the Learning Zone to figure out better strategies and systems to lead and to strengthen employee engagement and collaboration. When people thrive, the organization thrives.

When David Tashjian opened himself up to learning and growing in his style of leadership, he broke out of chronic performance and saw dramatic results. He stepped into the Learning Zone and learned from his mistakes. He approached the people he'd hurt and asked for forgiveness and feedback as he worked to change his ways. He decided to move beyond his tight circle of trusted confidants and try to transform his detractors into partners by having open communication with them and finding common ground. He felt strong enough to be vulnerable; he became more transparent. Employee satisfaction and effective collaboration soon followed.

Any of us can enter the Learning Zone to improve, expand, and strengthen our leadership toolkits—the set of tools we can use to envision and communicate the future we are driving toward, develop a strong culture, and organize, inspire, and support people to achieve the change we want to see in the world. In this and the next chapter, we will meet leaders who model the way. Remember that the goal is not for you to copy everything they do, but to develop a vision for how you want to lead and identify a few things to work on.

As always, all practices are rooted in the two core principles: always portray abilities and qualities as malleable, and set up mechanisms for the two zones. More holistically, the goal is to foster the *cornerstones of change* introduced in Chapter 4, along with the social context that reinforces them. You want to foster the belief that people can learn, an understanding of how to do so, a shared purpose that generates energy and direction, and a sense of belonging in a learning community.

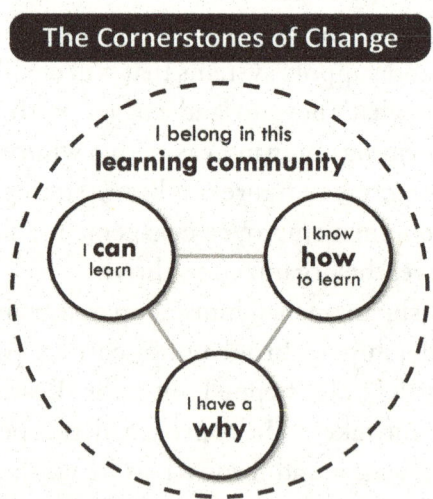

So, how can we lead for growth?

START WITH CARE AND DEVELOP TRUST

Francesca Lenci has worked for Siemens for sixteen years. She started out as a junior financial analyst in Lima, where she was born and raised. Over time, she took on significant challenges, moving to foreign countries and joining operations that were often in crisis. She earned many promotions along the way.

Francesca was working in Germany when a new opportunity arose to become the chief financial officer of Siemens Mobility in Italy. She took on the challenge, but when she arrived in Italy, she sensed that her team didn't believe it could become high achieving.

An ambitious professional and leader, Francesca wanted to transform her team. She sought to show her colleagues that they could be recognized as exemplary. But she didn't take a command-and-control approach.

Siemens holds a yearly contest within finance departments called the Cash Award, for exemplary management of cash. The award is given to countries that hold the highest cash management metrics, based on things like how quickly customers pay and how well supplier contracts and bills are handled. Italy ranked toward the bottom, but Francesca saw this as an opportunity to inspire her team members to reimagine what they could achieve together. She told her team she wanted them to go for the award and that, while they may not win it in the first year, she believed they could win in the future.

But she didn't start with a hard focus on performance and metrics. She started with care and trust.

After she joined the organization, Francesca took time to meet with each of her reports to get to know them, not only professionally, but also personally. This was significant Learning Zone work for her. She made sure to remember details of what was important to each person, such as the name of a special pet or a family member who lived far away or who was struggling with a health issue. She checked in with them about how they were doing.

She emphasized her desire to support their career development and helped them clarify their growth goals, encouraging them to devote thirty to sixty minutes to their personal development plan each month.

When the COVID-19 pandemic hit, Francesca noticed that people were struggling. In Italy, it wasn't a standard part of the culture to openly discuss mental health, but she created a weekly thirty-minute meeting where anyone could talk about anything—except for work. This deepened relationships and opened up communication for peers to support one another.

Different regions have different norms for how much information people tend to share about their personal lives. Francesca observed that in Italy, people in group settings tended to share more about events in their lives and less about their personal feelings and deeper struggles. But when she met with people one-on-one, they opened up much more.

After Francesca created social bonds and fostered team habits for the two zones, a year after she arrived in Italy, her team was recognized as a top-three finalist worldwide for the Cash Award. The same was true the second year. In the third year, they were a finalist and were also formally recognized as the "winners of the heart" due to their "sustainable and promising cash performance."

Clearly, the team has been transformed. They got there by searching for strategies to better manage financial systems and processes in the Learning Zone and by implementing them in the Performance Zone. But it started with Francesca's thoughtful and observant leadership and her genuine care for her people and their development.

Belonging can be fostered in any team, anywhere, even remotely. It's the result of genuine care, explicit communication, support, shared experiences, and emotional bonds.

Fostering a sense of belonging is not always a lengthy process. Sometimes just letting someone know that their contribution is valued can be deeply affirming. In his book, *Belonging,* Stanford psychology professor Geoffrey L. Cohen relates the story of a female executive at a major Silicon Valley company who shared with him a defining moment from early in her career. She was about to give a presentation to shareholders and was feeling apprehensive. At the time, there were few rising female leaders in the industry, and she was acutely aware of her outsider status. Just before she was introduced, the CEO of her company came up to her, looked her in the eye, and said, "You are changing this company." She told Cohen that those five words gave her a powerful sense of belonging. She knocked the presentation out of the park.

While care and trust are essential, they are not sufficient for driving growth, as Francesca Lenci knows.

A company I consulted with, a producer of fine goods, brought me in because, despite having made significant investments in the development of its culture, including working with external trainers and systems, the company was not achieving high performance or strong growth.

Looking at its employee engagement data and additional data from a survey I ran, it was clear to me that the company had developed a culture of care, trust, and safety. Employees had positive relationships, felt safe, enjoyed their work, and looked up to their leaders. The company had many strengths to build on, but it was missing other key ingredients for fostering a culture of learning and high performance. One of them was clear framing and guidance.

FRAME LEARNING AND PERFORMANCE TO PROVIDE CLEAR GUIDANCE

When Ian MacGregor, co-founder and CEO of Skratch Labs, a sports hydration and nutrition company, was having lunch with his new chief operating officer, he was surprised to hear his new colleague say that joining Skratch Labs was the riskiest thing he had ever done in his life.

Ian couldn't help but burst out laughing.

He didn't discount what his new COO was feeling, but it struck him as funny, because at that point in his life, starting Skratch Labs was the *safest* thing Ian had ever done.

Earlier in his life, Ian had been a pro cyclist. Twice, he was the United States' under-twenty-three national champion, before suffering a leg injury that forced him to retire at twenty-six. Prior to becoming a cyclist, he was a downhill ski racer, hurtling down mountains at incredible speeds.

Ian was so struck by the dramatic difference in their perspectives that he later described the conversation as one of the most memorable learning moments in his time as founder and CEO. It helped him better understand how differently people perceive risk.

Ian realized that if he wanted people at Skratch Labs to take risks, he needed to explicitly encourage and guide them, and to ensure they felt safe. They needed to know what behaviors he wanted, and that if they took a risk and it didn't pan out, they would be okay; in fact, they would be rewarded for taking appropriate risks.

Upon reflection, Ian recognized that his prior risk-taking as a pro cyclist and downhill ski racer had been made possible by the safety his parents had provided. He knew that if he got injured and became unable to continue his athletic career, he could move back in with his parents while figuring out what to do, and he was confident that he could learn something else and pursue a different path.

Skratch Labs' staff needed to know that the path to success would involve taking risks, not for the sake of recklessness, but for the sake of innovating and improving. They needed to know that things would not always go according to plan—that's risk, by definition—but that doing so was the path to advancing capabilities and expanding what's possible.

Ian developed ways to frame risk-taking for his staff and board of directors to generate alignment and cohesiveness.

When talking with his stakeholders about Skratch Labs' approach to innovation, Ian draws a horizontal line. He labels one end of the line *seed and nurture* and the other *launch and learn*.

Seed and nurture refers to a more methodical, cautious way of innovating. It involves coming up with ideas, conducting significant research to get smart about those ideas, and testing prototypes with small groups to reduce risk and improve products before launching them. It entails more of the pure Learning Zone before moving into the Performance Zone.

At the other end of the spectrum, launch and learn involves much less time devoted to research or lab-based experimentation. It's about quickly implementing ideas and learning from what happens next. It gets more—but less perfected—ideas to market faster. While more of them fail, more bets means that there are greater chances for a product to become a big hit. It's a lot more learning while doing.

Ian then shows where on that spectrum Skratch Labs wants to be: much closer to launch and learn than to seed and nurture. He wants staff to have a bias to action and taking risks. While this doesn't mean eliminating research or small experiments, it does mean launching promising ideas quickly and learning while doing.

"It's not spray and pray," he told me. "There is a process in place where we've got a funnel. We look at risk and reward. We look at brand fit, and we track it. There is a research element. But we lean heavily toward the launch and learn side, as opposed to deep consumer research."

Skratch Labs gathers elite athletes in its training camps in Boulder, Colorado, to closely interact with them, run ideas by them, and get feedback. The team then moves quickly to get promising products out into the world.

A launch and learn bias wouldn't work well in all contexts, but it works for Skratch Labs. A lot of its sales are direct to consumer through its website and Amazon, rather than through physical retailer distributors that take months to analyze and decide which products to display on limited shelf space. This strategy enables Skratch Labs to quickly put products on the virtual shelf, take them off, or add other varieties when new concepts prove successful. Frequent news about new product launches promotes Skratch Labs' brand as an innovator. And since the company's target customer is highly engaged with the brand, the company learns quickly what works and what doesn't.

To reduce the risk that throwing stuff out there may create significant damage, Ian makes an analogy: Skratch Labs is like a boat and the team is like its crew.

On a boat, he explains, if a fire starts on deck, it creates a crisis, but one that tends to be easy to resolve. Someone on deck sees the fire, grabs an extinguisher, and puts the fire out. This may create a bit of damage, but it's fixable and won't affect the boat's ability to stay afloat or navigate.

On the other hand, if a fire starts below the waterline—say in the engine room—it can be devastating. If structural wood is damaged and water starts pouring in, the boat may capsize.

Ian tells his teammates that when they're operating above the waterline, they should run with it. Launch and learn on your own. Take the risks. Experiment. But when they're operating below the waterline, they should bring in colleagues and share their ideas. Think things through together. Consider whether there's a way to mitigate risk, such as by gathering more feedback or running a small pilot.

Providing that clear picture of how to behave is an example of *framing*. Operating within this frame, Skratch Labs' staff can much more confidently and effectively engage in the two zones, knowing they're doing what they're supposed to.

Framing guides people. It provides parameters and shape to activities that can feel amorphous or overwhelming. It also helps them develop their understanding of the drivers of growth, such as competence, transparency, agency, challenge, feedback, mistakes, and community. It strengthens their growth propellers.

Framing is done proactively—as Ian MacGregor does—but also in response to events.

For example, when construction technology company Versatile developed its first product, CraneView, it identified a precious opportunity to launch it at a large and visible project. The Chase Center in San Francisco—the home venue for the Golden State Warriors—was being built at a construction cost of $1.4 billion.

The construction company involved was interested in Crane-View. Versatile spent months building a relationship and educating the company about the product, but for internal reasons, ultimately the builder decided against using the product. It was a significant setback for Versatile.

What did CEO Meirav Oren tell her staff? "Okay, this will be counted as tuition. What have we learned?"

That is *framing*. In doing so, Meirav impacted how people view mistakes. Yes, mistakes might be costly, but so is tuition. Rather than brush mistakes under the rug, we think through what we can learn from them to become smarter and work more skillfully moving forward.

Feedback must also be framed. Many people fear feedback and think of it as a sign of disrespect or ineptitude—actual or perceived. To prevent people from reacting defensively, share *why* you're giving feedback and define what feedback is: information for consideration that anyone can benefit from and that we desire, too.

Recall the *false consensus bias,* which leads us to overestimate the extent to which people think like us. It makes us think that others clearly understand what we mean when we say something to them, when in fact they may interpret it very differently than we intended.

By making what's implicit in our minds—such as our views on feedback or mistakes—explicit through our words, we help others build their growth propellers and we create alignment for effective communication, collaboration, learning, and performance. By making our goals, desired behaviors, and logic explicit to others—and doing so repeatedly and consistently—we ensure alignment on collective beliefs, habits, and community.

The need to frame is particularly important when communicating to groups—as leaders often do—because people may not have an opportunity to ask clarifying questions or may not feel comfortable doing so. They may then come away with an inaccurate understanding and venture further down the wrong path.

FRAMING FOR A LEARNING CULTURE

In 2017, Carol Dweck published a unified theory of motivation, personality, and development, based on all she knew about psychology. In it, she identified what she sees as universal human needs: acceptance, predictability, competence, trust, control, self-esteem/ status, and self-coherence.

As leaders, we need to create the conditions for people to be able to meet these needs within our organizations, but the way we go about doing so can make all the difference.

Consider the messages you use related to each of these needs and how those messages can create a know-it-all culture or a learning culture. In the table that follows, I have renamed a couple of these needs to better align with the language most often used in organizations.

HOW TO FRAME FOR A LEARNING CULTURE		
	MESSAGES THAT PROMOTE A KNOW-IT-ALL CULTURE	MESSAGES THAT PROMOTE A LEARNING CULTURE
BELONGING	You belong here because you are a genius, a natural, gifted.	You belong here if you care about our mission, have the competence needed to get started, and are committed to working hard and collaborating to develop ourselves and make a big impact.
PREDICTABILITY	Our job is to predict the future with certainty so that we can operate with full conviction.	We can learn about trends, develop hypotheses about what is likely to happen, and engage in scenario planning, but we can't predict the future with certainty. We can predict how we will behave with one another, following our values and agreements.
COMPETENCE	We should know how to do our jobs without making mistakes.	We are competent in our craft and in our ability to learn and improve further.
TRUST	We trust one another to always have the right answers, never make mistakes, be the best, cover one another's backs, and beat other teams.	We trust one another to do what we say we're going to do, to behave in the ways we have agreed on, and to challenge and support one another in our journey. If we have conflicts, we use fair and constructive processes to work them out and learn from them.

AGENCY	We have full control over our future and the direction in which our industry is going.	What we most control is our own behavior. Through effective teamwork in the two zones, we can impact the world.
STATUS	Here, the people who succeed and get promoted are the smartest in the room and the surest of themselves.	Here, the people who gain status are those who live our values, and in doing so strengthen our team and organization. They model learning behaviors and as a result are highly competent and continue to become more competent every day.
PURPOSE	We strive to show we're the best.	Our purpose is to improve the lives of our customers, our communities, and society. We also strive to create a working environment that enriches the lives of the whole staff and provides opportunities to continue to grow and develop.
OVERARCHING LOGIC	All messaging and mental lenses are aligned with the idea that abilities are fixed and that we strive for flawlessness.	All messaging and mental lenses are aligned with the idea that abilities can be developed through the Learning Zone and applied through the Performance Zone.

REGULARLY HIGHLIGHT THE DESIRED BEHAVIORS

Look for ways to reinforce desired behaviors by sharing stories of people and teams that exemplify them. This helps everyone get clearer about how the principles work in practice. It also provides memorable stories that help employees connect emotionally, remember, and communicate effectively.

Recall from Chapter 4 how Sonatype encouraged its staff to nominate colleagues who exemplified their core values. Anyone could submit a video explaining their nomination and sharing a story of the person who exemplified the values. Carlos Moreno Serrano nominated Richard Panman. Sonatype showcased the winners and their stories at a company-wide event.

Other companies send regular emails to all their staff, celebrating and highlighting exemplary behaviors.

The opposite of rewarding desired behaviors is punishing them. I've seen leaders encourage risk-taking, but then if the experiments don't work out as hoped, the leaders get disappointed, and the people involved may get a bad review or lower bonus, or be passed over for a promotion. This does not provide safety or true encouragement for taking real risks—quite the opposite. It leads people to be cautious and do what they know works. If we want to encourage challenge-seeking and risk-taking behavior, we have to reward challenge-seeking and risk-taking efforts, not only when the risks work out as hoped. We have to learn from the outcomes and value the lessons. If people see that the team or organization is learning from failure and applying the new insights going forward, they will feel more motivated and supported to continue taking risks.

Keep your messages concrete, focused, and clear, and keep in mind that even brief messages go a long way. When Rich Lesser was CEO of Boston Consulting Group, he would post videos he called "Two Minutes on Tuesday," in which he would discuss a variety of topics, such as the importance of growth mindset. In one video, he shared that "knowing what you don't know is more valuable than knowing what you do know," and explained why, which is not intuitive for many high-achieving management consultants. He also guided people to "look for opportunities to grow laterally . . . look for people who bring different skills than you." In these messages, he framed how BCGers go about learning and performing. He helped people see work as a way to foster growth. This enabled colleagues to show up to meetings and projects on the same page, understanding that acknowledging what they didn't know was valued, and being intentional about learning from one another.

This is how we lead with care, trust, and clarity. As leaders, we also need to set up systems and routines for the two zones, and we need to model the way. That is the subject of the next chapter.

REFLECTION QUESTIONS

- What do I want my team culture to be?
- Do my colleagues feel I care for them, and do they trust me? Do I trust them?
- Do I hold command-and-control assumptions that might be getting in the way of my goals?
- Am I celebrating and reinforcing the desired behaviors?

LOOKING FORWARD

What systems and routines might help our team engage in the two zones, and how might I lead the way?

Chapter 12: Great Leaders Are Great Learners

BIG IDEA *Great leaders put structures in place to support the two zones, and they visibly lead the way as learners.*

When Skratch Labs introduced Skratch Crispy—a healthy, convenient rice cake for athletes that doesn't melt in pockets—the company decided to use a new vendor for the film used in the packaging. As always, it erred on the side of "launch and learn" rather than "seed and nurture."

The product launch didn't go well.

The detailed images the company designed for the film turned out to be beyond the supplier's capabilities. The packaging looked blurry.

After conferring, the Skratch Labs team decided to still release the product while searching for a different film supplier. As soon as the company transitioned to the new packaging, it donated its remaining original inventory.

What does Skratch Labs do when things don't go smoothly?

The same thing as when they enjoy big successes.

Each quarter, the whole company gets together for a "state of the company" meeting, which typically lasts an hour and a half. They pick a couple of significant failures and big successes to openly discuss, which is very useful Learning Zone work.

Each analysis follows the same process, in which they discuss four things:

1. *The known costs.* In the Skratch Crispy example, this included the inventory that was donated.

2. *The unknown costs.* The company decided to release a product with blurry packaging, which might have negatively impacted customers' or journalists' impressions of the brand. Other unknown collateral damage might have occurred as well. The team acknowledges this explicitly—that there are things they don't know.

3. *The decision point.* The company brings the team back to the moment in time when a decision was made, identifying what information was then available. CEO Ian MacGregor tries to highlight something the team did well that reflects the company's core values, and then there's a discussion about what the team might have done differently.

4. *Process changes.* Lastly, Skratch Labs decides what process changes they'll make going forward, if any, given the lessons learned from the experience. In the case of the Skratch Crispy launch, the team decided that no process changes were called for. The supplier had assured them they could print the film accurately. Given their philosophy to launch and learn, with a bias to action, the team took an acceptable risk, above the waterline.

Skratch Labs follows this process regardless of whether significant projects fail or succeed. There are lessons to be learned from both.

Thanks to a new film supplier, Skratch Crispy is now a commercially successful product. Most important, Skratch Labs' staff continues to launch and learn, confident that's what their colleagues really want them to do.

SET UP SYSTEMS AND ROUTINES FOR THE TWO ZONES

Skratch Labs' quarterly meetings are an example of a system designed to support the two zones—in this case, to regularly examine and learn from failures and successes. The company also has daily stand-up meetings for each department that last between one and twelve minutes—a learning while doing forum where colleagues share important information and promote alignment so that they can later divide and conquer.

Other companies and teams conduct *after-action reviews*, a practice borrowed from the military that's used to reflect, learn, and identify what to do differently in future cycles.

Ashley Good, CEO of consultancy Fail Forward, assists people and organizations in using failure as an opportunity to learn and grow. She points out that we can learn more from short, regularly scheduled meetings to assess a project while it is ongoing—a *mid-action review*—rather than only going back and doing a postmortem when the project concludes.

"The after-action review is useful, but I say that hesitantly because some organizations do it and that is great, but for most organizations it is too late to change anything," Ashley told me. "After-action reviews are painful. People avoid them because they feel like root canals. So, it's better to have the conversations throughout and schedule them so that they are not in response to something going awry."

These are all sample structures for learning that enable higher performance.

Changing the agenda is an easy way to change the conversations that take place during meetings. That is what Tomer Cohen, chief product officer at LinkedIn, instituted in the company's weekly meeting for its top hundred or so leaders. He changed the agenda so a section of the meeting is now dedicated to having participants share lessons learned with other leaders across the company.

"My goal is both from a language standpoint, and also from a direction standpoint, to bring learning front and center, templated so that the expectation is the sharing of lessons learned as the norm," Tomer told me.

At first, during the new section of the meeting, people would share data or results of what went right or wrong, but without identifying a concrete lesson or takeaway. To help them sharpen their thinking and identify the generalizable lesson that peers could take away and apply going forward, Tomer would ask follow-up questions until the person sharing identified the "So what?" at the heart of the matter. With practice, people got used to this new way of thinking. Tomer would also encourage all leaders who attended the meeting to reflect on what they could learn and apply to their work. This not only reframed the meeting to be more focused on learning, but also shifted how leaders approached their daily work so that they would engage in more learning while doing.

After Tomer instituted this change, other people beyond top leaders started expressing interest in attending the weekly meeting—even if just to listen—having heard from participants that they felt the meeting made them smarter and more effective in their jobs.

It's not enough just to give people marching orders. Effective leaders are also effective teachers. They guide people along the way, not as know-it-alls, but as leaders with a vision of how to work, always open to considering others' perspectives.

Individuals, too, can identify ways to work more effectively by scheduling regular reflections and by seeking out periodic feedback from supervisors, colleagues, mentors, and customers. These are all systems and routines for the two zones.

Consider, also, how much you're systematically using collaborative work as an opportunity to develop others. For example, if a more novice colleague drafts a report and sends it to you for review, simply improving the report and delivering it is a missed opportunity. Rather, when reasonable, you can ask your colleague whether she would like to join you while you revise the report. As you make edits, you can explain your thinking to help her develop her mental models, or you can coach her as she makes the revisions. These approaches might take a little longer in the beginning but will have huge dividends moving forward, as future reports will need fewer revisions and take less time.

In your regular conversations with direct reports or teammates, ask people to share what they want to work on, after you share yours. Make that a habit so it becomes a system for regularly identifying opportunities for mutual support. To aid the development of a particular skill, you may decide to collaborate more closely on specific types of work, or have a junior person join some client pitches or conversations with senior leaders, or have a senior leader shadow a frontline worker for a day. Also consider how you or your team could benefit from more closely collaborating with people in a different function or product line for mutual benefit and learning. And if you have ideas for ways your leaders might better support your growth, describe them and ask if they are possible or if there are other ways to accelerate your development.

The key takeaway is that it's important to identify what systems you want your team to use, not only to perform, but also to learn. This may include what you talk about in different meetings with peers, superiors, and direct reports, as we have discussed here, or it may be systems for experimentation, role-playing simulations, or customer feedback.

Here are some additional systems and routines to consider:

- Pick a measurable goal and regularly track, analyze, and discuss data to generate ideas, run experiments, and evaluate results.
- Regularly invite other departments to join your team meeting to answer questions about what they do, solicit feedback, and explore ways to better collaborate.
- Schedule a recurring monthly or quarterly meeting to come together as a team and discuss challenges and ideas aimed at improving how you work together.
- Set up an annual 360-degree feedback process for everyone to gain information about what others find helpful and identify potential areas of improvement.

NEVER LET CHANGE GO TO WASTE

New initiatives or changes in your industry, company, or team are an opportunity to shift mindsets and habits. This also applies to any challenge your team is taking on or a mistake you are recovering from. Consider how you can leverage the situation to further strengthen growth propellers.

Remember Douglas Franco, the CEO of iEduca whom we met in Part One? Douglas faced a challenge when he joined the higher education company and was tasked with significantly accelerating its growth.

"At the beginning it was tough, because when I started as CEO, almost everyone in the company, and especially the executive team, was trying to look good," he told me. "It was terrible because then it was all about justifying themselves. And I was like, 'I don't care where we've been. I only care where we're going now.'"

That's another example of framing.

He wanted them to realize that if they weren't able to identify things that could be improved, they would not be able to change the trajectory.

"If we find issues and fix them, we will grow. If we don't find anything, we're f**ked. I'm sorry for my French, but we're in deep because if we don't have any opportunity to address an issue, how are we going to improve from where we are right now?" he said. "So that took time. And it also took some people. I had to make a couple of changes in the team, because there were a couple of people that wouldn't change."

Douglas also discovered he was making mistakes as a leader. He had an intimidating presence, which he exacerbated by doing things like not letting people finish their sentences. He would interrupt them when he thought he knew what they were going to say, or pose difficult questions to which he knew they didn't have the answers.

While his intention was not to create fear, the pressure *he* felt to perform was leading him to push his team toward chronic performance.

"They felt that they were put on the spot," he said. "I realized that dynamic I was fostering at the meetings was not good and it was not promoting the right culture. So, I also had to adjust my style, be more patient, listen with intent, and then teach by example. And say, 'Okay, let me explain why that hypothesis I think is not gonna work. I'm gonna share why. And let's look at what the numbers say.' I tried to be more of a coach, to bite my tongue and start asking questions, and adjust my leadership style to make it work. And it worked."

Despite needing to reduce its workforce by 17 percent during the COVID-19 pandemic, the company was able to weather the crisis and come out stronger. In less than two years, the leadership ran more than seventy experiments to test ideas for new products, target customer demographics, and promote channels and messages. Twenty of them failed, but on aggregate, these experiments led to the doubling of financial results—both revenue and income—within that time frame. After two years, they were back to the same number of employees they'd had pre-pandemic, but with record financial results.

When approving iEduca's yearly budget and target plan, the board of directors is presented with a base plan and an Everest plan. Management is evaluated according to the base plan, but in every board meeting they discuss their progress toward both plans, and everyone at the company talks about their Everest goals—the big, audacious goals tied to the company's strategic goals—which they pursue through experimentation.

When iEduca prepared to refresh its core values and guiding language and asked employees for input, staff chose names like "Base Camp" and "8,850 Meters" for the company's headquarters and offices. These names serve as shorthand daily reminders to be bold and to experiment beyond the known.

This is when we know that a cultural transformation is taking hold: when everyone in the organization—not just the leaders—starts living and owning the culture. After all, that is the end goal: shifting how everyone in the organization thinks and behaves and changing the culture every employee experiences.

MODEL THE WAY

Sometimes, as leaders, we see ourselves as learners and effectively engage in the Learning Zone regularly, but we do so privately, when others can't see us. Framing is important, but if our visible behaviors don't match our language, our actions will speak louder than our words. People emulate the behaviors they see, especially in leaders and role models. If we act like leaders should have all the answers, people will learn that's what the organization values, and what gets people promoted.

"You as the leader need to share your 360 evaluations with your teams, especially the really candid stuff about all the things you do poorly," Netflix co-founder and former CEO Reed Hastings writes in his book, *No Rules Rules*. "It shows everyone that giving and receiving clear, actionable feedback isn't so scary."

One of the most popular and longest running recurring bits on Jimmy Kimmel's late-night show is "Mean Tweets," in which celebrities are invited on air to read aloud the most insulting things posted about them on Twitter. Some years ago, a group of MBA students at Wharton, where organizational psychologist Adam Grant teaches, riffed on the "Mean Tweets" format, creating a comic video of faculty members reading critical comments about themselves from their end-of-semester student evaluations. In his book *Think Again: The Power of Knowing What You Don't Know*, Grant describes what happened to the dynamic between professors and students as a result of the video, which was so notable, he started sharing it with students at the beginning of every fall semester.

He observed that students became much more willing to offer constructive criticism to their professors once they saw the video, in which one professor reads an eval that says, "This professor is a b*tch. But she's a nice b*tch," and Grant himself cheerfully reads one of his own: "You remind me of a Muppet."

The video, Grant reports, allowed students to see that "although I take my work seriously, I don't take myself too seriously." It was so successful that years later, Grant wondered whether something similar would work to create the kind of psychological safety that the Gates Foundation was looking for on their teams. When he sent the video to Melinda Gates, she was completely on board. She even volunteered to go first.

"Her team compiled criticisms from staff surveys, printed them on note cards, and had her react in real time in front of a camera," Grant writes. "She read one employee's complaint that she was like Mary F***ing Poppins—the first time anyone could remember hearing Melinda curse—and explained how she was working on making her imperfections more visible."

It was effective—but *how* effective? To evaluate that, Grant and his colleagues divided employees into three groups: the first watched the "Mean Tweets"–style video, the second watched a different video of Gates discussing the culture she wanted to foster at the organization, and the third, a control group, didn't watch either. Grant found that it was indeed the first group who "came away with a stronger learning orientation—they were inspired to recognize their shortcomings and work to overcome them." And further, Grant observed that those employees were more likely to reach out to Gates for all kinds of reasons—with their concerns but also with compliments. Some of the inhibiting effects of power and hierarchy had dissolved.

Grant includes this comment from an employee: "In that video Melinda did something that I've not yet seen happen at the foundation: She broke through the veneer. It happened for me when she said, 'I go into so many meetings where there are things I don't know.' I had to write that down because I was shocked and grateful at her honesty. Later, when she laughed, like really belly-laughed, and then answered the hard comments, the veneer came off again and I saw that she was no less of Melinda Gates, but actually, a whole lot more of Melinda Gates."

To lead learning cultures, we need both actions and words to align. When there are mixed messages, actions speak louder than words, but without words, our actions can easily be misinterpreted in many different ways.

Julia Barbaro is a life and marriage coach who co-hosts the *Multi Family Zone* podcast with her husband, Gino (the former pizzeria owner who co-founded a thriving real estate investment company).

Years ago, she knew a group of married women in her neighborhood who seemed to have it all together. For a decade, she felt "less than" because she faced struggles in her life and she thought they didn't.

"I looked at them from the outside thinking these moms are perfect," she told me. "They got it together. Their kids are winning every spelling bee. I could never live up to them. I went through that for years. I really thought that they had it all together—marriage, family, homeschooling, education, all of it."

Until one day, when she was sitting in a coffee shop, she overheard some of the women at a table behind her, talking about the very struggles she imagined they'd never had.

"I thought, 'Holy cow, I never knew that,'" she said. "Because I never asked. I never approached them, because I felt that I wasn't even close to being as good as them. And I thought, 'My gosh, I never want to create that feeling in other people.'"

Now, when others see her and Gino leading a "perfect life" with their large, beautiful house, six kids, and financial independence, Julia makes it a point to talk about all the struggles and the learning along the way. She doesn't want people to make up stories in their mind and measure themselves against her as she had once done.

"When people started saying, 'Oh, you guys have the perfect marriage,' I'm like, no, no, no, we don't," Julia said. "We struggle, too. I want people to know that. That life is difficult. Raising children is difficult. We go through a lot of things. We just have to work at it. We have to apply ourselves. We have to learn from our mistakes."

Making assumptions about others is a common way fixed mindsets are formed. If we see a top athlete perform, we may assume it all comes naturally for her, because we haven't seen her process off the field or court. If we see a company executive present onstage engagingly or run a meeting masterfully, we may think that she's a natural and that she didn't have to work at it over time or prepare for the session. We see only the Performance Zone.

As leaders, we can remind others of the process we have gone through and continue to go through in the Learning Zone: our trajectory over the past, present, and future. And when we see others who appear flawless and gifted, we can remind ourselves that we are seeing only a snapshot in time and that everyone gets better through regular engagement in the Learning Zone.

I sometimes work with teams of executives who see themselves as strong learners. When I speak and interact with them, I think they're correct about this. But when I survey them and others on several dimensions, senior leaders consistently tend to think that they're modeling learning much more than the people who report to them perceive.

I also ask people I work with how they want to come across to their colleagues. While they list very positive things, seldom do they write that they want to come across as a work in progress—as someone who is continuing to develop.

If we want to create a culture of growth, we have to develop the intention to be perceived as learners, and we have to visibly model learning behaviors, making our implicit thinking explicit, so others understand what we're doing and why.

At some point, when our teammates get to know us well, we don't need to be fully explicit every time we model a behavior. But to get to that point, we first need to become a broken record. We have to consistently make transparent our thinking, logic, and assumptions, so that others understand where we're coming from and can develop their own mental models—their own growth propellers—to be in harmony with ours.

Keep in mind that employees are more than nine times as likely to see their leaders as under-communicative than over-communicative. And leaders who are perceived as under-communicative also tend to be seen as uncaring and unclear, while those who are perceived to over-communicate tend to come across as caring, clear, and putting in effort.

When the organization is facing a significant challenge, as leaders we can be honest about our uncertainties and struggles while still sharing our belief that together we can overcome obstacles and achieve our aims. We can acknowledge the difficulties while affirming that our team and teammates have what it takes to succeed in this next stage. While we may not yet have all the answers, we have the required foundational knowledge and skills, as well as the learning dispositions to continue to improve and learn from adversity.

For a long time, I, like many others, described role modeling as visibly engaging in the behaviors we want others to practice. But that's actually not quite right, especially early on when a leader is building culture.

Instead, leaders need to engage in what I call *asymmetrical modeling*.

If we want people to talk and ask questions, as leaders we need to tell them that's what we want and explain that we'll give them space to talk—and then do just that. If we want people to voice their ideas and disagreements, we don't start by voicing our own ideas and disagreements. We start by listening and asking questions. That's the asymmetrical part. Our position of power results in our behavior being interpreted differently, so if we talk and challenge, this can lead others to remain quiet and wait for our decisions.

As leaders, we can coach others, focus on listening and asking questions, and invite them to practice the desired behaviors. We can then reward them when they engage in those behaviors.

If we want others to ask questions, we can ask, "What questions do people have?"

If we want them to share their disagreements, we can start by asking, "Does anyone have a different perspective on this?"

And when we're gaining new perspectives, we show that we're learning from them and changing our mind. It's critical to avoid coming across as a know-it-all.

Finally, when it comes to modeling, there is a caveat: Visibly modeling learning works best when others believe we're competent. If they think we're incompetent, modeling learning can backfire, because it can be interpreted as ineptitude or insecurity.

This is one reason it's important to regularly engage in the Learning Zone throughout our careers. We want to continuously build our competence. The more we do, the more confident and effective we can be, both in getting things done and in creating a culture of growth, including by modeling learning.

I call this the *flywheel of competence*. Flywheels are heavy and take a lot of effort to get turning. But with steady force, we can get them to go faster and faster, and when they're turning fast and have gained momentum, it's hard to stop them.

Competence is similar. The more we develop it—through the Learning Zone—the easier it is to develop it further, to apply it and use it to lead culture. With everyone becoming more well-versed in learning and performing, the effectiveness skyrockets, and we gain more time for the two zones. It's a self-reinforcing cycle. That's when we become unstoppable.

That's why, when the COVID-19 pandemic started, Lizzie Dipp Metzger felt completely comfortable reaching out to three peers to propose a weekly call to support one another and share strategies. Everyone knew she was excellent at what she did, so her proposal to learn together was seen as a sign of strength and capability—of knowing what to do in times of crisis. Lizzie's colleagues also trusted her air sense—remember that Learning Zone strategy from Chapter 4? They knew she had a keen intuition and they trusted her to make good decisions that would benefit others. Hence, COVID-19 didn't stop her, and she continued achieving top performance. She remained resilient throughout her career because she knew what to do in times of challenge and uncertainty: leap into the Learning Zone.

If you're in a tricky situation, feeling insecure about your competence yet wanting to build a culture of learning, engaging in the Learning Zone to develop your skills is a positive step. In addition, explain *why* you're engaging in your learning behaviors. Make the implicit explicit. Create alignment on how everyone should be behaving, and when you're modeling, refer back to those agreements. This way, your behavior is less likely to be interpreted as ineptitude or insecurity. You're helping others interpret the behavior as a sign of leadership, which it is.

As you advance in your career, the complexity and level of expertise needed will increase. But once you feel competent in your job, the flywheel will be rolling, and it will become easier for you to further accelerate if you continue engaging in the two zones. The smoothest path is to consistently, throughout your career, invest in yourself in the Learning Zone.

INCENTIVIZE AND REWARD

Within your team, do you reward, praise, and celebrate only success and getting things right? When people take risks, do you praise and celebrate only the instances when those risks lead to the desired outcomes? If that's all you're doing, you may be fostering a know-it-all culture and chronic performance.

When I use the terms *incentivize* and *reward*, I don't just mean compensation. Authentic praise and gratitude tend to be more powerful ways of reinforcing people's behaviors.

Mahan Tavakoli, a consultant and the host of one of my favorite podcasts, *Partnering Leadership*, describes how remarkably well his former boss, Dale Carnegie & Associates CEO Peter Handal, did this.

"He would never be first to speak, almost always last," Mahan told me. "He always wanted constant debate and disagreement with his own opinions. And after the meeting, he would pull me aside—as I am sure he would do others—when I had vigorously disagreed with him. And he would say, 'I love that. I want to see more of that out of you.' I would be floating up in the air, especially after those early meetings. This did not make sense—the CEO just pulled me aside and told me to disagree with him, in front of the other team members! But disagreeing with him is something he loves, and he wants to see more of it."

Handal was guiding, incentivizing, rewarding, and engaging in asymmetrical modeling.

Social cues and rewards from teammates, especially from leaders, affect us more positively than compensation, as does pointing out how our behavior benefits our work and magnifies our impact. As leaders and teammates, we can use this to our advantage to promote the culture we want to create.

RECRUIT AND HIRE FOR GROWTH

As your organization grows, you will need to hire new staff. This is an opportunity to recruit people who have developed the beliefs and habits you value. But hiring too quickly can erode the existing culture if not done thoughtfully. To assess job candidates' learning dispositions and skills, a good place to start is through interview questions like the following:

- What would you want in a work environment and culture? (Do they describe just the Performance Zone or also the Learning Zone?)
- What are some skills you'd want to work on, or look to change, as you approach this new role? (How thoughtfully do they describe what they want to improve in themselves and how they want to go about doing so?)
- If you have a choice between leading an ambitious project that involves skills you haven't mastered or a less ambitious project in which you have a high chance of success, what are some of the considerations you'd think about when making your decision? (What do the answers reveal about their goals and about their views on collaborating, taking risks, and pursuing the mission?)
- Over the last few months, is there anything you've been working to improve on? How have you gone about doing so?
- When you struggle, what do you do? Can you give me some examples?
- What have been your greatest mistakes or failures? Tell me what happened as a result. (Do they take responsibility? Learn from it? Did it affect a later decision?)
- When was the most recent time you received feedback, and what happened afterward?

- What is your approach to giving feedback? (Do they have a well-thought-out framework?)
- What is your approach to receiving feedback? (Do they have a well-thought-out framework? Do they mention the importance of frequently soliciting feedback?)
- Who are some people or colleagues you've learned from, and what have you learned from them?
- What do you want to get better at? How do you plan to go about it?

When assessing answers, consider the extent to which the candidates consider themselves a work in progress rather than naturally talented, how much they're open to feedback and opportunities for growth, and how thoughtful they are about their Learning Zone strategies and what they've learned along the way. Also consider asking similar questions of candidates' references to learn what other people think about their behavior patterns.

You can also give the candidate some homework that requires them to learn in order to accomplish a task. See how well they do on this. Or you can use *scenario-based questions* in an interview that prompt the candidate to share what they would do in a given situation so that they can't easily infer what you are looking for and are challenged to think more holistically.

Here's an example: Imagine that a direct report comes to you with a complaint that a colleague keeps excluding her from meetings where decisions that impact her job are made. What would you do? (Does the candidate come to a decision based on that information, or do they describe what questions they'd ask, how they'd assess the situation, and what considerations would enable them to decide what path to take?)

Meirav Oren, the CEO and co-founder of construction technology company Versatile, whom we met in earlier chapters, turns the tables on job candidates and has them ask *her* questions. Since these candidates have already been vetted by colleagues she trusts, she can take the opportunity to assess their dispositions.

"I want to know what questions they're asking, what they actually care about, what drives them," she told me. "I ask the candidates to prioritize the questions and send me a list of questions ahead of time. As we get on the call, I say, 'You tell me where you want to start, because we probably won't get to all your questions.' The questions they choose tell me a whole lot about them and their hunger for knowledge, right?"

Meirav has found her system to be extremely effective.

"I should really patent that," she said, chuckling. "I've hired incredible leaders, which has enabled my ability to fire myself from roles I should no longer be doing, with trust that I've hired the right person, that I can give them the freedom to grow."

As CEO of Moovweb, Ajay Kapur has had great success hiring more than 600 high-performing, enthusiastic learners using the same principle. He looks for candidates who are "constantly asking questions, about the hard stuff, the product, the market, about the substance of the work."

But even if we don't have the benefit of hiring new team members and selecting people who are already further along in developing their growth propellers, we can always help strengthen—and even transform—the growth propellers of our current teammates, along with our own.

START WITH YOURSELF

Francesca Lenci, the CFO of Siemens Mobility in Italy, does a lot to support the growth of every person on her team. As we saw earlier, she leads with care, including care for people's growth.

But she doesn't neglect her own growth. She is disciplined about investing in her own development, and she wouldn't have gotten to where she is without deliberately working in the Learning Zone throughout her career.

On one occasion, Francesca noticed a pattern: She thought everyone was against her.

In some meetings, decisions were made that Francesca considered unfair, yet everyone else seemed okay with them. She continued advocating for her perspectives despite feeling she was on her own.

She wondered whether she might be holding some incorrect assumptions, and she decided to check. She went to her boss and requested a leadership coach. She knew that some of her colleagues were working with coaches, and she decided to give some sessions a try, hoping an external, unbiased guide could help her figure things out.

"I wanted to confirm whether what I was thinking was correct, or whether maybe there was another point of view that I was not taking into consideration," she told me.

The coaching sessions were transformative. Francesca realized that her boss had been telling her things she hadn't believed, but which in fact were true. She had been taking a competitive stance with her peers and advocating for her department against theirs, not seeing how they were all part of the same larger organization. She recognized that she sometimes needed to make sacrifices in her division for the benefit of the whole and find ways to negotiate and make compromises.

"The coaching sessions were life-changing for me, because after them I felt a little bit stronger in the discussions. I felt more empowered to reconcile and not just to fight to win," she said. "I try to share the lessons I learned with my team."

To become an effective leader, Francesca had to work on herself. All leaders do. This is work that never ends, because the world changes, challenges shift, and as we progress in our responsibilities, new skills are needed.

To this day, Francesca takes thirty minutes each month to review and update her personal development plan. She has regularly scheduled meetings with her mentor and frequently messages with her whenever she wants her opinion on a complex situation or decision. She is also methodical about reaching out to people with whom she can develop valuable relationships or partnerships, and those she can contribute to or learn from. Before networking events, she reviews who will be there and identifies the people she wants to speak with and the topics she will broach. While she often ends up meeting other people there and makes great discoveries, she is proactive about expanding her network with those who can strengthen her community strategically for both learning and performing.

When we first become interested in fostering a growth mindset and the Learning Zone in our teams and organizations, there's a tendency to look at others first: How are our employees stuck in a fixed mindset? How are our managers unwittingly creating a culture of chronic performance?

But we can't effect change in others without first effecting change in ourselves. Before we look around us, we need to look inward.

Let's not focus on changing others if we ourselves are not conscious, on a daily basis, of what we are working to improve, or if we are not soliciting feedback at least a few times per week from a variety of people, or if we brush aside mistakes rather than examine and discuss them to learn from them.

We are not likely to get others to do things that they don't see us doing. As we become more aware of our own opportunities for improvement and start making progress, we are better equipped to become change agents and influence others.

TOWARD A CULTURE OF GROWTH

To develop a strong culture of growth, start with care and trust, frame and guide, set up systems for the two zones, and regularly communicate, incentivize, reward, and model. In the process, you and your colleagues will form personal bonds with one another and with the two zones.

The tools described in this and the previous chapter are just some of the ways any of us can help shape and strengthen the growth propellers of the people we lead, formally and informally. Through continued engagement in the Learning Zone—both on its own and together with the Performance Zone in learning while doing—we can continue to expand and strengthen our leadership toolkit to advance cultures of growth and impact.

REFLECTION QUESTIONS

- How often am I explicitly modeling learning behaviors?
- To what extent do our team's structures and routines make using the two zones the easy default?
- Might I benefit from sharing the ideas in this book with others in my team and starting a strategic conversation about the two zones?

LOOKING FORWARD

Once we are equipped with strong Learning Zone habits, how might we promote top performance?

Part Three:
From Individual Transformation to Global Impact

Chapter 13: The Flywheel of Competence—In Motion and Unstoppable

> **BIG IDEA** *The Performance Zone enables you to get things done and contribute. To perform at your best, ensure that you're working in pursuit of your highest-level goals and that you're putting proven routines on autopilot so you can focus on what can take you to the next level.*

It's showtime! The stage lights are on—and they're shining on you!

It's time to execute. Time to perform. How do you best apply the knowledge and skills you have developed?

Over time, your regular engagement in the Learning Zone will equip you to answer that question. While everyone's circumstances are unique, I *can* point you to a couple of key strategies to consider as you prepare to deliver.

Before we dive in, let's check back in with Anjali, the consultant we met at the beginning of the book. When we last saw her in Chapter 6, she and her manager, Salma, were at odds because each had differing ideas of what feedback was for. Salma's well-intended feedback was misfiring because she was unintentionally sending the message that Anjali's abilities were due to innate talents, while Anjali was bristling over the implication that she was unable to learn some aspects of her job. Anjali was trapped in chronic performance, working as hard as she could, and Salma's feedback made her feel overwhelmed and defensive. They were deadlocked. So what happened next?

Fortunately, they worked at an organization that was learning to foster a growth mindset culture, and the executive leadership was committed to integrating Learning Zone and Performance Zone strategies to advance everyone's development and productivity.

While Anjali had interpreted Salma's feedback as a statement of ineptitude, Salma was actually trying to clarify that they didn't want Anjali to try to grind her way through problem-solving on her own, but to ask for help when needed. Having worked independently for years prior to coming on board, Anjali had never asked for help because, well, who would she have asked? Once Salma learned how to frame her feedback so Anjali didn't feel she was being attacked, Anjali was able to hear that the feedback was intended to help support her growth and performance. At this new job, asking for help was not perceived as a sign of incompetence but as a way to elicit collaboration. Interdependence was valued.

"I'd been so used to solving all problems on my own as an independent consultant for a decade, I was like, 'Oh, right, I'm part of a team now, I don't have to do this all on my own!'" Anjali told me.

When it came to her career, Anjali struggled with balancing her efforts; she always felt she was focusing on one area at the expense of another, or that she needed to pick between what she knew and what she was curious about. Working with a coach helped her set goals and get in touch with what most energized her about her work. Embracing collaboration with colleagues allowed her to find ways to spend more time on the things she loved and wanted to further develop. She realized that her obsession with productivity and control had actually mired her in stagnation. She learned how to take on big new challenges that had seemed overwhelming at first and break them up into actionable steps.

Soon she was performing so skillfully that she was promoted to a management position less than a year after joining the company. Salma helped her figure out which parts of her job she wanted to keep in her new role and which she wanted to transition to others. Ultimately the solution was a specially tailored role where Anjali still does some of the hands-on client work she loves, but also plays a bigger role in the company's long-term strategic planning, logistics, hiring, and team support.

She told me, "What was so special was that they really listened when I shared about the components of the job where I needed support. Salma and I worked together on the job description, and now we've brought on another staffer to provide additional mentoring and support for our team. It really is a 'pinch me' situation."

Working at an organization that fostered a culture of continuous learning and improvement changed Anjali's idea of what work could be; she'd been on the hamster wheel of chronic performance for years. Now she looked forward to going to work. The collaboration and teamwork in which she was engaged awakened her creativity and gave her a sense of belonging.

Today, not only is Anjali a rock star at her consultancy, but she has also taken the lead on launching a series of experiments to explore new project management technology. She's also mentoring younger colleagues in the Learning Zone strategies that helped her break out of the performance paradox, which trapped her for so long. Her *flywheel of competence* is in motion and unstoppable.

Anjali is just one of the many great performers we have met in this book. We know that they all regularly engage in the Learning Zone, but what are their Performance Zone habits? That's what this chapter is about. Read on to learn about the strategies and tools these performers use to execute at their best.

START WITH CLARITY

Always begin at the end—your end goal, that is. Before jumping into execution, make sure you and your colleagues are clear about what you're seeking to accomplish. Don't get ensnared in the performance paradox! Before working, make sure you're working on the right thing.

Instead of starting with discussing tasks to be done, identify the most important goals, ensure everyone is clear and aligned on them, and discuss strategies to achieve them. That way, everyone knows what matters most and can benefit from the knowledge and perspectives of colleagues on how to get there.

This applies not only to leaders, but also to individual contributors. If you feel you and your manager haven't aligned around goals, make sure to communicate the goals and timeline as you see them and ask if they make sense. Consistently delivering what you promise will build trust between you and your manager and may lead to more autonomy over how you do your work. But it starts with clarity and alignment on the goal.

GET YOUR ACT TOGETHER!

"Failing to prepare is preparing to fail," wrote legendary basketball coach John Wooden in his book *Wooden: A Lifetime of Observations and Reflections On and Off the Court.*

Preparation involves regularly engaging in the Learning Zone, to proactively develop your skills, as well as developing healthy habits—such as eating well and getting enough sleep—so your body and mind have what they need to function their best. But it also means strategizing about how you'll approach a specific performance. This can be as simple as taking one minute before each conference call to think through who you will be speaking with, how you want to show up, and what you want to accomplish during the call. Many athletes visualize the game they'll play, which helps them warm up mentally and achieve higher levels of performance. Salespeople run mental simulations of what prospects or customers might say or do and how to respond; they may also research information on the person and their company.

Preparation is the on-ramp to the Performance Zone. It allows us the time and cognitive resources to make a plan instead of trying to figure everything out on the spot. It also allows us to identify what skill we'll work on when learning while doing, or what we'll test— like the patient education consultants at ClearChoice Dental who identify beforehand in which part of the consult they'll try something different.

Winston Churchill was in the habit of preparing for speeches by practicing in front of a mirror. But if video had been available in his time, you can bet he would have used it. Record yourself on video and watch how you come across, which will replicate the conditions you'll face come showtime better than a mirror. As I prepared my first TEDx Talk—my first ever public speaking event—I was aware that I tended to get nervous when people watched me, and I wanted to avoid blanking out with so many eyes on me. So I printed photos of a crowd and practiced with them in front of me. Using pictures of people didn't perfectly replicate the conditions I'd face, but it was better than having no eyes on me at all. I video recorded each attempt and sent the recording to friends and colleagues for feedback, and then I adjusted and repeated the process.

Rehearsing is performing in a low-stakes setting. It can help us identify precisely what we need to work on. At times we can choose to engage in deliberate practice for a bit before going back to rehearsing.

To prepare for a difficult conversation, you may clarify the key points you want to make, envision how the conversation could get tricky, and plan how you would react. Or you might enlist a friend or colleague to role-play with you and offer scenarios, ideas, and feedback.

Once you become better versed in public speaking (or having difficult conversations), you'll need less preparation, but beware of getting trapped by the performance paradox. To reach new heights, you need to consistently engage in the Learning Zone and in learning while doing, always tweaking your approaches to getting things done.

Preparation is not about doing something hard before a performance. It's about building habits that enable great execution as the easy default.

PUT PERFORMANCE ROUTINES ON AUTOPILOT

Because most of our behaviors are driven by our habits and environment rather than by rational decisions, we need to thoughtfully design our routines and systems to best support both zones. That way, when we're executing, we can fully concentrate on the sub-stance of the work, knowing that we have established effective ways of working.

When Lizzie Dipp Metzger decided to sell life insurance, she set a daily habit of making twenty-one phone calls to potential clients. Establishing this habit saved her from spending time each day hav-ing to think up a new plan of action.

Anjali has also developed new habits to go along with her new role. She's learned she needs to be deliberate about how she struc-tures her time because the new managerial work can be fatiguing, so she makes sure to start off each day with a brief team check-in, a habit she finds rewarding and energizing.

Many high performers also have pre-event rituals to get into their desired mental and emotional state. Many athletes listen to their favorite music, run through self-talk scripts, or meditate. Be-fore presentations, many speakers and executives breathe deeply, stand tall, and remind themselves to raise their energy level. Before sales calls or meetings, many high performers review a standard document or record that contains key information about the client, prospect, or opportunity.

There are also team systems and frameworks that support skilled execution. Every Monday, Gino Barbaro, Jake Stenziano, and their colleagues follow the Level 10 Meetings framework—which is part of the EOS (Entrepreneurial Operating System) toolkit—to review their progress, plan their upcoming week, and keep one another ac-countable. Other companies use the Agile methodology, 4DX (4 Disciplines of Execution), OKR (Objectives and Key Results), Scaling Up (formerly known as the Rockefeller Habits), or the MIND (Most Important Number and Drivers) methodology. You can create your own personal or team systems for planning, execut-ing, and tracking progress. Then, you can use the Learning Zone to continue to improve from there.

Take the proven strategies and systems that enable you to per-form well and put them on autopilot so you can free your mental resources to focus on creativity, personalization, problem-solving, and improvisation. This is what Traca Savadogo did at Starbucks:

Eliminating the mental effort required to remember orders freed her to focus on engaging customers in conversation.

Automating deliberately is what the airline and healthcare industries have done through checklists used in cockpits and operating rooms before, during, and after high-stakes performances. As Atul Gawande describes in his book *The Checklist Manifesto*, checklists allow the performers—in this case, doctors and pilots—to be present and fully focused on what they're doing, knowing that their systems will ensure they cover the basics.

Do take note when a mistake arises and reflect on how the autopilot systems can be altered to prevent errors in the future. Also schedule periodic meetings or reflections to examine whether the systems could use some tweaking.

Just like the greatest accomplishments are achieved by teams rather than by individuals, the best performers act in partnership with the environment they have created rather than in isolation from the world around them. They don't rely on only their brains to make sure everything gets done. They set up systems so they can focus their attention on what can take them to the next level.

FOCUS, FOCUS, FOCUS

The human brain is capable of doing a lot of remarkable things, but it's pretty terrible at trying to do two conscious things at once, whether in the Learning Zone or in the Performance Zone. You may think you are accomplishing two things simultaneously because you take your effort as a proxy for output, but in fact your intelligence plummets and you get exhausted just trying to understand what is happening—without even being able to think critically about it.

Don't believe me? Try reading something—even a children's book—while listening to a podcast. Or try to write an email while keeping track of a movie you're watching. You'll notice that you completely lost the plot of one of the two activities. Dual-consciousness multitasking just doesn't work! Yet most of us still can't resist checking email or social media or the news while attending a meeting or watching a video—and when we come up for air, we realize we missed most of what was being said.

As Cal Newport recommends in his book *Deep Work*, create routines that allow you to focus on just one thing while working on anything complex that requires deep thought. Block your calendar, silence device notifications, close windows unrelated to the task at hand, and signal to colleagues and family that you're doing deep work and shouldn't be interrupted unless something is urgent.

More than once, I have facilitated conversations in which CEOs realize that colleagues aren't engaging in deep work because they think they need to constantly monitor emails and texts from higher-ups and jump on requests right away. The CEOs then recognize the need to be clearer about default ways of working and to communicate when things are truly urgent. Ask your colleagues whether deep work is important to them and whether they feel they have what they need to engage in it.

When motivating others to perform, focus on the value and purpose of the work rather than on carrots and sticks. Studies have found that it is not a good idea to use financial or social pressure to try to motivate and foster focus in yourself or others, especially with work involving critical thinking, because doing so draws cognitive resources away from the work. Instead, compensate and treat people fairly and equitably so that money and belonging are *not* concerns. As Neel Doshi and Lindsay McGregor recommend in their book, *Primed to Perform*, draw attention to the activity or work itself—how enjoyable, interesting, or important it might be, what problems need to be solved next, what strategies will get you to the next milestone. Sometimes leaders need to absorb and filter the financial and emotional pressure *they* feel and shield the people they lead from it so they can best perform.

If you want to execute at your best, do what Shannon Polson did when her life was at stake in the Apache helicopter over Bosnia: Turn down the volume on other things so you can focus on the one important thing. Cultivating your ability to focus deeply will allow you to rock the Performance Zone when you want to.

REGULATE PERFORMANCE ANXIETY BY PRIMING A GROWTH MINDSET

Most of us tend to get a little anxious when we're executing something important—that's normal. But too much anxiety can negatively impact performance by reducing the cognitive resources available for the task at hand. It also makes it harder to think creatively and to express positive emotions, which are helpful for effective teamwork.

One strategy to regulate performance anxiety is to prime a growth mindset.

Remind yourself that anyone—even Olympic gold medalists—can improve, and that any performance can be bettered. This calms you down and frees your cognitive resources to focus fully so you can perform at your best. Then, whatever hiccups there are during the performance are less likely to flood you and knock you off your game.

Reflect on whether your culture and team habits remind teammates that anyone can improve, using the techniques discussed in prior chapters. Remember that great performers act in partnership with their environment.

In the Performance Zone, we are working not to improve but to execute. Yet, knowing that we *can* improve—later, in the Learning Zone—helps us stay in the mental and emotional states that elicit our top game.

HANDLE MISTAKES LIKE A PRO

We all make mistakes, even when trying not to, because we're human, the world is complex, and any of us can further improve. Learning how to respond to mistakes we make in the Performance Zone is key to top performance.

The highest performers use struggle, mistakes, or failure as cues to flip to the Learning Zone, but not necessarily right away. If you're in the middle of a high-pressure, time-sensitive performance, you might want to make note of the mistake—mentally or by writing it down—and then go back to performing as best you can. Later, when the stage lights go out, you can reflect on your mistake and figure out what to do differently moving forward. You may want to spend some time in the Learning Zone before your next high-stakes performance.

Consider what you want your self-talk to be. If you make a mistake, you don't want that to flood you with anxiety and throw you off. So, how do you want to respond instead? Maybe you tell yourself, "I'll work on that later," or give it a light mental "Oops" and go back to doing the best you can for the time being.

Depending on the circumstances and your goals, you might want to use mistakes as an opportunity to model being a learner. If you're with colleagues and you've aligned with them on fostering a learning culture, you can acknowledge your mistake and verbalize what you might do differently next time—or mention that you'll work on it later. This helps build psychological safety and a learning culture, and it opens up a channel of communication in which you can solicit feedback afterward.

If it's a high-stakes performance with a client or external partner and you want to focus solely on projecting high domain competence rather than on fostering a learning culture, you may want to conceal the mistake or recover as quickly as possible—like a gymnast who lands a jump slightly off-balance. But my hope is that as we all collaborate to cultivate a world of learners and foster transparency, we will feel less pressure to hide our mistakes.

SET UP ACCOUNTABILITY FOR LEARNING AND PERFORMING

If we want to perform skillfully, we need to set up accountability systems for ourselves and our teams. Accountability is about aligning on goals and timelines—both performance and learning goals—and setting up processes to track them and troubleshoot when needed. We clearly define roles, responsibilities, and expectations, identify how to measure progress and success, and set in place periodic check-ins to examine how things are going. We problem-solve as needed, coordinate, and extract lessons learned to foster ongoing development. With clarity, social commitments, and systems to ensure follow-through, we feel more motivated to put in our best effort and persevere, and we are best positioned to deliver and reach new heights.

When possible, it is helpful to share these goals and timelines and to make our progress transparent to others, like Lizzie Dipp Metzger, Gino Barbaro, and so many others do with their colleagues. The established systems and tools mentioned earlier—in *Put performance routines on autopilot*—foster social accountability, usually through periodic team check-ins. Aim for a consistent structure for these meetings that includes reviewing progress, celebrating wins, surfacing challenges, aligning on who should work together to problem-solve or collaborate, and making next steps transparent. The check-ins are also a way for anyone to solicit support when needed and to spread lessons learned so others may benefit from them.

While teams benefit from structure, anyone can do this individually, in a less formal setting, or with an accountability partner. You can simply draft an agenda for a regular meeting with key items to discuss. Some of this can also be done asynchronously, such as by implementing OKR tools that make goals and progress transparent throughout the organization.

When setting up accountability systems, ensure that there are feedback loops. That is, the Performance Zone should always be generating information about what went well, what didn't, and what could be improved. You can use that information to identify what to work on in the Learning Zone and in *learning while doing*, so that you're continuing to develop and advance performance.

ADJUST IN REAL TIME LIKE VIRTUOSOS DO

While preparing for a live concert in Cologne, Germany, in 1975, pianist Keith Jarrett imagined he'd be performing on one of the world's best instruments. Instead, he had to rely on a very different tool: his creativity.

According to German radio station WDR 3, the opera house had agreed to provide him with a Bösendorfer Imperial concert grand piano that he'd requested for his show.

But when the staff couldn't find the piano, they brought out another instead—and it was a far cry from the model he'd requested.

"It was like half a piano," author and economist Tim Harford told NPR. "And the keys were sticking. The pedals didn't work. The felt was all worn away in the upper register, so the upper register sounded very harsh and tinny. And because it's not a grand piano, it's not loud enough."

Exhausted from travel and faced with an instrument that simply didn't work, he refused to play and left the opera house.

But as he got in his car, he noticed that someone had followed him outside.

It was Vera Brandes, the eighteen-year-old concert promoter whose love for jazz had inspired her to book Jarrett in the first place.

Standing in the rain, she begged him to come back and play. The show was sold out, and it was the most important event she had ever organized.

"I think at that moment, he just feels sorry for her," said Harford. "And he realizes she's just a kid. Fourteen hundred people are about to show up at this concert, and there's going to be no concert. And he says, 'Never forget. Only for you.' And he agrees to play."

Up against greater challenges and constraints than he had ever encountered in his career, Jarrett had no choice but to improvise. As he started to play, the opera house became completely silent as people listened in awe.

The live recording went on to become the best-selling solo jazz album of all time.

Virtuosos and masterful practitioners of any craft can perform while simultaneously engaging their creativity, adjusting, and improvising on the spot—like Keith Jarrett did when a subpar instrument inspired him to perform at new heights of his ability. As record producer Manfred Eicher told *The Wall Street Journal* when he was describing that night, because Jarrett did not love the sound of the piano he was forced to play, "he found another way to get the most out of it."

What enables top performers to pivot in the middle of a performance? And what can any of us learn from that? Great performers can adjust mid-performance because of the mastery they have developed over time through the Learning Zone, which gives them a diverse and nuanced set of skills to apply in different situations. Their mastery also frees up their cognition to improvise.

But they can also adjust because of their willingness to change what isn't working and try something else, whether in their self-talk, game plan, or focus. While you may not be facing an opposing team across the field or have an audience watching you, real-time adjustments may be needed to reach completely different levels of effectiveness.

Whether in the arts, sports, or business, the path toward brilliance requires the Learning Zone, the Performance Zone, and learning while doing. It also requires a willingness to leap beyond the known, adjust to what the moment requires, and improvise. The more expertise we develop, the better prepared we are to assess when it is the right time to leap into the unknown and engage in *learning while doing*, even while delivering masterful work.

As you expand your expertise, don't forget to enjoy the process. Have fun and lean in to creativity. Push your ability to go beyond the known—even during performances—with greater confidence that you have developed better and better intuitions about what tends to work. Sprinkle in some improvisation to generate awe and delight.

REMEMBER TO LEARN WHILE DOING AND REVISIT WHAT'S MOST IMPORTANT

As you focus on executing, don't get trapped by the performance paradox!

Remember that unless your Performance Zone involves very high stakes—like that of a Cirque du Soleil acrobat—most of your Performance Zone time should be spent *learning while doing*. Try a different way of doing things, observe how it works, solicit feedback, and identify what to adjust. Make integrating the two zones, and alternating between them, the way you live and the air you breathe.

Finally, beware of being so narrowly focused on what you're doing that you lose sight of why you're doing it—that's tunnel vision. Periodically reflect on your higher-level goals and consider whether you should change strategies in order to stay on the learning edge so you can achieve what's most important.

REFLECTION QUESTIONS

- How might improving my performance benefit me and others?
- What Performance Zone strategies might be most helpful, and how will I work at them?
- Can I put a system in place that could help me and my team leap to a whole new level?

LOOKING FORWARD

How might overcoming the performance paradox change my life and the lives of others?

Chapter 14: Overcome the Paradox, Change Lives

BIG IDEA *When we overcome the performance paradox and break out of chronic performance, we change both our journey and the destination. By embracing the two zones, we change lives, starting with our own.*

When Mariana Costa Checa and her partners decided to start a web development company in Lima, Peru, they were faced with the task of recruiting a team of software developers. Finding tech talent was challenging enough, but Mariana wanted a team that included a significant number of women. She soon discovered that finding female software developers in Peru was nearly impossible.

Many entrepreneurs would have thrown in the towel, yielded to the performance paradox, and simply hired male developers—the way things were usually done. But Mariana and her partners got curious and reflected.

Most of the developers they *did* find didn't come from traditional higher education backgrounds in computer science. They either studied something else in college or were entirely self-taught. This led Mariana to recognize that in software design and development, skills are more important than degrees, particularly since tech frameworks change so frequently.

"The most valuable asset really is a lifelong learning mindset—the ability to drive your learning," she told me.

For several decades, the tech sector worldwide had struggled to find enough software developers, but it had remained stuck in chronic performance, treading water, hiring the way it always had from the same pool of candidates.

In contrast, Mariana and her partners saw an opportunity and felt a calling. They could scratch their previous idea and instead start a nonprofit to help women develop skills to begin professional careers in tech—particularly women from economically under-served backgrounds who hadn't been able to access higher educa-tion. Their idea would generate well-paying jobs for those women and expand the pool of talent available to the tech industry.

They called the nonprofit Laboratoria. Using design thinking, the team came up with a recruiting process to find women who had the will, disposition, readiness, and commitment to go through a six-month immersive learning experience aimed at making them front-end developers or user experience (UX) designers.

Again, with design thinking, Laboratoria explored what the training should look like. How might they prepare these women promptly and cost-effectively to successfully jump into a tech ca-reer?

The organization came up with a project-based learning ap-proach. That is, from day one, while being guided by coaches, stu-dents are assigned real-world tech challenges in which they are given a month or so to figure out how to design and create software to solve a real problem.

They always work together in groups—even if the project is individual—so that they can get feedback and support from their peers. Laboratoria considers it important for the training boot camp to resemble a real-life workplace so participants can feel they're on an actual software team. The feedback from users, peers, and coaches mirrors that of a workplace. The result is that the women constantly need to be in the Learning Zone and the Performance Zone simultaneously. They're *learning while doing*.

"Project after project, this is obviously quite challenging, be-cause it's very different from a traditional educational setting where students are expecting to hear a lesson," Mariana said. "This is more like a challenge. You have the internet, you have your peers, and then you have your coaches, but we want to see that you are really trying to make the best out of it."

The setup trains students to be their own teachers and to learn through research, experimentation, and collaboration—all skills that will help them become learners for the rest of their careers.

Continuous improvement is also the default for Laboratoria staff. They learn lessons from every cohort to continue to hone the process. They experiment with adjustments to their recruiting, on-boarding, and training processes, and with new ways to reach women in more rural areas. They develop insights into what types of projects work best at different stages of the six-month experience and how to better connect students with alumni.

After they were forced to transition to Zoom sessions during the pandemic, Laboratoria discovered that conducting virtual instead of in-person training allowed the organization to recruit more women from remote villages who didn't have the resources to move to the city. The nonprofit decided to continue to operate the program virtually even after the pandemic ended.

The results are impressive. The participating women dramatically increase their income. While the majority of them are unemployed prior to starting the program, even those who start out with jobs nearly triple their salaries.

"If you talk to any of our alumni, yes, they're super happy that they have a job that will change their lives," Mariana said. "But really, I think the most important thing that they get is that they change the way they view themselves, they change the way they view learning, they change the way they view life. There's a lot of this feeling of agency, you know—'I can build the future I want for myself. If I don't have the skills, I will build them to accomplish my goals'—and that's really powerful."

Many of the companies that hire Laboratoria graduates are so impressed by the women—particularly their collaboration and experimentation—and by the organization's method of teaching that they ask Laboratoria to assist them in infusing their company with a learning culture. Laboratoria does this by helping companies source diverse talent and by facilitating workshops for other personnel.

Along with transforming the lives of the women who participate, the program also dramatically improves the trajectories of their families and communities and strengthens the companies they join. An assessment of Laboratoria's impact prepared by the organization shows that having the nonprofit's alumni as role models in their communities opens the eyes of many other women to the possibility of establishing professional careers.

With programs now in Brazil, Chile, Colombia, Mexico, and Peru, Laboratoria has trained thousands of women and placed 85 percent of them in tech jobs in Latin America and beyond.

This was all made possible because the founders got curious, broke out of the performance paradox, and embraced the two zones.

CHANGING LIVES AND COMMUNITIES

It may seem ironic that companies in the tech sector, while dedicated to innovation, were stuck in chronic performance when faced with a significant challenge. As they struggled to find enough software developers, rather than pioneer new ways to expand their pool of candidates, they largely kept using the same approach, time and again. But the performance paradox has fooled our entire society into chronic performance. It's our default. It permeates our homes, teams, organizations, and communities.

The good news is that any of us can break out of it.

Throughout the previous chapters, we met people who have used the two zones to transform their lives. As a result, they have also impacted their communities and beyond.

Gino Barbaro joined Jake Stenziano to form a real estate company, engaging in the Learning Zone to become enormously successful. But they didn't stop there. They created a company called Jake & Gino that is solely dedicated to providing learning opportunities for others who also want to become multifamily real estate investors.

Linda Rabbitt used the Learning Zone to transform herself, first from a teacher to a homemaker and mom, then, when forced to enter the workforce as a single parent, into an administrative assistant and eventually the founder of one of the most successful woman-owned construction companies in the United States. But she wanted to do even more. For twenty-five years, Linda has regularly met with a group of other women in her industry who learn from and support one another, thus extending their influence to become powerful forces for good.

Alex Stephany decided to do something about London's homelessness problem after he realized that occasionally giving his new friend a meal wasn't truly supporting him. Alex's work in the Learning Zone led him to found the crowdsourcing platform Beam, which has enabled more than 1,400 people to find jobs and launch careers, putting them on a path to stability.

Angelou Ezeilo used the Learning Zone to leave her job as an attorney and create a nonprofit that changes the way young people of color interact with the environment. Along the way, she formed a pipeline to direct hundreds of young people toward environmental careers, bringing desperately needed diversity to the field and generating a new source of workers.

While delivering to the public an app that helps people quickly pay bills—adding considerable convenience to our lives—Patrick Kann and his colleagues leaped beyond the known to find ways to increase the percentage of underrepresented groups working at Papaya. After starting out with half a dozen white guys, the company now has a workforce made up of 60 percent people from underrepresented groups. The company's success demonstrates the value of diversity to other companies.

The Learning Zone alone has not enabled all of this change; without the Performance Zone, there would be no results. What generates change and impact is the intentional use of the two zones.

That's true of Embrace and the hundreds of thousands of babies they've protected. It's true of d.light and the increased quality of life they've brought to more than 100 million people. It's true of Willy Foote and Root Capital, Lizzie Dipp Metzger, Microsoft, Skratch Labs, Versatile, the airline industry, and so many others.

And it can be true for any of us. Tapping into the power of the two zones enabled me to go from feeling chronically stressed and dissatisfied to feeling deeply alive and a good steward of my life. My health crisis triggered a learning journey that made me realize I saw my work as only a way to earn a paycheck. But there was so much more for me to gain from work. As I explored other routes, I eventually developed a path where I can continue to grow and contribute to others' growth. The two zones also enabled me to learn what was happening in my body and to drastically change my lifestyle to turn around my health and well-being.

But without the Performance Zone, I wouldn't have made any impact, and I'd still feel dissatisfied. It is the combination of both zones that has deeply enriched my life and allowed me to help enrich the lives of others. This is how the zones can change our lives, no matter where each of us is starting from.

Like Gino Barbaro, I discovered the need for the two zones as the result of a crisis, but we don't need to wait until things break down. When we proactively engage in the two zones, we set ourselves up to achieve much greater growth and outcomes. And as we embark on a completely new journey, we start to see immediate benefits.

THE JOURNEY ALONG THE WAY

Breaking out of chronic performance changes our lives not only because it leads us to better competence, life situations, jobs, and impact, but also because, as research shows, engaging in learning comes with its own benefits. We gain a sense of wonder and awe from our explorations and discoveries; a decrease in anxiety from knowing that we can overcome challenges; personal satisfaction from the growth of our skills and contributions; and greater happiness and well-being as we learn to brush off hiccups and deepen relationships.

It's not just about the destination; it's also about the journey.

In fact, even when it's not for an immediately practical purpose, the process of exploration and discovery can be a deeply enriching part of life. From the comfort of our homes, any of us can explore the depths of the oceans, the planet Mars, Renaissance Florence, ancient civilizations, fictional depictions of possible realities, the insides of our bodies, the way our brains work, the grandeur of nature, or anything else we're curious about. In the process, we experience wonder, increased understanding, and more curiosity.

Awe and wonder are not the only benefits. In the process of discovery, we also enhance our health and well-being.

Studies have found that when we adopt a learning orientation, we experience lower levels of stress, anxiety, and depression, because it enables us to see our current struggles as temporary. Equipped with the Learning Zone, we feel greater agency over our lives because it enables us to ask, "What can I do to fix or improve this?"

Many studies show that adopting a learning orientation leads people to be more persistent and resilient. This is because they understand that through the Learning Zone, they can adapt, overcome obstacles, and achieve their goals.

The Learning Zone also leads to more constructive conflict resolution. Céline Darnon and colleagues found that when people are more interested in learning than in outperforming others, they tend to resolve conflict by looking for ways to integrate both points of view, rather than just proving their own case.

Studies by David Yeager and others have found that when people experience exclusion, bullying, or other forms of aggression, their belief that people can change helps them respond less through retaliation and more by sharing constructive feedback, thus achieving better relationships and life satisfaction.

Karina Schumann, Jamil Zaki, and Carol Dweck conducted a study showing that when people see empathy as a quality that can be developed rather than as an innate characteristic, they tend to behave more empathetically in challenging situations. That is, when others look, think, or behave differently than we do, we are better able to get in their shoes when we believe that empathy can be cultivated.

The Learning Zone not only enables us to more successfully meet our goals, reach higher performance, and attain better health, relationships, and communities, but it also leads us to previously unimaginable capacities.

We live in a learner's paradise and a non-learner's swamp. Avoid learning—the basic literacy skill of the twenty-first century—and you're left behind, or worse. Embrace learning and the world is your playground, with fertile ground for thriving and contributing.

TACKLING THE WORLD'S GREATEST CHALLENGES

Esther Duflo and her husband, Abhijit Banerjee, grew up in different worlds—Duflo in Paris and Banerjee in Kolkata, India—but they both developed an interest in helping to alleviate poverty.

According to *Vogue India*, Banerjee's parents were professors of economics. As a young child, when he would play soccer with kids from the Kolkata slums, his mom would comment on the dynamics that led to such poverty. This sparked his curiosity.

Duflo's father was a professor of mathematics, but it was her mother, a pediatrician, who ignited in her an interest in helping others. Her mother would travel to El Salvador, Haiti, and Rwanda, and return to Paris with stories of what she saw. Duflo became aware of how fortunate she was and grew interested in doing something for those most in need.

Flash forward a couple decades: Both became academics interested in development economics but frustrated by how theoretical the field was. They wanted to effect real change.

"We didn't want to simply do our own thing and discover some private truth. We wanted to institute change in the entire way development economics is studied. That was our ambition," Banerjee told *Vogue India*.

But they first had to figure out how.

As Duflo shared in her TED2010 talk, the pair realized that randomized controlled trials—a powerful tool in science and medicine—were not being used in development economics. But what if social innovation could go through the same testing process that scientists use to assess efficacy?

"In this way," she said, "you can take the guesswork out of policy-making."

They began conducting randomized controlled trials—not in labs but in people's everyday environments—to understand what policies would make substantial impacts on the lowest-income communities.

In their early work, together with their colleague Michael Kremer, they studied which interventions would improve educational outcomes at the lowest cost. More textbooks (which were often nonexistent)? Free school meals (since many children were hungry)? Teaching assistants (given how many children were far behind)? To find out, they partnered with local organizations in Kenya and India and performed field experiments.

The team randomly divided schools into different groups that received different kinds of extra support at different times.

Basically, they did the same thing that Simon Tisminezky— whom we met in Chapter 3—did to grow Ipsy: experiment, test, and iterate. But Duflo, Banerjee, and Kremer used this method to find out what would decrease poverty and improve quality of life for entire populations.

Studies showed neither textbooks nor free school meals had an impact on learning outcomes (other than possibly some gains for the highest-performing students when children were given textbooks). On the other hand, teaching assistants for the children furthest behind made a big difference.

They expanded their experiments to other countries and issues, such as nutrition, access to credit, consumer choices, fertility rates, and the usefulness of new technologies.

Most important, they helped the field of development economics break out of a pattern of chronic performance in how research had always been done. Now, conducting randomized controlled trials has become an additional established method for assessing policy ideas, and it has led to real impact.

Since 1995, due in part to the impact this work has had in development economics, per capita GDP in the world's poorest countries has doubled. Child mortality has halved, and the proportion of children attending school has increased from 56 to 80 percent.

For their work, Esther Duflo, Abhijit Banerjee, and Michael Kremer were awarded the 2019 Nobel Prize in Economic Sciences. Duflo was the second and youngest woman to be awarded the recognition. She and Banerjee were the sixth couple to win a Nobel Prize and thereby join the "Partners in Life and Science" club, whose first members were Pierre and Marie Curie.

Despite the positive impact on many populations, great challenges remain and new ones continue to emerge. To overcome these challenges, we must crush the performance paradox and stay on the learning edge.

If we just do what we think works best, without subjecting our thinking to testing and experimentation, we stagnate. Whether it is in education, in government more broadly, or in the policies and structures we use within our teams and organizations, it's tempting to form strong opinions of what works best and just run with that without engaging in further examination.

If there are differences of opinion on what will work best, we often let power dictate who gets to choose.

We are, as a society, largely stuck in chronic performance.

Throughout this book, we have explored the many ways that individuals, teams, and organizations have used the Learning Zone to bring about change and growth. Tomoe Musa brought together neurosurgeons and orthopedists in the Learning Zone to improve spinal cord care, and achieved better healthcare outcomes for patients.

Traca Savadogo saw that orders were not being efficiently and correctly filled at Starbucks, so she came up with the idea to write the orders on the sides of cups, leading Starbucks stores to become calmer places with increased focus on customer interactions.

When Keith Jarrett leaped into the Learning Zone and figured out how to use an inferior piano to play at the Cologne Opera, he uplifted the 1,400 attendees in memorable delight—and many others who have since enjoyed the recording.

Willy Foote and Root Capital found ways to offer farmers—especially women—around the world a path to prosperity by giving them the capital, training, and access to markets they needed to build profitable livelihoods.

Any of us can effect change from where we sit if we come to understand the performance paradox and how to overcome it.

CROSSING DIVIDES NEAR AND FAR

Let's more deeply consider the problem of increasing societal polarization. Are we choosing to try to better understand people who think differently than we do? Are we reading or listening to respected intellectuals who are representative of other ideologies in order to understand their rationales? Are we interacting with people from other political parties, asking questions, and engaging in learning-oriented conversations to understand what they think and what life experiences have led them to think the way they do?

I'm not asking you to do anything you don't feel safe doing, but any of us can become more curious and expand our understanding. It can be as simple as listening to podcast interviews of people with diverse points of view.

We can work on this from wherever we sit.

Like a lot of us, Tiy Goddard, an MBA classmate of mine who works in higher education in Illinois, would find herself standing in line to cast her ballot and realize that she knew very little about the candidates and the referenda she was about to vote on. As she moved closer to the voting machine, she'd frantically text her friends to get their take on how she might vote. Tiy and a few friends from her book club decided that they had the power to change this all-too-common scenario. They began to meet up a few days or weeks before an election to talk about candidate positions, look up information together, send questions out to others who might add useful perspectives, and figure out what questions they still had. It transformed the voting experience for each of them. Instead of stepping into line with whatever their preferred party or family members were telling them to do, they gave themselves the power to make up their own minds. This is one small way engaging in the Learning Zone can help us do our part to strengthen our democracies.

To address polarization, Stanford professors James Fishkin and Larry Diamond developed a method of *deliberative democracy* called America in One Room, which centers on the Learning Zone. It entails gathering random groupings of Americans composed of a variety of racial, ethnic, and political backgrounds and having them deliberate on major issues that currently divide the country: the economy, taxes, immigration, healthcare, foreign policy, climate change, and the like. Each of the participants is given balanced briefing papers with no political orientation presenting the pros and cons of each issue. Then, the group comes together to deliberate, either in person or online, with one rule: Members must respect one another and let one another speak.

"We have found both in the in-person deliberations we organized and in the online deliberations . . . that people really like this," said Diamond. "They not only often narrow their differences on policy issues, but they also transcend some of that emotional dislike or even disgust that they have for members of the other party. So, it narrows partisan deliberation, and it discovers common ground on the issues."

Fishkin and Diamond started the Deliberative Democracy Lab to continue their research and find ways to eventually scale up the method so that millions of people can participate and help narrow polarizing divisions.

When we learn to love proactive learning and growth and internalize it as a part of who we are, we start asking more questions, listening more carefully, empathizing more, and understanding where people who think differently are coming from. When we do this, we discover that we have a great deal in common, yet we go about pursuing these commonalities in different ways, based on different beliefs, habits, and communities.

Almost everyone, for example, desires agency, belonging, trust, and care, but pursues them in different ways. Many people on the political left seek a sense of care by developing widespread societal structures that provide a safety net for everyone. By contrast, many people on the political right go about it by forming strong relationships, rooted in understanding, trust, and mutual support, with the people physically closest to them. They tend to seek self-sufficiency as a community to become less dependent on people far away in political centers or in other countries, who might not understand or serve them. If you're driving in a snowstorm in rural Alaska and your car breaks down, you'd better be prepared with firewood in your car and hope that somebody drives by, because you may not be able to call 911.

Both sides have a theory of how care and safety nets are established: one through self-reliance and close relationships, the other through government-driven structures.

As Jonathan Haidt describes in his book *The Righteous Mind*, most people on both sides of the political spectrum are driven by the same moral foundations of human emotion and behavior—care, fairness, loyalty, authority, sanctity, and liberty—but prioritize and pursue them in different ways.

Right now, if you're feeling an urge to make an argument or take a side, I invite you to pause. How could you apply some of the principles of design thinking and the Learning Zone? How could you bring a beginner's mind, defer judgment, and focus on observing, inquiring with open-ended questions, and seeking to uncover insights to empathize with others? You'll get smarter—something we all can do.

When we come to understand our shared humanity more deeply, we connect, communicate, and collaborate more effectively. The Learning Zone also helps us better understand the systems we are a part of—be it our teams, organizations, communities, or the wider world—giving us greater wisdom to seek a worthy purpose and effective ways to pursue it.

PATHS TO PURPOSE

Thinking about the world's challenges can feel overwhelming, in part because humanity has been fooled by the performance paradox and is largely stuck in chronic performance. But once we learn how to get unstuck, we can feel optimistic, resourceful, and able to take action to contribute to change.

If we allow ourselves to dwell on being one of billions of people—just an insignificant drop in the ocean—we can feel helpless and devoid of agency. Instead, we can focus on the things we can influence and the progress we can make. We all have agency over ourselves, our actions, our choices, and the way we live. Any of us can swim parallel to the shore to find and develop currents that can carry us to new destinations.

We all contribute to the world's challenges, so we can all be a part of the solutions. And we can all exert influence with our loved ones, our colleagues, and others with whom we interact, while simultaneously learning from and with them.

If we haven't found effective ways to do this, we can engage in the Learning Zone to get better at it. The more we strengthen our growth propellers, the more effective we will be at improving ourselves and helping others grow. Any of us can also learn to influence our organizations and communities, because at the end of the day, the ones who do are people just like us.

When we grow older and get closer to the end of our life, we want to look back and feel proud of the life we crafted, the person we became, and the contributions we made to others. To make sure that this happens, it is worthwhile for us to pause now and reflect on our identity and purpose. Who am I? Who do I want to become? What do I care about most? What purpose do I want to pursue?

And how can I grow my effectiveness so I can feel great about how I am spending my precious time on Earth?

REFLECTION QUESTIONS

- How might breaking out of chronic performance improve my life and the lives of others?
- Am I regularly seeking out perspectives and knowledge to expand my wisdom and my understanding of others?
- When I am exposed to a different perspective, do I wonder what truth there may be in it?
- Might people from my team or organization benefit from reading this book to advance our shared understanding and practices? What about my family and friends?

LOOKING FORWARD

What insights have I generated?
What will I do and when?
Who will I become?

AFTERWORD: NEVER FINISHED

As Walter Isaacson describes in his biography of Leonardo da Vinci, the Renaissance Man was one of the most curious people who ever lived. He loved to learn, which is how he became a self-taught polymath.

Having received almost no schooling, he never got trapped in chronic performance.

He was also notorious for not finishing what he started, to the great frustration of his patrons, because he so loved to explore, ponder, and tinker.

For at least fourteen years he worked on the *Mona Lisa,* which was still in his studio when he died. As far as da Vinci was concerned, his greatest masterpiece is incomplete. In fact, all of his paintings are.

He believed that "Art is never finished, only abandoned."

I agree. I think this is true of paintings, poems, plays, and so many other works, including books.

I could have continued working on this book my entire life. I would have enjoyed doing so. But at some point, authors need to publish. Software developers need to ship code. Designers need to implement.

The Performance Zone is how we scale impact. It can also be a precious source of feedback for us to continue to learn and grow—if we solicit it.

So, I'd love to learn from you. If you have any feedback on this book or ideas on how I could further contribute to learning and high performance, please email me at feedback@briceno.com.

ACKNOWLEDGMENTS

People say that publishing a book is like giving birth. I wouldn't know, but I can say that this book involved a lot more people. It wouldn't even exist without Carol Dweck, Chip Conley, Doug Abrams, or Jennifer Hershey.

Carol Dweck's groundbreaking research is a cornerstone of this entire body of knowledge. Beyond her scholarship, without her commitment to making an impact, belief in others, mentorship, and support, I would not be doing this work, nor would many others. I'm eternally grateful.

I was not planning to write a book. I reached out to Chip Conley—whom I didn't know at the time—with an unrelated question, and he generously suggested we speak. During that call, he felt inspired to connect me with Doug Abrams at Idea Architects, who became my literary agent and catalyzed a book deal with Jennifer Hershey at Ballantine. Without Chip's unsolicited initiative, Doug's engagement, or Jennifer's leap to take a chance on me, this book would not exist. I'm so thankful. Chip has since become a treasured mentor and guiding light. This is yet another example of how engaging in the Learning Zone—asking a question—can lead to unforeseen adventures, relationships, and growth.

I was privileged to work with experts who collaborated on what was very much a team effort. Many people contributed to the beauty of the writing in this book, starting with my collaborative writer, Nick Chiles, who was a joy to work with and whose craft, curiosity, teamwork, and resilience brought ideas to life in a compelling and engaging manner. Several editors helped shape the writing—most centrally, Sarah Rainone, whose edits were magical. Tai Moses, Doug Abrams, Rachel Neumann, Lara Love Hardin, Emily Hartley, Drummond Moir, Davi Sherman, Toni Sciarra

Poynter, Renata Dolz, and Alyssa Knickerbocker also contributed skillful editing and developmental feedback at various stages. It took a village over two and a half years to co-create this manuscript, reinforcing for me the African proverb, "If you want to go fast, go alone. If you want to go far, go together."

While writing this book was a team effort, no one contributed more to its quality than Mary Reynics, my editor at Ballantine. Her care, expertise, dedication, collaboration, patience, and perseverance were unparalleled. She has been a partner from heaven, and this book would not be what it is without her. I'm forever thankful.

Many friends, colleagues, clients, and partners read drafts and provided valuable feedback, including Katie Robertson, Sue Bevington, Kelly Woltornist, Gary Shoesmith, Kirsten Wenz, Tomer Cohen, Alicia Ginsburgh, John Chiodo, Jeff Schwartzman, Susan Potter, Erik Allebest, Chip Conley, Liz Cohen, Ron Berger, Javier Osa, Manuel Calero, Mawi Asgedom, Ali Parnian, Peter Winick, Bill Sherman, Jessica Duffield, Ree Soesbee, Todd Cherches, Mahan Tavakoli, Arthur Woods, Jezza Ong, and Doug Bromley. There were others, as I gathered feedback using a tool that allowed for anonymous input. Thank you all.

I interviewed over one hundred exemplary learners and performers who generously made time to speak with me. The interviews made for a fun and fruitful Learning Zone and greatly enriched the book's insights and stories. People mentioned in the book also took the time to review text to ensure it was accurate and helpful. Many fellow authors and consultants spoke with me and shared their advice. I am grateful to everyone and to the connectors who put us in touch.

Many others have supported me in meaningful ways throughout my career and life. Particularly impactful to the knowledge I share in this book were Ron Berger, Lisa Blackwell, Angela Duckworth, and the late Anders Ericsson, a kind and humble man whose work I am honored to build on. Beyond those already mentioned, many other researchers, disseminators, and practitioners have contributed to this body of work, including Peter Senge, Warren Bennis, Amy Edmondson, Adam Grant, John Kotter, Robert Kegan, Lisa

Laskow Lahey, Greg Walton, David Yeager, Mary Murphy, Heidi Grant, Dave Paunesku, Camille Farrington, David Rock, Steve Blank, Eric Ries, Marshall Goldsmith, Patrick Lencioni, and Dan Pink.

Ballantine's and Penguin Random House's author development, design, production, marketing, publicity, and other teams have been a joy to work with and were instrumental in creating a high-quality book that can be accessible to anyone. I also appreciate the support from the rest of the crew at my literary agency, Idea Architects, including Ty Love, Janelle Julian, Bella Roberts, Staci Bruce, and Mariah Sanford.

Illustrators Manuela Gutierrez Montoya and Anastasiia Matviienko co-created clear and compelling images, for which I'm thankful.

I am deeply grateful to my parents, Alberto and Beatriz Briceño, who gave my sister, Isabel, and me every opportunity they could think of, and who made us their highest priority. The three of them have always provided support, stability, love, and encouragement.

I cherish my friends, who ground me and inspire me with models of what I want the world to evolve toward.

Foremost, I am thankful for my greatest guide, reading teacher, constructive critic, love, and life partner, Allison Briceño. Our conversations on nature hikes in New Mexico were a memorable cradle for many of the ideas in this book. Throughout the project, Allison coached me and helped me problem-solve when challenges arose. She read many iterations of the manuscript and provided feedback. Most significantly, I would not have written this book were it not for the twenty-five years we've spent together, as I would be a different person. I am a lucky man.

While this book is written, our stories are not. I look forward to exploring new adventures with current and future collaborators.

And I am grateful to all the readers who, while appreciating the present, persist on the learning edge to enrich their lives and the lives of others.

NOTES

CHAPTER 1: THE PERFORMANCE PARADOX

3 *Anjali felt her palms grow sweaty* Personal interview with "Anjali," February 2, 2022. Anjali's and Salma's real names have been altered to protect anonymity.

4 *Gino Barbaro always leaped to answer it* Personal interviews with Gino Barbaro, January 18, 2021; Gino Barbaro and Jake Stenziano, November 22, 2021, and December 13, 2021.

4 *Douglas Franco was tapped* Personal interview with Douglas Franco, November 2, 2022.

9 *more than one hundred people drown in rip currents* B. Chris Brewster, Richard E. Gould, and Robert W. Brander. "Estimations of rip current rescues and drowning in the United States." *Natural Hazards and Earth System Sciences* 19, no. 2 (2019): 389–397.

14 *study mindset in depth* See Carol S. Dweck. *Mindset: The New Psychology of Success*. Random House, 2006.

15 *it is not a silver bullet* See Camille A. Farrington, Melissa Roderick, Elaine Allensworth, Jenny Nagaoka, Tasha Seneca Keyes, David W. Johnson, and Nicole O. Beechum. *Teaching Adolescents to Become Learners: The Role of Noncognitive Factors in Shaping School Performance—A Critical Literature Review*. Consortium on Chicago School Research, 2012.

15 *what role growth mindset played* Maria Cutumisu. "The association between feedback-seeking and performance is moderated by growth mindset in a digital assessment game." *Computers in Human Behavior* 93 (2019): 267–278.

Maria Cutumisu and Nigel Mantou Lou. "The moderating effect

of mindset on the relationship between university students' critical feedback-seeking and learning." *Computers in Human Behavior* 112 (2020): 106445.

CHAPTER 2: THE TOURNAMENT AND THE RANGE

21 *countless hours typing away* See Nina Keith and K. Anders Ericsson. "A deliberate practice account of typing proficiency in everyday typists." *Journal of Experimental Psychology: Applied* 13, no. 3 (2007): 135–145.

21 *they analyzed sixty-two research studies* Niteesh K. Choudhry, Robert H. Fletcher, and Stephen B. Soumerai. "Systematic review: The relationship between clinical experience and quality of health care." *Annals of Internal Medicine* 142, no. 4 (2005): 260–273.

21 *playing a lot of games of chess* Neil Charness, Michael Tuffiash, Ralf Krampe, Eyal Reingold, and Ekaterina Vasyukova. "The role of deliberate practice in chess expertise." *Applied Cognitive Psychology* 19, no. 2 (2005): 151–165.

21 *Serena and Venus, didn't play junior* See Richard Williams. *Black and White: The Way I See It.* Simon & Schuster, 2014.

22 *making sure we engage in two distinct* See John G. Nicholls. "Achievement motivation: Conceptions of ability, subjective experience, task choice, and performance." *Psychological Review* 91, no. 3 (1984): 328–346.

Carol S. Dweck. "Motivational processes affecting learning." *American Psychologist* 41, no. 10 (1986): 1040–1048.

Timothy Urdan. "Achievement goal theory: Past results, future directions." In Martin L. Maehr and Paul P. Pintrich (eds.), *Advances in Motivation and Achievement* 10 (1997): 99–141.

23 *say you're a pro golfer* K. Anders Ericsson. "The path to expert golf performance: Insights from the masters on how to improve performance by deliberate practice." *Optimising Performance in Golf* (2001): 1–57.

K. Anders Ericsson and Len Hill. "Digging it out of the dirt: Ben

Hogan, deliberate practice and the secret: A commentary." *International Journal of Sports Science & Coaching* 5, no. 2 (2010): S23–S27.

23 *the tournament* and *the range* K. Anders Ericsson. "Deliberate practice and acquisition of expert performance: A general overview." *Academic Emergency Medicine* 15, no. 11 (2008): 988–994.

24 *Lizzie Dipp Metzger showed up* Personal interview with Lizzie Dipp Metzger, July 29, 2022.

25 *"I went to every class"* Lizzie Dipp Metzger, "Impossible things are happening every day," New York Life 2017 Chairman's Council (keynote address, The Venetian, Las Vegas, NV, USA, February 23, 2018).

25 *Four years after that, she was ranked by* Forbes This was in 2021. Data provided by SHOOK Research, LLC. Source: Forbes.com. Neither SHOOK nor *Forbes* receives any compensation in exchange for placement on its Top Financial Security Professional (FSP) rankings (including the Best-in-State Financial Security Professional rankings), which are determined independently. FSP refers to professionals who are properly licensed to sell life insurance and annuities. FSPs may also hold other credentials and licenses that would allow them to offer investments and securities products through those licenses. Investment performance is not a criterion. SHOOK's research and rankings provide opinions intended to help individuals choose the right FSP and are not indicative of future performance or representative of any one client's experience. You can find the full methodology here: forbes.com/sites/rjshook/2022/07/28/methodology-americas-top-financial-security-professionals-2022/.

26 *we don't get better at selling insurance* Sabine Sonnentag and Barbara M. Kleine. "Deliberate practice at work: A study with insurance agents." *Journal of Occupational and Organizational Psychology* 73, no. 1 (2000): 87–102.

27 *In his book* No Rules Rules Reed Hastings and Erin Meyer. *No Rules Rules: Netflix and the Culture of Reinvention.* Penguin, 2020.

28 *executed by more than 1,000 artists* See "Press Room: About Cirque," Cirque du Soleil, cirquedusoleil.com/press/kits/corporate/about-cirque.

28 *into one of the training studios* Personal interview with Marie-Noëlle Caron, September 14, 2016.

29 *practice brainstorming every day* Melanie S. Brucks and Szu-Chi Huang. "Does practice make perfect? The contrasting effects of repeated practice on creativity." *Journal of the Association for Consumer Research* 5, no. 3 (2020): 291–301.

Patrick J. Kiger. "Practice Does Not Necessarily Make Perfect When It Comes to Creativity." Insights by Stanford Business, September 10, 2020, gsb.stanford.edu/insights/practice-does-not-necessarily-make-perfect-when-it-comes-creativity.

30 *who have cross-cultural competence* Graham Jones, Bernardita Chirino Chace, and Justin Wright. "Cultural diversity drives innovation: Empowering teams for success." *International Journal of Innovation Science* 12, no. 3 (2020): 323–343.

30 *ideating in isolation* Vicky L. Putman and Paul B. Paulus. "Brainstorming, brainstorming rules and decision making." *Journal of Creative Behavior* 43, no. 1 (2009): 29–40.

30 *focusing on quantity* Paul B. Paulus, Nicholas W. Kohn, and Lauren E. Arditti. "Effects of quantity and quality instructions on brainstorming." *Journal of Creative Behavior* 45, no. 1 (2011): 38–46.

See also:

Melanie S. Brucks. "The Creativity Paradox: Soliciting Creative Ideas Undermines Ideation." PhD diss., Graduate School of Business, Stanford University, 2018.

31 *playing games before brainstorming* Alan R. Dennis, Randall K. Minas, and Akshay P. Bhagwatwar. "Sparking creativity: Improving electronic brainstorming with individual cognitive priming." *Journal of Management Information Systems* 29, no. 4 (2013): 195–216.

32 *performance alone can appear* See Michael A. McDaniel, Frank L.

Schmidt, and John E. Hunter. "Job experience correlates of job performance." *Journal of Applied Psychology* 73, no. 2 (1988): 327–330.

Rick Hayman. "The Role of Deliberate Practice in Developing Adolescent Golfing Excellence." PhD diss., University of Central Lancashire, 2012.

K. Anders Ericsson. "Deliberate practice and the acquisition and maintenance of expert performance in medicine and related domains." *Academic Medicine* 79, no. 10 (2004): S70–S81.

K. Anders Ericsson. "Deliberate practice and acquisition of expert performance: A general overview." *Academic Emergency Medicine* 15, no. 11 (2008): 988–994.

35 *behavioral economists call* present bias George Ainslie. *Picoeconomics: The Strategic Interaction of Successive Motivational States Within the Person.* Cambridge University Press, 1992.

Ted O'Donoghue and Matthew Rabin. "Present bias: Lessons learned and to be learned." *American Economic Review* 105, no. 5 (2015): 273–279.

36 *Tim Cook put it this way* David M. Rubenstein. *How to Lead: Wisdom from the World's Greatest CEOs, Founders, and Game Changers.* Simon & Schuster, 2020.

"Apple CEO Tim Cook on The David Rubenstein Show," *The David Rubenstein Show: Peer-to-Peer Conversations,* YouTube, May 2018, youtube.com/watch?v=2ZfGBGmEpRQ.

36 *according to founder Jeff Bezos* David M. Rubenstein. *How to Lead: Wisdom from the World's Greatest CEOs, Founders, and Game Changers.* Simon & Schuster, 2020.

"Amazon CEO Jeff Bezos on The David Rubenstein Show," *The David Rubenstein Show: Peer-to-Peer Conversations,* YouTube, September 2018, youtube.com/watch?v=f3NBQcAqyu4.

CHAPTER 3: INTEGRATING THE LEARNING ZONE AND THE PERFORMANCE ZONE: LEARNING *WHILE* DOING

38 *cosmetics subscription service Ipsy* Personal interview with Marcelo Camberos, February 9, 2021.

Personal interview with Esteban Ochoa, February 24, 2021.

Personal interview with Trey Reasonover, June 2, 2021.

Personal interview with Simon Tisminezky, June 25, 2021.

40 *documentary* Free Solo Elizabeth Chai Vasarhelyi and Jimmy Chin. *Free Solo*. United States: National Geographic Documentary Films, 2018.

44 *John Dewey, Kurt Lewin, and David Kolb* Robert Kegan. "What 'form' transforms? A constructive-developmental approach to transformative learning." In *Contemporary Theories of Learning*, pp. 29–45. Routledge, 2008.

45 *as a barista at a busy Starbucks* Personal interview with Traca Savadogo, February 8, 2021.

CHAPTER 4: SIX ESSENTIAL LEARNING ZONE STRATEGIES

51 *their idol's eighty-one* Billboard *hit songs* "Beyoncé," *Billboard*, billboard.com/artist/beyonce.

51 *she has other plans* Amy Wallace. "Miss Millennium: Beyoncé," *GQ*, January 10, 2013, gq.com/story/beyonce-cover-story-interview -gq-february-2013.

51 *She has earned more Grammy Awards* Anastasia Tsioulcas and Hazel Cills. "Beyoncé Sets a New Grammy Record, While Harry Styles Wins Album of the Year," NPR, February 6, 2023, npr.org/ 2023/02/05/1152837932/2023-grammy-awards-winners-beyonce.

52 *displayed at the start* "Beyoncé—***Flawless ft. Chimamanda Ngozi Adichie," Beyoncé, YouTube, November 24, 2014, youtube .com/watch?v=IyuUWOnS9BY.

52 *the most influential female musician* "Turning the Tables: Your List of the 21st Century's Most Influential Women Musicians,"

NPR, November 20, 2018, npr.org/2018/11/20/668372321/turning
-the-tables-your-list-of-the-21st-centurys-most-influential-women
-musicia.

52 *Foo Fighters invited to the stage* Jessica Shalvoy. "Foo Fighters
Bring Rock Back to the Forum But 11-Year-Old Drummer Nandi
Bushell Steals the Show: Concert Review," *Variety,* August 27,
2021, variety.com/2021/music/news/foo-fighters-nandi-bushell
-los-angeles-forum-concert-1235050726.

53 *had tweeted at the Foo Fighters front man* Nandi Bushell
(@Nandi_Bushell), August 17, 2020, twitter.com/nandi_bushell/
status/1295419281073672195.

53 *at first, Grohl thought the message was cute* "Dave Grohl Finally
Conceded Defeat in His Drum Battle with a 10-Year Old," *The
Late Show with Stephen Colbert,* CBS, November 19, 2020,
cbs.com/shows/video/5bWmWSe4Wfe_4z3uZ5BO7X5hwL6gH
AgG.

53 *For months, they went back and forth* See Isabella Bridie DeLeo.
"The Complete Timeline of Dave Grohl and Nandi Bushell's Epic
Drum Battle," *Fatherly,* updated December 15, 2021, fatherly.com/
play/the-complete-timeline-of-dave-grohl-and-nandi-bushells-epic
-drum-battle.

53 *the two of them spoke over video* "Dave Grohl meets Nandi
Bushell—BEST DAY EVER—EPIC!!!—*New York Times,*"
Nandi Bushell, YouTube, November 9, 2020, youtube.com/watch
?v=rS4ZBM1_UlM.

53 *"I play it slowly, bit by bit"* Christi Carras. "On a Winning Streak
Against Dave Grohl, There's Nothing Nandi Bushell Can't Do,"
Los Angeles Times, October 12, 2020, latimes.com/entertainment
-arts/music/story/2020-10-12/nandi-bushell-interview-drum-battle
-dave-grohl.

53 *"experts are always made"* K. Anders Ericsson, Michael J. Prietula,
and Edward T. Cokely. "The Making of an Expert," *Harvard
Business Review,* July–August 2007 Issue, hbr.org/2007/07/the
-making-of-an-expert.

54 *"Not all practice makes perfect"* Ibid.

54 *To engage in deliberate practice* Eduardo Briceño, "How to get better at the things you care about," TED Talk, November 5, 2016, ted.com/talks/eduardo_briceno_how_to_get_better_at_the_things _you_care_about. Special thanks to professors Carol Dweck and K. Anders Ericsson for helping me prepare this talk.

54 *category called* purposeful practice K. Anders Ericsson and Robert Pool. *Peak: Secrets from the New Science of Expertise.* Eamon Dolan, 2016.

54 *"you can probably gain"* Jonathan Fields, "Anders Ericsson: Dismantling the 10,000 Hour Rule," *Good Life Project,* podcast audio, May 16, 2016, goodlifeproject.com/podcast/anders -ericsson.

54 *there isn't anything magical* Anders Ericsson and Robert Pool. "Malcolm Gladwell Got Us Wrong: Our Research Was Key to the 10,000-Hour Rule, but Here's What Got Oversimplified," *Salon,* April 10, 2016, salon.com/2016/04/10/malcolm_gladwell_got_us _wrong_our_research_was_key_to_the_10000_hour_rule_but_heres _what_got_oversimplified.

55 *Olivier Perrin's colleagues* Personal interview with Olivier Perrin, February 18, 2021.

56 *Luke's Lobster* Patrick J. McGinnis. "Luke Holden—Wicked Lobstah: Vertical Integration and the Luke's Lobster Success Story." *FOMO Sapiens with Patrick J. McGinnis,* podcast audio, May 9, 2019, patrickmcginnis.com/luke-holden-wicked-lobstah -vertical-integration-and-the-lukes-lobster-success-story. Personal communications with Luke Holden, December 5, 2022, and March 14, 2023.

57 *iEduca began offering its courses online* Personal interview with Douglas Franco, November 2, 2022.

59 *"I look at what everyone else is doing"* Dax Shepard. "Celebrating the GOAT GOD." *Armchair Expert with Dax Shepard,* podcast audio, February 5, 2021, armchairexpertpod.com/pods/tom-brady -zxrhd.

60 *Carlos Moreno Serrano considers* Personal interview with Carlos Moreno Serrano, September 23, 2022.

61 *"several values involved in this nomination"* "Sonatype Core Values Champions Videos," performed by Carlos Moreno Serrano, July 19, 2022, San Francisco, video.

62 *As the alarm went off* Personal interview with Shannon Polson, February 17, 2021.

64 *"I was nine months pregnant"* Personal communications with Alicia Ginsburgh, April 9, 2021.

66 *"It really doesn't matter how long"* K. Anders Ericsson, Michael J. Prietula, and Edward T. Cokely. "The Making of an Expert," *Harvard Business Review*, July–August 2007 Issue, hbr.org/2007/07/the-making-of-an-expert.

66 *scientists who have won the Nobel Prize* Robert Root-Bernstein, Lindsay Allen, Leighanna Beach, Ragini Bhadula, Justin Fast, Chelsea Hosey, Benjamin Kremkow et al. "Arts foster scientific success: Avocations of Nobel, National Academy, Royal Society, and Sigma Xi members." *Journal of Psychology of Science and Technology* 1, no. 2 (2008): 51–63.

66 *limit their engagement in deliberate practice* K. Anders Ericsson, Ralf T. Krampe, and Clemens Tesch-Römer. "The role of deliberate practice in the acquisition of expert performance." *Psychological Review* 100, no. 3 (1993): 363–406.

67 *Some people like to set a timer* Francesco Cirillo. *The Pomodoro Technique: The Acclaimed Time-Management System That Has Transformed How We Work.* Currency, 2018.

68 *Jean Monnet, the French entrepreneur* Jean Monnet. *Memoirs: Jean Monnet.* Doubleday & Company, 1978.

68 *"totally lost in thought"* Liam Viney. "Good Vibrations: The Role of Music in Einstein's Thinking," *The Conversation*, February 14, 2016, theconversation.com/good-vibrations-the-role-of-music-in-einsteins-thinking-54725.

68 *To be effective and motivated learners, we need to* Camille A. Farrington, Melissa Roderick, Elaine Allensworth, Jenny Nagaoka,

Tasha Seneca Keyes, David W. Johnson, and Nicole O. Beechum. *Teaching Adolescents to Become Learners: The Role of Noncognitive Factors in Shaping School Performance—A Critical Literature Review.* Consortium on Chicago School Research, 2012.

68 *a reason to put in the effort to improve* Jacquelynne Eccles, Terry F. Adler, Robert Futterman, Susan B. Goff, Caroline M. Kaczala, Judith L. Meece, and Carol Midgley. "Expectancies, values, and academic behaviors." In Janet T. Spence (ed.), *Achievement and Achievement Motives.* W. H. Freeman, 1983: 75–146.

70 *We want to be the most growth-minded and persistent when it comes to* See Angela Duckworth and James J. Gross. "Self-control and grit: Related but separable determinants of success." *Current Directions in Psychological Science* 23, no. 5 (2014): 319–325.

71 *different Learning Zone strategies* See "The Science of Learning." Deans for Impact (2015).

CHAPTER 5: UNLEASHING THE POWER OF MISTAKES

73 *Robert Duke and his colleagues* Robert A. Duke, Amy L. Simmons, and Carla Davis Cash. "It's not how much; it's how: Characteristics of practice behavior and retention of performance skills." *Journal of Research in Music Education* 56, no. 4 (2009): 310–321.

74 *Andrew Huberman points out* Andrew Huberman, "Using Failures, Movement & Balance to Learn Faster," *Huberman Lab,* podcast audio, February 15, 2021, hubermanlab.com/using-failures -movement-and-balance-to-learn-faster/.

76 *Researchers from Michigan State University* Jason S. Moser, Hans S. Schroder, Carrie Heeter, Tim P. Moran, and Yu-Hao Lee. "Mind your errors: Evidence for a neural mechanism linking growth mind-set to adaptive posterror adjustments." *Psychological Science* 22, no. 12 (2011): 1484–1489.

76 *almost all of the major decisions* Personal interview with Marcelo Camberos, February 9, 2021.

77 *Tomoe Musa directs patient safety* Personal interview with "Tomoe Musa," March 4, 2021. Tomoe's real name has been altered to protect anonymity.

78 *"If the only tool you have is a hammer"* Abraham Harold Maslow. *The Psychology of Science: A Reconnaissance.* Gateway / Henry Regnery, 1966.

80 *I even keep a blog where I share them with others* "Joy of Mistakes," Eduardo Briceño, joyofmistakes.com.

81 *In a TED Talk, Damberger told the story* David Damberger, "What happens when an NGO admits failure," TED Talk, March 13, 2014, ted.com/talks/david_damberger_what_happens_when _an_ngo_admits_failure.

82 *It built a website called admittingfailure.org* "Admitting Failure," Engineers Without Borders Canada, admittingfailure.org.

84 *relating to unconscious biases, we tend to withdraw* Robin DiAngelo. *White Fragility: Why It's So Hard for White People to Talk About Racism.* Beacon Press, 2018.

85 *Dona Sarkar is a software engineer* Personal interview with Dona Sarkar, January 25, 2021.

87 *in 1912, eight of fourteen U.S. Army pilots* Matthew Syed. *Black Box Thinking.* Portfolio, 2015.

87 *Flash forward to 2019* ICAO *Safety Report, 2022 Edition.* Montréal: International Civil Aviation Organization, 2022.

89 *some hospitals are now beginning to use black boxes* Nina Bai. " 'Black Boxes' in Stanford Hospital Operating Rooms Aid Training and Safety," Stanford Medicine News, September 28, 2022, med.stanford.edu/news/all-news/2022/09/black-box-surgery.html.

89 *records all meetings* Ray Dalio. *Principles.* Simon & Schuster, 2017.

89 *ClearChoice Dental similarly records* Personal interviews with Andrew Kimball, October 20, 2020, January 21, 2021, and July 26, 2021.

89 *one of the biggest mistakes of his career* Personal interview with Dipo Aromire, November 9, 2020.

91 *incorporates an awareness of different kinds of mistakes* Personal interview with Tomer Cohen, July 16, 2021.

93 *Remember Gino Barbaro, the pizzeria owner* Personal interview with Gino Barbaro, January 18, 2021.

   Personal interviews with Gino Barbaro and Jake Stenziano, November 22, 2021, and December 13, 2021.

95 *portfolio of more than $225 million in assets* "Welcome to Jake & Gino," Jake and Gino, jakeandgino.com.

CHAPTER 6: SIX COMMON MISCONCEPTIONS ABOUT LEARNING

97 *"The Tortoise and the Hare"* Aesop. "The Tortoise and the Hare," Project Gutenberg, gutenberg.org/files/45384/45384-h/45384-h.htm#link2H_4_0034.

99 *the ideas in the book* The Secret Rhonda Byrne. *The Secret.* Simon & Schuster, 2006.

99 *A growth mindset is not a wishing well* Carol Dweck. "What Having a 'Growth Mindset' Actually Means." *Harvard Business Review* 13, no. 2 (2016): 2–5.

99 *"potential is nurtured, not predetermined"* Microsoft 2018 Corporate Social Responsibility Report. Redmond, WA, USA: Microsoft Corporation, October 23, 2018.

100 *Research tells us the opposite* K. Anders Ericsson. "Deliberate practice and the acquisition and maintenance of expert performance in medicine and related domains." *Academic Medicine* 79, no. 10 (2004): S70–S81.

101 *My friend Rajeev asked me* Rajeev's real name has been altered to protect anonymity.

102 *the unintentional consequences of well-intended praise* Claudia M. Mueller and Carol S. Dweck. "Praise for intelligence can undermine children's motivation and performance." *Journal of Personality and Social Psychology* 75, no. 1 (1998): 33–52.

103 *he was too direct in his criticism* Personal interview with Marcelo Camberos, February 9, 2021.

104 *one of the leaders of the EL Education network* Personal interview with Ron Berger, March 8, 2021.

104 *"I'm not a good writer"* See Karla M. Johnstone, Hollis Ashbaugh, and Terry D. Warfield. "Effects of repeated practice and contextual-writing experiences on college students' writing skills." *Journal of Educational Psychology* 94, no. 2 (2002): 305–315.

104 *"I can't do math"* See Jo Boaler. *Mathematical Mindsets: Unleashing Students' Potential Through Creative Math, Inspiring Messages and Innovative Teaching.* John Wiley & Sons, 2015.

104 *"I'm not a social person"* See John W. Hunt and Yehuda Baruch. "Developing top managers: The impact of interpersonal skills training." *Journal of Management Development* 22, no. 8 (2003): 729–752.

106 *Learning environments prime a growth mindset* David S. Yeager, Jamie M. Carroll, Jenny Buontempo, Andrei Cimpian, Spencer Woody, Robert Crosnoe, Chandra Muller et al. "Teacher mindsets help explain where a growth-mindset intervention does and doesn't work." *Psychological Science* 33, no. 1 (2022): 18–32.

CHAPTER 7: THE GROWTH PROPELLER: FIVE KEY ELEMENTS THAT DRIVE GROWTH

108 *Lizzie Dipp Metzger, the newbie insurance agent* Personal interview with Lizzie Dipp Metzger, July 29, 2022. She is an insurance agent with New York Life Insurance Company.

108 *and financial planner* Lizzie Dipp Metzger is a financial planner with Eagle Strategies LLC.

108 *Emilio, the father* Emilio's real name has been altered to protect anonymity.

110 *When Linda Rabbitt's husband* Personal interview with Linda Rabbitt, May 20, 2021.

Mahan Tavakoli, "Succeeding Against All Odds to Become a Profile in Success with Linda Rabbitt | Changemaker," *Partnering Leadership,* podcast audio, February 9, 2021, www.partneringleadership .com/succeeding-against-all-odds-to-become-a-profile-in-success -with-linda-rabbitt-changemaker.

111 *"Absolutely nothing, but I can learn"* Mahan Tavakoli, "Impactful Leadership with a Genuine Drive to Help with Steve Harlan | Greater Washington DC DMV Changemaker," *Partnering Leadership,* podcast audio, February 2, 2021, partneringleadership.com/ impactful-leadership-with-a-genuine-drive-to-help-with-steve -harlan-changemaker.

111 *as having multiple identities* Richard M. Ryan and Edward L. Deci. "Multiple identities within a single self: A self-determination theory perspective on internalization within contexts and cultures." In Mark R. Leary and June Price Tangney (eds.). *Handbook of Self and Identity.* 2nd ed. Guilford Press, 2012: 225–246.

Peter J. Burke. "Relationships among multiple identities." *Advances in Identity Theory and Research* (2003): 195–214.

111 *Various scholars* See Beth Crossan, John Field, Jim Gallacher, and Barbara Merrill. "Understanding participation in learning for non-traditional adult learners: Learning careers and the construction of learning identities." *British Journal of Sociology of Education* 24, no. 1 (2003): 55-67.

111 *Stanton Wortham* Stanton Wortham. *Learning Identity: The Joint Emergence of Social Identification and Academic Learning.* Cambridge University Press, 2005.

111 *and Alice and David Kolb* Alice Kolb and David Kolb. "On becoming a learner: The concept of learning identity." *Learning Never Ends: Essays on Adult Learning Inspired by the Life and Work of David O. Justice* (2009): 5–13.

Andrew Wojecki. " 'What's identity got to do with it, anyway?' Constructing adult learner identities in the workplace." *Studies in the Education of Adults* 39, no. 2 (2007): 168–182.

112 *call someone a "born leader"* See Tamarah Smith, Rasheeda Brumskill, Angela Johnson, and Travon Zimmer. "The impact of teacher

language on students' mindsets and statistics performance." *Social Psychology of Education* 21 (2018): 775–786.

Claudia M. Mueller and Carol S. Dweck. "Praise for intelligence can undermine children's motivation and performance." *Journal of Personality and Social Psychology* 75, no. 1 (1998): 33–52.

112 *"The self is not something one finds"* Thomas Szasz. *The Second Sin*. Anchor Press, 1973.

112 *Meirav Oren spent a lot of time pretending to be sick* Personal interview with Meirav Oren, April 16, 2021.

113 *Rather than think about* finding *your purpose* Paul A. O'Keefe, Carol S. Dweck, and Gregory M. Walton. "Implicit theories of interest: Finding your passion or developing it?" *Psychological Science* 29, no. 10 (2018): 1653–1664.

114 *"It's all about your beliefs"* Lizzie Dipp Metzger, "Impossible things are happening every day," New York Life 2017 Chairman's Council (keynote address, The Venetian, Las Vegas, NV, USA, February 23, 2018).

116 *"the conviction that you shape your own future"* Angela Duckworth. "Guided Mastery," *Psychology Today*, October 18, 2021, psychologytoday.com/us/blog/actionable-advice-help-kids-thrive/202110/guided-mastery.

116 *Alex Stephany, a London-based technology entrepreneur* Personal interview with Alex Stephany, August 18, 2022. Lucas's real name has been altered to protect anonymity.

117 *"I am not inauthentic, but I was sounding that way"* Personal interview with Linda Rabbitt, May 20, 2021.

118 *We need to exercise judgment and inhibit some of our impulses* Lisa Rosh and Lynn Offermann. "Be Yourself, but Carefully." *Harvard Business Review* 91, no. 10 (2013): 135–139.

120 *belonging—the feeling that your community is your home* See Marco Antonsich. "Searching for belonging—an analytical framework." *Geography Compass* 4, no. 6 (2010): 644–659.

See also:

Kaisa Kuurne, and M. Victoria Gómez. "Feeling at home in the neighborhood: Belonging, the house and the plaza in Helsinki and Madrid." *City & Community* 18, no. 1 (2019): 213–237.

CHAPTER 8: PILLARS OF A LEARNING ORGANIZATION

127 *As Nadella describes in his book,* Hit Refresh Satya Nadella, Greg Shaw, and Jill Tracie Nichols. *Hit Refresh.* Harper Business, 2017.

130 *the company even posts the surf report* "Perks: Surf's Up at Patagonia," Bloomberg, August 31, 2011, bloomberg.com/news/photo-essays/2011-08-31/perks-surf-s-up-at-patagonia.

130 *"Sometimes people just need to call and talk"* Alaina McConnell. "Zappos' Outrageous Record for the Longest Customer Service Phone Call Ever," Business Insider, December 20, 2012, businessinsider.com/zappos-longest-customer-service-call-2012-12.

132 *"I think the archetype myth of the twenty-two-year-old founder"* Marc Andreessen and Balaji Srinivasan, "Startups and Pendulum Swings Through Ideas, Time, Fame, and Money," *a16z Podcast,* podcast audio, May 30, 2016, future.com/podcasts/startup-technology-innovation.

133 *When Kevin Mosher joined ClearChoice Dental* Personal interviews with Andrew Kimball, October 20, 2020, January 21, 2021, and July 26, 2021.

137 *researchers led by Elizabeth Canning and Mary Murphy* Elizabeth A. Canning, Mary C. Murphy, Katherine T. U. Emerson, Jennifer A. Chatman, Carol S. Dweck, and Laura J. Kray. "Cultures of genius at work: Organizational mindsets predict cultural norms, trust, and commitment." *Personality and Social Psychology Bulletin* 46, no. 4 (2020): 626–642.

138 *When Jake and Gino began their real estate company* Personal interview with Gino Barbaro, January 18, 2021.

Personal interviews with Gino Barbaro and Jake Stenziano, November 22, 2021, and December 13, 2021.

138 *PVPs—Purpose, Values, and Principles* See "Policies & Practices:

Purpose, Values & Principles," Procter & Gamble, us.pg.com/policies-and-practices/purpose-values-and-principles.

139 *Get rid of forced rankings* Peter Cappelli and Anna Tavis. "The Performance Management Revolution." *Harvard Business Review* 94, no. 10 (2016): 58–67.

140 *Dona Sarkar, the software engineer* Personal interview with Dona Sarkar, January 25, 2021.

141 *Microsoft Inclusion Journey website* "Microsoft Inclusion Journey: Work in Progress," Microsoft, microsoft.com/en-us/inclusion -journey.

141 *Liquidnet is another company that has many structures* Personal interview with Jeff Schwartzman, February 11, 2021.

142 *every employee is given forty hours of paid work time* "Learning and Development," Telenor, telenor.com/career/culture/learning -and-development.

142 *to break the Guinness World Record* "New World Record: Telenor Employees Write E-learning History," GlobeNewswire, November 11, 2021, globenewswire.com/en/news-release/2021/11/11/ 2332231/0/en/New-world-record-Telenor-employees-write-e -learning-history.html.

142 *One, called the Internal Mobility Program* "Engage and Inspire on Employee Appreciation Day," New York Life, newyorklife.com/ newsroom/people-employee-appreciation-day.

142 *From agent surveys, New York Life estimates that* Personal communications with Mark Scozzafava, December 12, 2022. The surveys were administered in 2020.

143 *the best insurance agents engage in learning at least once a week* Sabine Sonnentag and Barbara M. Kleine. "Deliberate practice at work: A study with insurance agents." *Journal of Occupational and Organizational Psychology* 73, no. 1 (2000): 87–102.

144 *Deloitte launched Deloitte Ventures* "Deloitte Ventures," Deloitte, deloitte.com/uk/en/pages/innovation/solutions/ventures.html.

144 *Coats created Innovation Hubs* Gary James. "Coats Thrives

Through Innovation, Sustainability," *BedTimes*, November 19, 2019, bedtimesmagazine.com/2019/11/coats-thrives-through-innovation-sustainability.

144 *Microsoft implemented massive hackathons* Ei Pa Pa Pe-Than, Alexander Nolte, Anna Filippova, Christian Bird, Steve Scallen, and James D. Herbsleb. "Designing corporate hackathons with a purpose: The future of software development." *IEEE Software* 36, no. 1 (2018): 15–22.

145 *when Brad Willoughby, Oracle Cloud Infrastructure director* Personal communications with Brad Willoughby, November 15, 2022.

147 *"The goal is not to teach them a script"* Personal interviews with Andrew Kimball, October 20, 2020, January 21, 2021, and July 26, 2021.

148 *Accenture onboards more than 150,000 new employees* Jason Warnke. "Going Beyond with Extended Reality," Accenture, March 16, 2022, accenture.com/us-en/about/going-beyond-extended-reality.

148 *Peter Handal, fostered trust and belonging* Personal interview with Mahan Tavakoli, January 15, 2021.

149 *Claude Steele coined this phenomenon* stereotype threat Claude M. Steele. *Whistling Vivaldi: How Stereotypes Affect Us and What We Can Do.* W. W. Norton & Company, 2010.

149 *Eugene Baah and Patrick Kann roomed together* Personal interview with Patrick Kann, May 28, 2021. Personal communications with Eugene Baah, October 27, 2022.

152 *raise more than $65 million in funding* Mary Ann Azevedo. "Papaya Raises $50M to Give You a Way to Pay Bills via Its Mobile App," TechCrunch, December 15, 2021, techcrunch.com/2021/12/15/papaya-raises-50-million-to-give-you-a-way-to-pay-bills-via-its-mobile-app.

152 *Environmental activist and social entrepreneur Angelou Ezeilo* Personal interview with Angelou Ezeilo, July 7, 2021.

152 *As Ezeilo wrote in her book* Engage, Connect, Protect Angelou Ezeilo and Nick Chiles. *Engage, Connect, Protect: Empowering*

Diverse Youth as Environmental Leaders. New Society Publishers, 2019.

CHAPTER 9: GETTING TEAMS IN THE ZONES

157 *Razmig Hovaghimian, took a course called* Personal interview with Razmig Hovaghimian, August 15, 2022.

158 *the students sent one of their teammates, Linus Liang, to Nepal* Tom Kelley and David Kelley. *Creative Confidence: Unleashing the Creative Potential Within Us All.* Currency, 2013.

159 *Embrace has saved more than 350,000 lives* Embrace Global, embraceglobal.org.

159 *Sam Goldman and Ned Tozun, took the same course* Personal communications with Sam Goldman and Ned Tozun, December 8, 2022.

159 *They have now sold more than twenty-five million products* Jessica Pothering. "D.light Raises $50 Million in Debt as Investors Warm Up (Again) to Off-Grid Solar," ImpactAlpha, July 25, 2022, impactalpha.com/d-light-raises-50-million-in-debt-as-investors-warm-up-again-to-off-grid-solar.

159 *They have impacted the lives of more than 140 million people* "Our Impact," d.light, dlight.com/social-impact.

160 design thinking *or* human-centered design—*foster learning teams* See Maria Orero-Blat, Daniel Palacios-Marqués, and Virginia Simón-Moya. "Team-Based Learning Through Design Thinking Methodology: A Case Study in a Multinational Company." In *INTED2020 Proceedings.* IATED, 2020: 3712–3719.

160 *was pioneered by the design firm IDEO* "History," IDEO, designthinking.ideo.com/history.

160 *has led to breakthrough innovations from leading companies* See Esther Han. "5 Examples of Design Thinking in Business," Harvard Business School Online, February 22, 2022, online.hbs.edu/blog/post/design-thinking-examples.

161 *inspired from design thinking* See "Design Thinking," IDEO, ideou.com/pages/design-thinking.

161 *d.school executive director Sarah Stein Greenberg's* Sarah Stein Greenberg. *Creative Acts for Curious People*. Ten Speed Press, 2021.

162 *alternate between divergent thinking and convergent thinking* "Human-Centered Design Sits at the Intersection of Empathy and Creativity," IDEO, ideo.org/tools.

164 *it's essential to develop trust among teammates* David L. Paul and Reuben R. McDaniel, Jr. "A field study of the effect of interpersonal trust on virtual collaborative relationship performance." *MIS Quarterly* 28, no. 2 (2004): 183–227.

165 *the* false consensus bias Brian Mullen, Jennifer L. Atkins, Debbie S. Champion, Cecelia Edwards, Dana Hardy, John E. Story, and Mary Vanderklok. "The false consensus effect: A meta-analysis of 115 hypothesis tests." *Journal of Experimental Social Psychology* 21, no. 3 (1985): 262–283.

165 *"The executives listened. They learned together"* Satya Nadella, Greg Shaw, and Jill Tracie Nichols. *Hit Refresh*. Harper Business, 2017.

167 *"laser-sharp focus on the essential needs of the user"* Kara Platoni. "Baby, It's Cold Outside," *Stanford Magazine*, January/February 2009, stanfordmag.org/contents/baby-it-s-cold-outside.

167 *"desperate parents in a remote village"* Jane Chen, Razmig Hovaghimian, Linus Liang, and Rahul Panicker. *Team Embrace Final Report*. Stanford University. May 9, 2007.

171 *particularly when we are working with others* For some individuals (such as those with low levels of the hormone DHEAS—dehydroepiandrosterone sulfate), negative situations and moods can feed certain types of creativity, such as individual artistic creativity.

Modupe Akinola and Wendy Berry Mendes. "The dark side of creativity: Biological vulnerability and negative emotions lead to greater artistic creativity." *Personality and Social Psychology Bulletin* 34, no. 12 (2008): 1677–1686.

Some renowned artists were known to suffer from depression, including Vincent van Gogh, Sylvia Plath, Charles Dickens, Virginia Woolf, Pyotr Ilyich Tchaikovsky, and Frida Kahlo, among others. Nadra Nittle. "The Link Between Depression and Creativity," Verywell Mind, updated February 20, 2023, verywellmind.com/the-link-between-depression-and-creativity-5094193.

But for collaborative, problem-solving-oriented creativity, a positive mood tends to be beneficial for most people and teams. Yuhyung Shin. "Positive group affect and team creativity: Mediation of team reflexivity and promotion focus." *Small Group Research* 45, no. 3 (2014): 337–364.

More recent research suggests that in teams, promotion-focused affect—whether positive like happiness or negative like anger—may foster creativity, while prevention-focused affect like tension or fear may reduce it. Kyle J. Emich and Lynne C. Vincent. "Shifting focus: The influence of affective diversity on team creativity." *Organizational Behavior and Human Decision Processes* 156 (2020): 24–37.

CHAPTER 10: THE COLLABORATION SUPERPOWER: HOW TO FORGE MIGHTY TEAMS

173 *Willy Foote fell in love* Personal interview with Willy Foote, March 25, 2021.

174 *It reinforces the performance paradox and fools us into chronic performance* See John G. Nicholls. "Achievement motivation: Conceptions of ability, subjective experience, task choice, and performance." *Psychological Review* 91, no. 3 (1984): 328–346.

See also:

Damon Burton. "Winning isn't everything: Examining the impact of performance goals on collegiate swimmers' cognitions and performance." *The Sport Psychologist* 3, no. 2 (1989): 105–132.

175 *Collaboration drives better learning and better performance* François Chiocchio, Simon Grenier, Thomas A. O'Neill, Karine Savaria, and J. Douglas Willms. "The effects of collaboration on performance: A multilevel validation in project teams." *International Journal of Project Organisation and Management* 4, no. 1 (2012): 1–37.

175 *"Today one of my top priorities"* Satya Nadella, Greg Shaw, and Jill Tracie Nichols. *Hit Refresh*. Harper Business, 2017.

177 *"Honestly, we didn't really know each other yet"* Personal interview with Razmig Hovaghimian, August 15, 2022.

178 *My mentor Chip Conley was a seasoned hotel executive* Chip Conley. *Wisdom at Work: The Making of a Modern Elder*. Currency, 2018. Personal interview with Chip Conley, December 29, 2020.

179 *Cindy Eckert, CEO of Sprout Pharmaceuticals* Tim Ferriss, "Cindy Eckert—How to Sell Your Company For One Billion Dollars (#314)," *The Tim Ferriss Show*, podcast audio, May 10, 2018, tim .blog/2018/05/10/cindy-whitehead.

181 *Ethan Bernstein studied the second-biggest phone factory in the world* Ethan S. Bernstein. "The transparency paradox: A role for privacy in organizational learning and operational control." *Administrative Science Quarterly* 57, no. 2 (2012): 181–216.

182 *instituted monthly meetings at General Mills* Personal interview with Jenny Radenberg, February 11, 2021.

183 *Bridgewater Associates, the largest hedge fund in the world* Avery Koop. "Ranked: The World's 20 Biggest Hedge Funds," Visual Capitalist, December 7, 2022, visualcapitalist.com/worlds-20 -biggest-hedge-funds-2022.

183 *The recordings become a tool* Ray Dalio. *Principles*. Simon & Schuster, 2018.

183 *question your superiors, admit your weaknesses* Richard Feloni. "Employees at the World's Biggest Hedge Fund Spend a Couple Hours Every Week Studying Each Other's Meetings," Business Insider, August 30, 2016, businessinsider.com/bridgewater -associates-management-principles-training-2016-8.

183 *In his TED Talk, he did just that* Ray Dalio, "How to build a company where the best ideas win," TED Talk, April 24, 2017, ted.com/talks/ray_dalio_how_to_build_a_company_where_the_best_ideas_win.

185 *As a first-year doctoral student, Amy Edmondson* Amy C. Edmondson. *The Fearless Organization: Creating Psychological Safety in the Workplace for Learning, Innovation, and Growth.* John Wiley & Sons, 2018.

186 *the higher-performing teams didn't make more errors* Amy C. Edmondson. "Learning from mistakes is easier said than done: Group and organizational influences on the detection and correction of human error." *Journal of Applied Behavioral Science* 32, no. 1 (1996): 5–28.

186 psychological safety, *which she defined as the shared belief* Amy Edmondson. "Psychological safety and learning behavior in work teams." *Administrative Science Quarterly* 44, no. 2 (1999): 350–383.

186 *"When psychological safety is high, candor no longer feels risky"* Henrik Bresman and Amy C. Edmondson. "Exploring the relationship between team diversity, psychological safety and team performance: Evidence from pharmaceutical drug development." No. 22-055. Harvard Business School Working Paper, 2022.

186 *promote psychological safety by using* framing *and* inquiry Ibid.

189 *David Bradford and Carole Robin explain in their book,* Connect David L. Bradford and Carole Robin. *Connect: Building Exceptional Relationships with Family, Friends, and Colleagues.* Currency, 2021.

190 *neurons that fire together wire together* Nathan Collins. "Pathways," *Stanford Medicine Magazine*, August 21, 2017, stanmed.stanford.edu/carla-shatz-vision-brain.

190 *countries might have different communication norms* Erin Meyer. *The Culture Map: Breaking Through the Invisible Boundaries of Global Business.* PublicAffairs, 2014.

CHAPTER 11: LEADING FOR GROWTH

194 *When Mike Stevenson was a young man* Personal interview with Mike Stevenson, January 14, 2021.

195 *we need to extend trust to others* See Stephen M. R. Covey. *Trust and Inspire: How Truly Great Leaders Unleash Greatness in Others*. Simon & Schuster, 2022.

See also:

Mahan Tavakoli, "168 How Truly Great Leaders Unleash Greatness in Others with Stephen M. R. Covey | Partnering Leadership Global Thought Leader," *Partnering Leadership*, podcast audio, June 16, 2022, www.partneringleadership.com/how-truly-great-leaders-unleash-greatness-in-others-with-stephen-m-r-covey-partnering-leadership-global-thought-leader.

196 *management theory was born in the Industrial Revolution* See Daniel A. Wren and Arthur G. Bedeian. *The Evolution of Management Thought*. 8th ed. John Wiley & Sons, 2020.

197 *"The most dangerous leadership myth is that leaders are born"* Warren Bennis. *Managing People Is Like Herding Cats: Warren Bennis on Leadership*. Executive Excellence Pub, 1997.

198 *When David Tashjian was moved into leadership* Personal interview with David Tashjian, January 12, 2022.

See also:

Sophia Kristjansson and David Tashjian. "Case study: Transparency and candor and a growth mindset." *People & Strategy* 39, no. 4 (2016): 26.

199 *managers account for at least 70 percent of the variance* Jim Harter and Amy Adkins. "Employees Want a Lot More From Their Managers," Gallup, April 8, 2015, gallup.com/workplace/236570/employees-lot-managers.aspx.

State of the Global Workplace: 2022 Report. Gallup, 2022, gallup.com/workplace/349484/state-of-the-global-workplace-2022-report.aspx.

199 *This has led to massive shifts* Sandro Formica and Fabiola Sfodera. "The Great Resignation and Quiet Quitting paradigm shifts: An

overview of current situation and future research directions."
Journal of Hospitality Marketing & Management 31, no. 8 (2022):
899–907.

201 *Francesca Lenci has worked for Siemens for sixteen years* Personal interview with Francesca Lenci, August 10, 2022.

202 *In the third year, they were a finalist and were also* Personal communications with Francesca Lenci, December 12, 2022.

202 *Belonging can be fostered in any team, anywhere* See Ellyn Shook and Christie Smith. *From Always Connected to Omni-Connected.* Accenture, 2022.

202 *Cohen relates the story of a female executive* Geoffrey L. Cohen. *Belonging: The Science of Creating Connection and Bridging Divides.* W. W. Norton & Company, 2022.

203 *Ian MacGregor, co-founder and CEO of Skratch Labs* Personal interviews with Ian MacGregor, March 11, 2021, and April 28, 2022.

206 *Versatile developed its first product, Crane View* Personal interview with Meirav Oren, April 16, 2021.

207 *In 2017, Carol Dweck published a unified theory* Carol S. Dweck. "From needs to goals and representations: Foundations for a unified theory of motivation, personality, and development." *Psychological Review* 124, no. 6 (2017): 689–719.

210 *"knowing what you don't know is more valuable"* Rich Lesser, 2021, linkedin.com/posts/richlesserbcg_twominutesontuesday -growthmindset-activity-6772559956769067008-3aLS.

CHAPTER 12: GREAT LEADERS ARE GREAT LEARNERS

212 *When Skratch Labs introduced Skratch Crispy* Personal interviews with Ian MacGregor, March 11, 2021, and April 28, 2022.

214 after-action reviews, *a practice borrowed* John E. Morrison and Larry L. Meliza. *Foundations of the after action review process.* Institute for Defense Analyses, Alexandria, VA, 1999.

Nathanael L. Keiser and Winfred Arthur, Jr. "A meta-analysis of the effectiveness of the after-action review (or debrief) and factors that influence its effectiveness." *Journal of Applied Psychology* 106, no. 7 (2021): 1007–1032.

214 *Ashley Good, CEO of consultancy Fail Forward* Personal interviews with Ashley Good, January 5, 2021, and February 8, 2021.

214 *Tomer Cohen, chief product officer at LinkedIn, instituted* Personal interview with Tomer Cohen, July 16, 2021.

217 *Douglas Franco, the CEO of iEduca whom we met* Personal interviews with Douglas Franco, April 12, 2021, and November 2, 2022.

219 *"You as the leader need to share your 360 evaluations"* Reed Hastings and Erin Meyer. *No Rules Rules: Netflix and the Culture of Reinvention.* Penguin, 2020.

219 *a group of MBA students at Wharton* Adam Grant. *Think Again: The Power of Knowing What You Don't Know.* Viking, 2021.

220 *Julia Barbaro is a life and marriage coach* Personal interview with Julia Barbaro and Gino Barbaro, February 4, 2021.

222 *likely to see their leaders as under-communicative* Francis J. Flynn and Chelsea R. Lide. "Communication miscalibration: The price leaders pay for not sharing enough." *Academy of Management Journal* (2022).

223 *it can be interpreted as ineptitude or insecurity* Elliot Aronson, Ben Willerman, and Joanne Floyd. "The effect of a pratfall on increasing interpersonal attractiveness." *Psychonomic Science* 4, no. 6 (1966): 227–228.

225 *Mahan Tavakoli, a consultant and the host* Personal interview with Mahan Tavakoli, January 15, 2021.

227 *turns the tables on job candidates* Personal interview with Meirav Oren, April 16, 2021.

228 *Ajay Kapur has had great success hiring* Personal interview with Ajay Kapur, January 29, 2021.

228 *Francesca Lenci, the CFO of Siemens Mobility in Italy* Personal interview with Francesca Lenci, August 10, 2022.

CHAPTER 13: THE FLYWHEEL OF COMPETENCE—IN MOTION AND UNSTOPPABLE

235 *let's check back in with Anjali* Personal interview with "Anjali," February 2, 2022. Anjali's and Salma's real names have been altered to protect anonymity.

238 *"Failing to prepare is preparing to fail,"* John Wooden and Steve Jamison. *Wooden: A Lifetime of Observations and Reflections On and Off the Court.* McGraw Hill, 1997.

238 *Winston Churchill was in the habit of* K. Anders Ericsson, Michael J. Prietula, and Edward T. Cokely. "The Making of an Expert," *Harvard Business Review,* July–August 2007 Issue, hbr.org/2007/07/the-making-of-an-expert.

241 *checklists used in cockpits and operating rooms* See Atul Gawande. *The Checklist Manifesto.* Metropolitan Books, 2009.

241 *pretty terrible at trying to do two conscious things at once* Kaitlyn E. May and Anastasia D. Elder. "Efficient, helpful, or distracting? A literature review of media multitasking in relation to academic performance." *International Journal of Educational Technology in Higher Education* 15, no. 1 (2018): 1–17.

242 *create routines that allow you to focus* Cal Newport. *Deep Work: Rules for Focused Success in a Distracted World.* Grand Central Publishing, 2016.

242 *not a good idea to use financial or social pressure* Dan Ariely, Uri Gneezy, George Loewenstein, and Nina Mazar. "Large stakes and big mistakes." *Review of Economic Studies* 76, no. 2 (2009): 451–469. Edward L. Deci, Richard Koestner, and Richard M. Ryan. "A meta-analytic review of experiments examining the effects of extrinsic rewards on intrinsic motivation." *Psychological Bulletin* 125, no. 6 (1999): 627–668.

242 *draws cognitive resources away from the work* Kou Murayama, Madoka Matsumoto, Keise Izuma, and Kenji Matsumoto. "Neural basis of the undermining effect of monetary reward on intrinsic motivation." *Proceedings of the National Academy of Sciences* 107, no. 49 (2010): 20911–20916.

242 *draw attention to the activity or work itself* Neel Doshi and Lindsay McGregor. *Primed to Perform.* Harper Business, 2015.

243 *too much anxiety can negatively impact performance* Bettina Seipp. "Anxiety and academic performance: A meta-analysis of findings." *Anxiety Research* 4, no. 1 (1991): 27–41.

245 *in 1975, pianist Keith Jarrett* Vera Brandes. Interview by Sabine Krüger. "Wie Keith Jarretts Welterfolg fast ausfiel. 'The Köln Concert,'" WDR 3, January 23, 2015.

246 *"It was like half a piano"* Tim Harford. Interview by Guy Raz. "Tim Harford: How Can Chaos Lead to Creative Breakthroughs?" NPR. May 10, 2019, npr.org/transcripts/719557642.

246 *whose love for jazz* Charles Waring. "'The Köln Concert': How Keith Jarrett Defied the Odds to Record His Masterpiece," uDiscover Music, January 24, 2023, udiscovermusic.com/stories/koln -concert-keith-jarrett.

246 *Manfred Eicher told* The Wall Street Journal *when* Corinna da Fonseca-Wollheim. "A Jazz Night to Remember," *The Wall Street Journal,* October 11, 2008, wsj.com/articles/SB122367103134923957.

248 *Periodically reflect on your higher-level goals* See Angela Duckworth and James J. Gross. "Self-control and grit: Related but separable determinants of success." *Current Directions in Psychological Science* 23, no. 5 (2014): 319–325.

CHAPTER 14: OVERCOME THE PARADOX, CHANGE LIVES

249 *When Mariana Costa Checa and her partners decided* Personal interview with Mariana Costa Checa and Andrew Kimball, January 21, 2021.

252 *having the nonprofit's alumni as role models* Daniela Sarzosa. *Analyzing the Social and Economic Returns of Laboratoria's Bootcamp.* Laboratoria, April 21, 2021.

254 *better competence, life situations, jobs, and impact* Jaideep Ghosh. "'Holy curiosity of inquiry': An investigation into curiosity and

work performance of employees." *European Management Journal* (2022).

254 *decrease in anxiety from knowing that we can overcome challenges* See Chuanxiuyue He and Mary Hegarty. "How anxiety and growth mindset are linked to navigation ability: Impacts of exploration and GPS use." *Journal of Environmental Psychology* 71 (2020): 101475.

254 *greater happiness and well-being* Hanwei Wang and Jie Li. "How trait curiosity influences psychological well-being and emotional exhaustion: The mediating role of personal initiative." *Personality and Individual Differences* 75, no. 3 (2015): 135–140.

254 *deepen relationships* Todd B. Kashdan and John E. Roberts. "Trait and state curiosity in the genesis of intimacy: Differentiation from related constructs." *Journal of Social and Clinical Psychology* 23, no. 6 (2004): 792–816.

255 *lower levels of stress, anxiety, and depression* Xu Jiang, Christian E. Mueller, and Netanel Paley. "A systematic review of growth mindset interventions targeting youth social–emotional outcomes." *School Psychology Review* (2022): 1–22.

255 *leads people to be more persistent and resilient* David S. Yeager and Carol S. Dweck. "Mindsets that promote resilience: When students believe that personal characteristics can be developed." *Educational Psychologist* 47, no. 4 (2012): 302–314.

255 *leads to more constructive conflict resolution* Todd B. Kashdan, C. Nathan DeWall, Richard S. Pond, Paul J. Silvia, Nathaniel M. Lambert, Frank D. Fincham, Antonina A. Savostyanova, and Peggy S. Keller. "Curiosity protects against interpersonal aggression: Cross-sectional, daily process, and behavioral evidence." *Journal of Personality* 81, no. 1 (2013): 87–102.

255 *Céline Darnon and colleagues found* Céline Darnon, Dominique Muller, Sheree M. Schrager, Nelly Pannuzzo, and Fabrizio Butera. "Mastery and performance goals predict epistemic and relational conflict regulation." *Journal of Educational Psychology* 98, no. 4 (2006): 766–776.

255 *helps them respond less through retaliation* David S. Yeager, Kali H. Trzesniewski, Kirsi Tirri, Petri Nokelainen, and Carol S. Dweck. "Adolescents' implicit theories predict desire for vengeance after peer conflicts: Correlational and experimental evidence." *Developmental Psychology* 47, no. 4 (2011): 1090–1107.

255 *when people see empathy as a quality that can be developed* Karina Schumann, Jamil Zaki, and Carol S. Dweck. "Addressing the empathy deficit: Beliefs about the malleability of empathy predict effortful responses when empathy is challenging." *Journal of Personality and Social Psychology* 107, no. 3 (2014): 475–493.

256 *Banerjee's parents were professors* Shahnaz Siganporia. "Into the Lives of Nobel Prize–Winning Economists Abhijit Banerjee and Esther Duflo," *Vogue India,* March 5, 2020, vogue.in/magazine -story/into-the-lives-of-nobel-prize-winning-economists-abhijit -banerjee-and-esther-duflo.

256 *the pair realized that randomized controlled trials* Esther Duflo, "Social experiments to fight poverty," TED Talk, February 12, 2010, ted.com/talks/esther_duflo_social_experiments_to_fight _poverty.

257 *they studied which interventions would improve educational outcomes* "Research to Help the World's Poor," The Nobel Foundation, nobelprize.org/prizes/economic-sciences/2019/popular -information.

258 *Since 1995, due in part to the impact this work* Ibid.

259 *would find herself standing in line to cast her ballot* Personal interview with Tiy Goddard, July 19, 2021.

260 *developed a method of* deliberative democracy *called America in One Room* James Fishkin, Alice Siu, Larry Diamond, and Norman Bradburn. "Is deliberation an antidote to extreme partisan polarization? Reflections on 'America in One Room.'" *American Political Science Review* 115, no. 4 (2021): 1464–1481.

260 *"We have found both in the in-person deliberations we organized"* Personal communications with Larry Diamond, March 20, 2023.

261 *political spectrum are driven by the same moral foundations* Jonathan Haidt. *The Righteous Mind: Why Good People Are Divided by Politics and Religion.* Pantheon, 2012.

AFTERWORD: NEVER FINISHED

265 *the Renaissance Man was one of the most curious people* Walter Isaacson. *Leonardo da Vinci.* Simon & Schuster, 2017.

265 *"Art is never finished, only abandoned"* Michael A. Conway. "Beyond sight: The artist and mystic intuition." *The Furrow* 65, no. 12 (2014): 592–599.

INDEX

ABOUT THE AUTHOR

Eduardo Briceño is a global keynote speaker, facilitator, and program provider who supports organizations in developing cultures of learning and high performance. Earlier in his career, he was the co-founder and CEO of Mindset Works, the first company to offer growth mindset development services. Previously, he was a venture capital investor with the Sprout Group. His TED Talk, *How to Get Better at the Things You Care About,* and his prior TEDx Talk, *The Power of Belief,* have been viewed more than nine million times. He is a Pahara-Aspen Fellow, a member of the Aspen Institute's Global Leadership Network, and an inductee in the Happiness Hall of Fame.

briceno.com/newsletter
linkedin.com/in/Eduardo-Briceno
Twitter: @ebriceno8

ABOUT THE TYPE

This book was set in Garamond, a typeface originally designed by the Parisian type cutter Claude Garamond (c.
1500–61). This version of Garamond was modeled on a
1592 specimen sheet from the Egenolff-Berner foundry,
which was produced from types assumed to have been
brought to Frankfurt by the punch cutter Jacques Sabon
(c. 1520–80).

Claude Garamond's distinguished romans and italics
first appeared in *Opera Ciceronis* in 1543–44. The Garamond types are clear, open, and elegant.